SERVANTS *of* EMPIRE

An Imperial Memoir of a British Family

F.R.H. DU BOULAY

I.B. TAURIS

LONDON · NEW YORK

Published in 2011 by I.B.Tauris & Co. Ltd
6 Salem Road, London W2 4BU
175 Fifth Avenue, New York, NY 10010
www.ibtauris.com

ISBN: 978 1 84885 571 7

A full CIP record for this book is available from the British Library
A full CIP record for this book is available from the Library of Congress

Library of Congress catalog card: available

Typeset in Perpetua by A. & D. Worthington, Newmarket, Suffolk
Printed and bound in Great Britain by CPI Antony Rowe, Chippenham

Contents

Illustrations

Acknowledgements

Bringing Robin's last work to publication has only been made possible through the generous help of his fellow historians and members of the Du Boulay family. My thanks are especially owed to Professor Francis Robinson, who first read the text and recommended it to the publisher, and to Professor Hugh Lawrence, Robin's friend and colleague for over 40 years, who wrote the Foreword and throughout provided invaluable advice and support as did Professor Caroline Barron. Professor Tony Stockwell provided us with the historical background.

Mr Giles H. du Boulay's archive of the whole Du Boulay family since c.1600 enabled him to produce the simplified family tree, together with detailed cvs of the Reverend James Du Boulay, his wife Alice Cornish and each of their 13 children. They give much added clarity to the narrative for which I am most grateful. Mr James Du Boulay provided remarkable photographs of his great-grandfather's time in India a century ago and for this I offer him my sincere thanks. Mrs Jackie Dixon-Payne has kindly allowed us to print her fine sketch of Robin in his last year.

Lastly, grateful acknowledgement is made to the administrators of the Isobel Thornley Trust who have been good enough to provide a subvention in aid of this publication.

Margaret Du Boulay

Foreword

The author of this book, Robin Du Boulay, was for 35 years a teacher and writer of medieval history, of which he was Professor at Bedford College in the University of London. His family traced its descent from a French Huguenot family, whose thoroughly anglicized descendants came to include a number of divines and dons as well as some outstanding servants of the British Empire.

Robin Du Boulay belonged to that generation of the family whose education was interrupted, and enlarged, by the Second World War. After winning a scholarship to read History at Balliol College, Oxford, he spent his first year in college, but then volunteered for the army, and served as an artillery officer in the fierce fighting in the Netherlands and north Germany with which the war ended. He returned to Oxford in 1945 to complete his degree, in which he was awarded First Class Honours. The many articles and books he wrote during his professorial career all display his extraordinary gifts as a scholar and a writer of limpid and elegant English. Among these, his *Lordship of Canterbury*, a study of the estates of the see and their occupants from the eleventh century to the Reformation, stands out as a major contribution to our understanding of medieval society; and the same can be said of his book *Germany in the Later Middle Ages*. But I would single out his later works, especially *The England of Piers Plowman*, as those that most strongly exemplify his fine gifts as a writer: his deep empathy with medieval people and his ability to bring to life the world of the distant past.

Du Boulay tells us in the first chapter of this book how it came to be written. It is the product of a rich family archive, comprising hundreds of letters exchanged between his grandfather, who was a housemaster at Winchester, and his 13 children, who together formed an extraordinary 'network of affection' extending over much of the world. The writers of these letters, the father, uncles and aunts of the author, made their careers and achieved eminence as soldiers, administrators, farmers and missionaries in the old lands of the British Empire, and they wrote home describing their work, adventures, hopes and fears. It was this remarkable cache of documents that, when it came into Du Boulay's hands, moved him in retirement to embark upon a book which is at once a family history and a vivid literary memorial of a past society. It was completed before his death in 2008.

As the author says, it is not a history of the later British Empire. It is a collection of biographies; but despite this disclaimer, it offers an important and fascinating contribution to our understanding of our imperial history. The letters on which it is based open windows upon the lifestyle, affections, political thinking and social assumptions of those who served the British Raj at ministerial level in its last days. The society of those who worked for the empire at this level has been explored by modern novelists such as Paul Scott. Here its inner history is brilliantly told from the *ipsissima verba* of some who formed its last generation.

C.H. Lawrence
Professor Emeritus of Medieval History
University of London

Historical Background

The Reverend James Du Boulay and his wife Alice had 13 children born between 1860 and 1883. James was not affluent but, as a house-master at Winchester College, he ensured that his seven sons and six daughters received a good education. The girls might be expected to marry (though only two did) and the eldest boy became a surgeon, but, at a time of poor prospects at home and widening opportunities in the empire, the others looked overseas.

This was not unusual in families like the Du Boulays. Benjamin Jowett, Master of Balliol, would readily recommend imperial service to the sons of such families who asked: 'What line of life should I choose, with no calling to take orders and no taste for the Bar and no connexions to put me forward in life?'[1] Thus, Noel Du Boulay joined the army and served in Egypt, the Sudan, the Far East and Mauritius. George entered the church and later became a mission-ary in Africa. James made a career in the Indian Civil Service. Ralph and Philip worked in Egypt. Dick and Mary, who were joined for a time by Philip and Phyllis, struggled to make ends meet in the Trans-vaal. Drawing upon a rich family archive, the late Professor Robin Du Boulay has vividly described the imperial lives of his father, uncles and aunts. Ever judicious in his assessments of their actions and atti-tudes, he has placed them in the context of their time of which they were as much the products as we are of ours.

As the Du Boulay family scattered, so the siblings led separate

---

1. Quoted in Anthony Kirk-Greene, *Britain's Imperial Administrators, 1858– 1966* (Basingstoke, 2000), p 16.

lives and approached imperial problems from different angles. They disagreed, for example, on self-determination for subject peoples. They even quarrelled from time to time, though they were 'too well-bred to shout'. Yet the solidarity of what Kipling referred to in his own case as 'the family square' was never broken by the tyranny of distance. Mutual support was refreshed by home leave and occasionally by family encounters while overseas. Of special importance for sustaining contact between siblings and parents were their letters which Ralph collected and disseminated round the family. Home thoughts from abroad colour this correspondence. Although a sense of exile tore some families apart, with women and children being particularly hard hit,[2] for the Du Boulays the remembrance of home strengthened their resolve abroad. Winchester remained their point of reference since Winchester, and particularly the College, had set them on course for work overseas.

In the 1860s, soon after the arrival of James Du Boulay *père*, Winchester College underwent reform under Dr George Ridding, headmaster and James's close friend. Ridding was at the forefront of the creation of the late Victorian public-school system which had been triggered by the report of the Clarendon commission of inquiry (1861–64) into nine leading schools including Winchester. These 'Clarendon Schools' were soon joined in the Headmasters' Conference by a growing number of others which were either recent or revived foundations. Such schools were neither run by the state nor accessible to all, and were public only insofar as they were open to the fee-paying public and were dedicated to public service. Much has been written, some of it sentimental, about their educational ideals, but the connection between public-school education and the preparation of 'prefects' or 'Platonic guardians' to run the expanding empire is clear.[3]

---

2. See Elizabeth Buettner, *Empire Families: Britons and Late Imperial India* (Oxford, 2004).

3. See, for example, Rupert Wilkinson, *The Prefects: British Leadership and the Public School Tradition* (London, 1964); Kirk-Greene, *Britain's Imperial Administrators*.

2. The Masters of Winchester College, 1884. Centre: Rev. James T. Du Boulay and Dr George Ridding, Headmaster.

Unlike Haileybury under the East India Company, late Victorian public schools did not instruct boys for imperial service by imparting technical knowledge or vocational skills. Rather they aimed to inculcate qualities for ruling. Thus Noel would acquire his professional training elsewhere, at the Royal Military Academy; Philip would teach himself Arabic after he arrived in Egypt; Dick would pick up farming in South Africa by trial and error. Public-school education, by contrast, rested on the humanities (especially the classics) and team sports. It was intended to foster health, character and the gentlemanly virtues of self-discipline, loyalty, team spirit and fair play. It produced 'generalists', such as Jim who, after Balliol, was ideally suited to the Indian Civil Service. By and large public-school boys were encouraged to choose a public career, however few its material rewards, rather than one in commerce or industry. They tended to be as mistrustful of businessmen who did well out of the empire as they were of popular jingoists. When the sons of the Reverend James

Du Boulay left school, they had what Professor Du Boulay has called 'Winchester-bred mentalities': reserve, a commitment to work and acceptance that a life devoted to the public good should be its own reward.

Winchester College was a seedbed for imperial servants. It supplied more recruits to the pre-1914 Indian Civil Service than any school (other than St Paul's and Clifton), more to the later Colonial Administrative Service (other than Marlborough) and 50 per cent more than any other school to the Sudan Political Service. This book shows how the 'the world of Winchester reached out for its own', passing on news or offering a helping hand. Indeed, 'old boys ... seem to have been encountered at every turn'. Phil met Winchester contemporaries at Port Sudan, Aden and the Dardanelles. Noel ran into Wykehamists throughout his time in the army. As commandant of the Summer Palace in Peking after the Boxer rising, he was assisted in the task of listing its valuables by another former pupil, Edmund Backhouse, the sinologist who years later would be exposed as a fraudster. A connection through the College with Lord Selborne assured Dick much needed sponsorship as he started farming in the Transvaal, though it failed to end Phil's unemployment in Egypt at a time when jobs were being reserved for locals. The Wykehamist circle by no means cut them off from others. A notable example of a new friendship was that between Noel and the anglophile Colonel Shiba Gorō at the time of the Sino-Japanese War of 1894–95. It outlasted Noel's posting in the Far East. Shiba later became military attaché to Great Britain, was decorated by King Edward VII and died following a suicide attempt after Emperor Hirohito's surrender in August 1945.

The Wykehamist network spread across an empire which itself was sometimes little more than a web of influence. Although the British Empire expanded to its greatest extent during the period covered by this book, it was neither monolithic nor centralized. Rather it was a ragbag of territories varying in size, wealth, ethnic composition, culture, political development and economic and strategic significance. They ranged from India, which was an empire in itself, to micro-states such as the fortress colonies of Gibraltar, Malta, Aden and Hong Kong, or the penurious islands of the Caribbean, Pacific and Indian Ocean. They included crown colonies where Britain was the sovereign power, protected states where the British were supposed to act merely in an advisory capacity, and dominions of white settlement which were already self-governing. In some of these dependencies the British presence was centuries old; in others it was recent and short lived. The exercise of British power depended on collaboration with local communities. It also became a matter for international negotiation, as in the partition of Africa, the government of Egypt (which was never formally part of the empire) and the 'opening' of China or rather its division into spheres of influence. By the end of the First World War Britain's resources were overstretched by its global commitments.

In common with similarly placed families, the Du Boulays' personal experience of this empire turned out to be relatively short lived. Du Boulays had not been pioneers and 'bushwhackers', or *boxwallahs* and *taipans*. While they had an ingrained sense of public service, they had no tradition of serving overseas, as had, for example, the Lawrences of India or the Maxwells of Malaya. Moreover, apart from Jim who had a term as private secretary to the viceroy, Du Boulays did not move in the highest circles, although they closely observed the captains and the kings. They were professional, conscientious and attentive to their surroundings without immersing themselves in local cultures. Nevertheless, the period of 'high imperialism' from the mid-1880s to the end of the First World War proved to be their 'imperial moment' when members of a single generation participated in campaigns in the Sudan and Middle East, in the administration of the Raj and of Egypt, and in education and farming in South Africa. And George moved beyond the British sphere altogether to become a missionary in German East Africa.

George, Professor Du Boulay has written, 'is perhaps the greatest absentee from these pages'. None of his letters from Africa to Winchester has survived. They would surely have illuminated the nature of the missionary project during the European 'scramble' and

3. The Rev. George Du Boulay (1866–95).
Missioner to Africa with the UMCA.

its relationship with late Victorian imperialism. A few of the letters he sent to the vicar of his former parish in Nottingham are, however, preserved in the archive of the Universities Mission to Central Africa (UMCA), and these, together with recent scholarship on missionaries, help to fill the void.[4]

The UMCA was launched in 1859 in response to David Livingstone's campaign to redeem 'the dark continent' at a time when missionary endeavour had begun to flag. Its founders were high-church Anglicans committed to the conversion of Africans, the extirpation of slavery and the promotion of 'civilized commerce'. Missionaries in the field, however, questioned the equation of Christianity with commerce and civilization. They made a virtue of close collaboration with Africans and were generally more sensitive than were missionaries of other organizations to indigenous customs and beliefs. By the late nineteenth century recruits to the UMCA were increasingly motivated by the desire to protect Africans against the spiritual and cultural despoliation which they associated with rampant commercialism and which they had experienced in Britain's deprived urban parishes.

In 1893 the Reverend George Du Boulay left the populous parish of Sneinton in Nottingham for Zanzibar. He was later transferred to the mainland to be priest in charge of Misozwe, a satellite of the mission's station at nearby Magila, some 35 miles inland from the port of Tanga and about 65 miles north-east of Zanzibar. Situated in wooded hills and well watered, the region reminded George of Switzerland. Magila had flourished under the leadership of John Farler (1875–87), and Africans had come to the station for its protection, hospital and boarding school. George's principal task at Misozwe was to build up its school but progress was hampered by meagre

---

4. Letters from Reverend G.H. Du Boulay to J.E. Nugee, UMCA, A (VI) B, Rhodes House Library, Oxford. See also Andrew Porter, *Religion versus Empire? British Protestant Missionaries and Overseas Expansion, 1700–1914* (Manchester, 2004); Justin Willis, 'The makings of a tribe: Bondei identities and histories', *Journal of African History*, 33 (1992), pp 191–208; Willis, 'The nature of a mission community: the Universities' Mission to Central Africa in Bonde', *Past & Present*, 140 (August 1993), pp 127–54.

resources, famine and pestilence. The death toll amongst servants of the UMCA was heavy. In 1895 alone Bishop Chauncy Maples was drowned in a storm on Lake Nyasa, the Reverend George Atlay was murdered by a raiding party and Herbert Ley de Ros, 'a young medical man of great promise', succumbed to 'the fatal African fever' at Magila. George himself was rarely free of fever and shortly before Easter 1895 he was brought to the hospital at Magila. He died on 1 April, his 29th birthday, and was buried alongside the graves of two other missionaries. George was unmarried – celibacy was a mission ideal – but, as Professor Du Boulay has recorded, he was surrounded by his flock and 'his altar prayer-book is inscribed in his hand with the names of Africans he had baptized'.

A.J. Stockwell
Professor Emeritus of Modern History
Royal Holloway, University of London

Preface

These memoirs are of my grandfather's family, which needs to be put in its setting.

We have been English since the eighteenth century but derive, with our complicated name, from Alençon in Normandy. In that community of French Calvinists (Huguenots) our large family called itself Houssemaine and practised various trades and professions as 'bourgeois d'Alençon'.

The first to become English was Benjamin François (1724–65). He is described in parish records as Sieur du Boullay, which is not easily translatable but means in effect 'Mr du Boullay' and denotes the place or district he came from. Benjamin François studied theology at the University of Leiden, qualified for admission to the ministry, went to Amsterdam, and from there was invited by the elders (*consistoire*) of the French church in Threadneedle Street to serve as their pastor in London. On arrival he altered his name to Houssemayne Du Boulay, which has endured to this day, with or without a capital D.

By the time Benjamin François came to England the French Protestants there were assimilating at varying speeds to English ways.[1] Some congregations, including Threadneedle Street, conformed to the Anglican Church. Benjamin himself was ordained in the Temple Church by Bishop Thomas Sherlock of London, as deacon in 1751, priest in 1753. He served as pastor in various churches in Spitalfields,

---

1. For all this see Robin Gwynn, *Huguenot Heritage* (Brighton: Sussex Academic Press, 2nd ed, 2001).

1

married Louise La Motte in 1756, lived with his growing family at 12 Fournier Street, and died at a relatively young age in 1765. His survivors were taken in and looked after by relatives in Wanstead, Essex.

It is not surprising that the vigorous family he began should be clearly Anglican. His grandson, the Reverend James H. Du Boulay (1801–36), became rector of Heddington in Wiltshire. His great-grandson – also the Reverend James Thomas H. Du Boulay (1832–1915) – married Alice Mead Cornish and founded and ran a 'Tutor's House' at Winchester College from 1862 to 1893. They had 13 children, some of whose letters are the subject of this memoir, and one of whom was the father of the present writer.

Authors who have been given permission to use copyright material or who have been helped in some way to knock their book into shape usually acknowledge such kindnesses at the outset. In the present instance my principal acknowledgements must be to my uncles and aunts and to my own father for the actual materials of this book.

First in time are the letters home by Lieutenant Noel Houssemayne Du Boulay, Royal Artillery, while he was taking part in the Nile Expedition of 1884–85 in the famous but vain attempt to relieve General Gordon besieged in Khartoum. The letters, written mostly in indelible pencil on coarse writing paper, still remain in the brown paper parcel among the files and boxes of my long-lived family.

The same subject-matter was covered, more cursorily but with some added detail, in Uncle Noel's field diary, a green thick exercise book half-filled with his own ink handwriting. This peters out on 13 February 1885, but there was evidently another diary which he lost on the return march at a moment when he was (unusually for him) feeling unwell. Just before getting back to Wadi Halfa in July they stopped for the night at Gemai, on the borders of Egypt and the Sudan,

> and to my horror I discovered I had left my writing-case behind. I had felt very seedy and had pulled it out of my saddle-bags to raise my pillow a bit, and when we started in the morning in the dark I left the packing-up entirely to my servant and lay flat on my back till the last moment. I asked him if he had put it in, but he misunderstood

me, and as it was not usual for me to have it out, he hadn't expected
it and didn't notice it, and so it was left behind.

When I discovered its absence I borrowed a trolley from the railway
station, hooked on behind a train, and with 3 men went back to the
exact spot, but found it gone, and then had to work back the seven
miles in time to start on the march to Halfa. I have lost my diary in
the writing-case, which is my chief regret.

The exactness of this account and of Noel's efforts to recover his
writings is a good sign of his natural practicality and care for detail.
Luckily most of the lost information was incorporated in his regular letters home. The surviving bit of diary shows that. The letters
were also so spontaneous that Colonel H.S. Hearn, who later read
everything Noel had written, thought they were the best basis for any
account of the battles.

The letters and the surviving diary enabled Noel to write a more
formal report entitled 'Reminiscences of the Sudan Campaign, 1884–
5', which he did in 1926 at the request of the 20th Light Battery, the
successor of his own original unit, the 1/1 Southern. The 20th Light
made a copy and returned the handwritten original which is in my
possession.

Noel's little private store of papers also included letters concerned
with his time in Japan and north China as a staff officer attached to
the Japanese Army at war in China (1894–95) and as commandant of
the Summer Palace in Peking after the Boxer risings in 1900. He had
an opposite number and special friend, artillery colonel and sometime Japanese military attaché in London, Shiba Gorō, four of whose
letters he preserved all his life. To these fragments should be added
Noel's important lecture to the Royal Artillery Institution at Woolwich in 1896.[2]

What happened to all the other letters home of this dutiful
correspondent is unfortunately unknown, but the Nile correspondence must have cried out at the time to be preserved, and in fact it
formed the model of the systematic family collection from which the

---

2. Captain N.W.H. Du Boulay, *Proceedings of the Sino-Japanese War.*

following chapters are written.

If Noel was the pioneer in a family of foreign correspondents, he was unique as a pictorial illustrator of his life. Among his effects now in my brother's keeping is a collection of some 55 watercolours and 65 pencil sketches made on his travels around the world between 1879 and 1935. The pictures are mostly small, often exquisite and always concerned with detail. In many cases they are dated and enable one to reconstruct a life which moved between England, the Mediterranean, Egypt and the Nile, the Punjab, China, Japan and the Rocky Mountains.

The original credit for keeping the Nile letters belongs to the main recipients, his father and mother and my grandparents, the Reverend J.T.H. and Mrs Du Boulay. When Alice Du Boulay was widowed in 1915 she took a lease of 26 St Thomas Street, Winchester, where she reserved an apartment for Noel between his retirement and her own death, that is, from 1922 to 1925. The papers were then kept by Noel in his bachelor lodgings at the Bridge Hotel, Shawford, until they passed on his death in 1949 to his youngest brother (and my father) Philip, and thence to the keeping of my brother George and me.

The habit of circulating the other brothers and sisters with the letters each of them wrote home from abroad grew up as several of them departed from England one by one to earn their highly various livings. In this way we have eyewitness commentaries between about 1908 and 1917 from the soldier in Mauritius and France, from the Indian Civil Servant at the centre of Indian government, from the tenant-farmer and his sister the school inspector in the Transvaal, and from the manager on the spot of Egyptian irrigation and salt production. They come and go, occasionally meet but always write, and depended with deep family feeling upon receiving news.

The circulation of typewritten copies became formalized from London by Uncle Ralph from 1908 after he had returned from Cairo to represent the Egyptian Salt and Soda Company in their London office in Fetter Lane, and to bring up his children in England. Ralph, almost absent from the correspondence itself, deserves special acknowledgement for his full and faithful copy-extracting as well as the quiet advice and practical help he so often gave his brothers and sisters abroad. Surviving autograph letters can be compared with their typescript copies to show how little of interest was left out. Family members did not use harsh words of each other but occasionally expressed doubts or hopes destined only for the recipient, and these would be omitted in the circulated draft. The letters also provide evidence that Ralph's services were appreciated. Dick, for example, was amused in September 1913 by getting one of his own letters back from Ralph, sent to the Transvaal in typed form, and wrote at once and eagerly that he enjoyed receiving the family letters and was grateful for them.

There should therefore have been several sets of this correspondence. I can only say that a single set came down to me and my brother on our parents' deaths, which exists in three files arranged in chronological order, and numbering some 800 letters in all.

It is not hard to see why it peters out in the middle of the Great War. Grandfather, who always wanted to know the factual details of his children's working lives, died in October 1915. Noel became a middle-aged staff officer in England after 1916 and had neither time nor the liberty to say very much. James and family returned from India with their retiring viceroy, Lord Hardinge, in 1916. My father withdrew into domestic life in 1917. In fact, the brothers and sisters went on working but the copying of letters faded out, and those written later and preserved by chance are mostly about private routine matters.

That these memoirs are put together by a historian might raise the expectation that they would be worked into some historical treatment of the British Empire's last days, but any such intention would be beyond a medievalist and in any case irrelevant to the purpose, which is to record the actual lives and interplaying personalities of a family. References to published works have occasionally been made, simply to clarify who or what the letters were talking about. The names of political and military leaders sometimes crop up because they entered the lives of these uncles and aunts, and sometimes they were friends and acquaintances as well as superiors. They help to frame the dramas in which the letter-writers were acting, but friendship is precious in its own right, irrespective of rank.

That said, these memorials are presented as eyewitness reports of lesser servants of empire, at a period of crucial change, taken from a level somewhat nearer the ground than that of commanders-in-chief, high commissioners and the like, and thus sharp in ground detail. It is their book, not mine, nor that of the top brass, and it is them I acknowledge.

Robin Du Boulay

4. George (aged four) and Robin (aged six) Du Boulay,
Alexandria, Christmas 1926.

5. Professor Robin Du Boulay, FBA, and Professor George Du Boulay,
CBE, at Robin's 85th birthday, 19 December 2005.

CHAPTER 1

A Letter-Writing Family

My grandfather was an incessant letter-writer and always knew the times when the mails went out and came in. Both he and Alice, my grandmother, wrote weekly to those of their many children who were out in the world, and he expected the same of them. He could be 'furious' even with those not of his own family who did not reply promptly to letters.

There was more to this correspondence than the formless talkativeness now catered for by the telephone. On his 70th birthday grandfather wrote to his youngest son, my father, not without a trace of self-pity, that he now lived upon memories rather than 'any actual joys except the interest of the lives of our scattered sons and daughters'. When he died in 1915 his eldest son observed that the old man had never really had any hobbies; but the collection of letters which lies before me makes it clear that the interest in his children and their doings was paramount in his life.

All this sounds patriarchal, the more so as the letters which have been carefully preserved were mostly written from distant parts of the world to the family home in Winchester. They are addressed turn and turn about to 'father' and 'mother' (never jointly) and signed always, with the Victorian formality, 'Your loving son' (or daughter), followed by initials and surname.

But the family and its collective mind was by no means a one-sided patriarchy. The children looked demandingly for their letters from home, to be delivered regularly whether to desert column on campaign, to a Transvaal farmhouse or to the frantic activity of the viceroy's camp somewhere in India. Sometimes they rejoiced collectively over a good 'budget' of Christmas letters from home, as in the South Africa of 1911, occasionally perhaps wept in a moment's solitary recollection of a distant family gathering, or admitted simply that a parent's letters had been, as to Phil in 1916, 'my only joy and recreation for the last month'.

The children wrote to each other also, though many of those letters are lost, and seized opportunities to meet each other, often at inconvenience, when their lines of travel seemed able to cross. They too were sad at missed mails and felt especially that Christmas and birthdays were incomplete without a sheaf of letters from the others. 'Jim is always most hurt when he does not get a letter from anyone,' wrote his wife Freda from Simla in 1914, 'and he complains that no-one loves him.' From Noel in Dongola after the gruelling Sudanese campaign of 1885 came thanks for newspapers, 'but above all for the letters which come every week most regularly and which I look forward to most eagerly'.

The family was therefore a network of affection extended over much of the world but never really ceasing to centre upon Winchester as home. Its members in their practical way wanted to know how the others were, what they were doing, even how they looked as ill health and recovery or the passage of years worked their changes.

There are many descriptions of routine life in the letters which show that regular letter-writing to catch the outgoing mail was so usual as to be almost universal among the literate classes who sought their living or served their country abroad. There are verbal snapshots of soldiers scribbling in bivouac or civilians sitting silently in clubs while they wrote against time on the same day of the week while the ship or the messenger waited.

But even though the family letter was a commonplace in the days before the First World War, this does not make the correspondence of my father's family too ordinary for general notice. This is partly because of the sort of people they were, and partly because of the places where they found themselves.

It was not a rich family but it could hardly avoid being an educated one. Both these descriptions fitted the clergyman-housemaster of Winchester College and his wife, the daughter of another clergyman and mother of 13 children.

The era covered by this account, roughly 1885 to 1917, was a bad time for finding suitable work in England for those with general education but few resources or professional qualifications. At the same time it was a society of friendships formed by families and schools and hence of connections and opportunities abroad, espe-cially where Englishmen were likely for historical reasons to find themselves: Africa, India, Egypt.

So the family scattered. A son qualified in medicine might stay at home, and so too girls who found themselves detained by marriage or ill health, but the boys after the school-days spent in their father's House departed to work considered appropriate but wryly accepted as not well paid. A colonel could not always afford leave at home. An Indian 'civilian' found promotion blocked by his very indispensabil-ity. A vigorous farmer was hopelessly under-capitalized, and so on. But none of them is explainable apart from origins.

In 1859 the Reverend J.T.H. Du Boulay, Fellow and Tutor of Exeter College, Oxford, fell in love with an 18-year-old beauty he had met in Oxford society called Alice Mead Cornish, daughter of another clergyman, George Cornish (friend of Keble), who had died in 1849. Uncertain of prospects, the widowed Mrs Cornish took her daughter to winter in Algiers, but Du Boulay pursued them, persuaded them and married Alice in Algiers in February 1860.

In the Oxford world of celibate dons this looked like the end of Du Boulay's Fellowship, but quite recently, in 1858, another Exeter Tutor, George Ridding, had himself got married but had been so much valued that for the first time the College waived the rule that tutors should resign on marriage. Ridding and Du Boulay were friends, and the College evidently gave my grandfather the same indulgence as Ridding, if only for a while. In 1861 Du Boulay was acting as pro-Proctor for Ridding, and their friendship clearly lasted into married life when the two men are found travelling Europe in all-male company. So marriage and Oxford could go together for a time, and indeed the first two children were born to the Du Boulays while he was still a don: Hubert, future medical doctor, in 1860, and Noel, soldier and subject of the next chapter, in 1861.

The family's future was bound up in another way with the Ridding connection, because George Ridding's first wife (who died tragically young) was Mary Moberly, daughter of Dr Moberly, Headmaster of Winchester and future bishop. It was Moberly who invited James Du Boulay to start a third house for non-Collegers at Winchester. This he did in 1862, evidently with his own money or that of his wife, and until 1893, when he retired, Southgate Hill, Winchester, became 'Du Boulays' and the home of all the sons and daughters who were born to James and Alice and brought up and educated there.

After Noel came Isabel (b. 1863) who married another school-master, Alfred Evans, and had a lively family including the A.J. Evans who played cricket for Kent and formed a habit of escaping from enemy prisoner-of-war camps. Mary (b. 1864) enters these memoirs as a school inspector in the Transvaal on the morrow of the Boer War. George (b. 1866) is perhaps the great absentee from these pages. Educated at Exeter College and ordained from Wells Theological College he is remembered by his family not through a single letter but by a tradition that he was loved as a curate at Nottingham, that he seemed to bring happiness into any room he entered, and through the fact that he went to East Africa as a missionary and died there of fever on his 29th birthday. His altar prayer-book is inscribed in his hand with the names of Africans he had baptized.

James (b. 1868) passed from Balliol College, Oxford, into the Indian Civil Service, and his correspondence forms the basis of the third chapter. After him came Ralph (b. 1869), man of business but also said by one of his daughters to have been in his day the best dancer in Cairo; his crucial role in the correspondence is explained above in the Preface. Beatrice (b. 1871) delicate and home-based, seemed an ideal maiden aunt, and lived also to be a Winchester City councillor. Harriet (Harty) (b. 1873) married Arthur Lance, West Country parish priest beloved of all who knew him; and Winifred (b. 1874) died young. None of these three girls contributes directly to the material of this memoir. Bringing up the rear and all at one time in the nursery together were Richard (b. 1877), Philip (b. 1880) and Phyllis (b. 1883) – sometimes 'the Philistines' in good-natured derision, yet as different from each other as could be, as will appear.

This is a family litany needed for the record and kept as short as possible. To point the obvious, it is their letters, especially of six of them, that provide the book's substance, and most but not quite all were letters home.

People do not write regular letters into the void or persevere when there are no answers. Of course the parents were the moving spirits behind the whole correspondence. Few of their letters have survived, but in a black pocket-book Philip treasured a few of them all his life.

Such was a 'letter-writing family' whose industry allows them to be remembered. This chapter is intended to do little more than perform the personal introductions required by politeness before asking the subjects to speak.

There is yet one matter upon which none of them would have thought of commenting, but which their heir or editor would be negligent in omitting. These sons and daughters of Southgate Hill were not only hard-working members of a scattered British community with some skill at description. They were brothers and sisters interested in each other's families within the wider family, and they stuck together. Undemonstrative to a fault, they might on rare occasion mock, not without irony, their inability to praise one another. But they were loyal, and they helped one another in practical ways when difficulties or misfortune made it seem necessary. Those who were able lent money – indeed gave money – to others in a tight spot. It was done almost silently, as a matter of accepted form. But the heir and the editor knows, because he has seen the documents and felt the benefit. In this way they were as a group not merely industrious and literate, but frugal with themselves and generous towards the others.

6. Major Noel Du Boulay, RA (1861–1949), centre,
with Battery officers, Sandown, 1906.

CHAPTER 2

Victorian Gunner: Noel Wilmot

In 1880 Noel was commissioned as lieutenant into the Royal Artillery after passing out of the Royal Military Academy at Woolwich. He was 19 and the oldest but one of his parents' already numerous family. In the same year my father, Philip, was born as number 12 out of a total of 13, so there is a pleasant kind of neatness that the stories the brothers and sisters could tell should begin here with Noel's and end in the last chapter with Philip's.

With the oldest brother at medical school and the others still to be educated, it is not surprising that Noel had to live on his pay and entered a regiment in which that was possible. But the fact never stopped him from enjoying the friendship and respect of those who were better off, whether officers from smart regiments, senior commanders or indeed anyone he met in the course of duty. An ease of relationships shines from his correspondence and seems to be owing both to his personal character and to the climate of his age. He may have been a professional soldier but he was also a man of peace who looked after his subordinates without arrogance and associated when asked with his superiors without fawning. The drawings and talented little watercolours with which he illustrated his letters express an inner tranquillity even in turbulent surroundings.

As to the temper of army life in the later nineteenth century, the letters of Noel suggest that above the routine brutalities of war there could reign a genial camaraderie among regimental officers on active service which created a sort of ever mobile club of tents and bivouacs. It was normal to invite any officer in the neighbourhood to your mess. It was not out of the ordinary for a general to ask a couple of lieutenants to dinner. The printed memoirs of famous commanders seem fuller of bitching about their peers than the private letters of unspoiled juniors like Noel.

People sometimes suppose that before the holocausts of the world wars the life of the peacetime army was an easy-going existence of walk-over expeditions punctuated by polo and cricket. This must be an illusion. Even apart from the horrors of the Crimean and the South African wars there was not very much relaxation for the small professional British Army.

Leaving aside the rights and wrongs of an empire policed by troops, there seem to be two big differences in attitude between the pre-wars army and the mass citizen forces of post-1914 Britain. Perhaps they are the two sides of the same coin. First is the absence of a highly charged emotional patriotism fed by the conviction (doubtless correct) that civilization was at stake. Second was the acceptance that a campaign was a precise job of work ordered by the government, which ought to be done competently and without fuss. Generals mostly had the confidence of their troops unless unlucky or grotesquely bad. But heroics were for the newspapers and civilians back in England.

The expedition of the winter 1884–85 up the Nile to rescue General Gordon besieged in Khartoum was one of these jobs of work.

It is a well-known story but quite hard to explain what British troops were doing anyhow in Egypt and the Sudan. It is even harder to visualize what day-to-day life was like to the men who took part, even though some of us living now can remember a participant as sharply as though he were in the room.

When Noel had joined his first battery and was serving in Portsmouth in summer 1882, the British were occupying Egypt, being torn between the fear that the French would do so otherwise and the fear that the collapse of Turkey's ancient power in Egypt would endanger British lives, commercial interests and imperial links with the East. Egypt was vital to most of the Great Powers of the day, and Alexandria especially was a microcosm of international society, full of British, French, Greeks, Italians, Germans and peoples from Near Eastern countries.

Egypt's considerable wealth derived from the Nile, and the Nile flowed down from the Sudan which had been captured in 1820 by Mohammed Ali, Egypt's national hero. So in 1882 the British made themselves military masters of Egypt for 40 years, and therefore also responsible for the Sudan. At the same time, Turkey was in theory the overlord with a sort of viceroy present in Egypt, called the Khedive. The country was governed by the Egyptian political classes who had to do what their British advisers told them.

Ever since then Egypt has been driven by the developing national sense of its own people. But in 1882 it was the Sudan which was affected. Here there was an Islamic revolution led by the Sunni Muslim known to history as the Mahdi. Ridiculed in English newspapers as leader of dervishes or 'fanatical fuzzy-wuzzies', this son of a Nile boat-builder was in fact a charismatic leader who believed the Turks had betrayed the true path of Islam, and who attracted the devotion of a brave and simple army.

General Gordon had been sent to the Sudan partly to suppress the slave trade, of which it was an age-old centre, but also to withdraw the Egyptian garrison to look after Egypt itself and to try and set up an acceptable successor government in the Sudan.[1]

The whole thing went wrong. Gordon had not understood the bravery and discipline of which the Mahdi's forces were capable and, having asked for a British expedition to 'smash up the Mahdi', found himself besieged in Khartoum. The British government did not like expense but was forced to vote the then large sum of £350,000 for an expedition to relieve Gordon.

This striking force was put into the hands of a well-known and

---

1. A succinct and up-to-date account of these complex events is given in *The Cambridge History of Africa*, vol. 6 (1870–1905), ed Roland Oliver and G.N. Sanderson (1985), esp. pp 592–679.

highly opinionated soldier called Lord Wolseley, who also happened
to be a personal friend of Gordon. He had had some success in a little
Canadian campaign by sending soldiers up a long river with tents and
thought he could do the same on the Nile. He nearly succeeded.

But before any relieving force could arrive, Khartoum fell to
the Mahdi, and Gordon was killed. It remained for Kitchener at the
slaughter of Omdurman in 1898 to recapture the Sudan for Egypt and
Britain jointly.

To most people this is an obscure campaign made famous only
in its relation to the 'eminent Victorian', General Gordon. Senior
commanders and regimental historians have also given their accounts.[2]
What follows is different. A subaltern's view expressed in his regular
letters home and his private diary may be thought by some historians
to be of little consequence. But it gives a more vivid picture than the
high-level accounts, it is free from the urge for self- justification, and
in this case was written by a man with sharp eyes and the education
to write exactly.

In August 1882 Noel's battery was sent from Portsmouth to
Malta as part of a larger movement of reinforcement for the British in
Egypt. The Queen in the royal yacht *Victoria and Albert* led the troopship *Malabar* out through Spithead. In Malta 18 months were spent
in continuous training on guns of all sizes from colossal siege-pieces
down to seven-pounder 'pop-guns'.

At last in February 1884 the battery was sent on to Egypt in the
troopship *Poona*. It went straight to billets in the Citadel, Cairo, and
quickly moved on to the Abbassiyeh Barracks outside the city to the
south, familiar to generations of British soldiers and at that moment
shared with other gunners and with their fast friends of the future,
the 19th Hussars.

Here the battery was re-equipped with the weapons they were
really going to use on the campaign – the 2.5-inch guns capable of
being taken rapidly to pieces for transport. Mountain gunners of

---

2. Notably Adrian Preston (ed), *In Relief of Gordon: Lord Wolseley's Campaign
Journal of the Khartum Relief Expedition, 1884–85* (London, 1967); and Colonel
Sir Charles Wilson, *From Korti to Khartum* (4th ed, 1886).

the Second World War were familiar enough with the slightly larger screw-gun firing a 20lb shell with great accuracy, transported on mules with silent ease. In 1884 the principle was the same but the order was suddenly given to re-equip the battery with camels. Not that the coming campaign was a secret. The absence of security seems extraordinary today, and as early as May 1884 the best route up the Nile was already being discussed in Cairo at very junior level by gunners and engineers. In fact the whole expedition was being equipped with camel transport for the great march south to Khartoum and the total number of animals to be bought was prodigious.

It fell to Noel's lot to go out and acquire the camels for his battery of six guns. To the neat list of the 115 camels purchased, with numbers and prices against the sellers' names, all in Noel's handwriting, he added his own story in diary and report: 'I was sent on 29 August [1884] to Minieh, about 6½ hours by rail south of Cairo, with a young vet, Mitchell (who had never seen a camel except in a zoo but proved himself an expert), Gunner A. Law to brand the camels, and my servant [batman], Gunner Owen, and an interpreter, Joseph Chepeney.'

At Minieh (now El Minya) they were met and lodged by officials on behalf of the Mudir, or local governor, in two filthy rooms. An interpreter also seems to have been provided by the Mudir, and this was Mr Mirza Hashum, the son of a Bombay indigo merchant and also rather strangely one of the principal owners of the crowd of camels paraded for inspection.

The first evening they dined with the Mudir – 'a most horrible meal', commented Noel. Next morning there was the preliminary bargaining. The conversation between the two interpreters and interventions by the others would have been interesting, but it was before the days of audio-tape and there were no clerks. In bazaar style the parties were provided with chairs and cigarettes in the town square, a general level of price was agreed, and then the beasts were rapidly reviewed and either bought or rejected. This went on from 10 a.m. to 5 p.m. As each camel was bought it was branded 1.S.R.A. (1st Battery Southern, Royal Artillery) by Gunner Law, who was the centre of an admiring crowd of native boys, with whom he kept up a continual conversation in broken English.

After buying 100 there seemed to be no more good ones. The transaction was not at all private and excited lively interest. Noel decided to go off publicly to telegraph Cairo for another £50, and this had the magical effect of producing more camels for sale. Noel's firm refusal to buy inferior animals from the Mudir also had the beneficial effect of making sellers see that good ones really were wanted.

In the upshot, 115 were bought for approximately £1,500 in English money of the time, and they proved in general the best ones in the whole expedition except for the private riding camels, expensive and reserved for key personnel, which in Egypt as in India were distinguished with red saddle-cloths.

Sir Charles Wilson, colonel in charge of the expedition's intelligence, later commented on the haphazard way in which the enormous number of camels required were bought between October and December, and no doubt he was right. Yet it is difficult to see how it could have been managed more effectively for units than in this decentralized fashion. Noel for his part was no doubt lucky in being ordered to buy as early as August, and certainly his team showed skill in rapidly acquiring the battery's transport at a fraction over £13 a head: 'Delta camels and accustomed to restraint' as he described them, 'and wonderfully responsive to the feeding and watering they received on the way up to Korti.'

In the café where they adjourned for meals, the buying-party met a French-speaking police officer who later marched the camels to Cairo with the loss of only one, which was killed by a railway tram on the road.

The day after their return to Cairo Noel developed a nasty eye infection which he had picked up at the sale, and had to spend ten days in hospital. This did not matter very much, for he and most of the battery were having anyhow to hang around while the guns and stores were sent on to Wadi Halfa, and while special camel saddles were being made in the Egyptian arsenal in Cairo, copied from the standard mule-saddle but designed to fit on the hump. This work too was excellently carried out.

The haggling, the eye trouble and the good performance of Noel's camels gave him quite a reputation. Later on he wrote from Wadi Halfa right up the Nile, just over the Sudan border, 'I am quite a celebrity on their account. Whenever I am introduced to a staff-officer he says, "Oh, you are the officer who bought the camels. How is your ophthalmia?" Three or four bosses have said the same, so I am notorious.'

In his more formal report, written up for the Battery History, Noel modestly attributed the good choice of camels to the vet, and to Captain Henry Sclater (later General Sir Henry Sclater) who had authorized his request for extra money in Cairo.

The thought of six little muzzle-loading guns with all the shells and kit strapped carefully on to 115 camels takes us back to a former age. The long slow column of beasts and men launched into distant desert country against its angry natives seemed even then a fearful hazard. Yet, with cool timing, devastation could be done by shrapnel which burst in the air and by case-shot like a vast shot-gun discharge straight from the muzzles against thick ranks of charging enemies.[3] The camels which carried the guns and ammunition were mostly ridden by natives, though two ammunition camels were ridden by gunners.

Noel himself got his first camel ride on 8 November 1884 at Aswan, taught by a friend called Marriott of the Egyptian Camel Corps. 'I managed him all right,' he wrote a little grimly.

> We take a lot of trouble with them [he explained later on], grooming and cleaning and exercising ... The cleaning process consists of taking the camel down to the Nile bank and making him sit down in shallow mud and water whilst the native drivers plaster him all over with mud. He then goes back to the lines for the day and the mud dries quite hard over him. Then he is taken down again to the Nile and pushed off the bank into deeper water and thoroughly washed

---

3. I am grateful to Brigadier John Lewendon, R.A., for his technical explanations, and also for telling me that battle-honours are still preserved in the title of the 176 Abu Klea Battery, Royal Artillery.

and rubbed, and he comes out quite clean. Most of the camels enjoy it very much, but some of them object strongly.

I have got a very good camel for myself now which was one of those given to us to march down here [Dongola] from Korti. It is No. 6000 and was ridden across the desert and back again by the Senior Commissariat Officer Nugent, who has gone down the Nile sick. But [the camel] ran away with me the other day and I had to hold on by the skin of my teeth till he chose to stop, for I was riding in a Dongolese pattern saddle, which is a sort of cup stuck on top of his hump, with no stirrups: a most comfortable sort of saddle for the ordinary walk or shuffle, but awfully unsafe the moment the camel begins to bound along, when it really becomes a case of cup and ball.

By the end of November at Wadi Halfa the gunners themselves were also proficient at camel riding. Quick as ever to defend their prowess, Noel wrote on 1 December that the authorities had laid down that the men must practise riding their camels as the infantry were doing, but in his view they could all manage much better than the Camel Corps even though they had only baggage camels and pack saddles instead of riding camels and riding saddles.

As the march developed southward from Wadi Halfa they pushed on quickly across the open plain, 'camels going very well and men helping them and encouraging them'.

This bond between men and animals was evident throughout. Letters and diary refer often to the quality of forage, the need to water the camels (after the battle of El Metemma they did not drink for six days) and with unveiled regret when they were dying at the rate of two a day from want of food as the march back began. 'Those that are left,' wrote Noel on 1 March 1885 of his original camels, 'have stood the hard times better than the others we have had, but we haven't many left.'

After a march of 21 miles back towards Korti in March he noted:

the men all marched capitally and so did the camels, though we went rather fast for them. It may be nothing for a man to walk 21 miles but with a rifle and bandolier to carry and bad sandy ground it is a stiff business, and though our men have not rifles to carry, they had what is perhaps worse, to drag and drive the camels, which is like towing a boat along a river — it sometimes comes along without your feeling it, at others you have to give it a pull, and at others you have to steer it round some difficult point. The gunners have come out in the march back splendidly … the way they have managed to make weak camels last by care and attention, and the way they have loaded them so as to have very few stoppages for readjustment are wonderful.

In July Noel was still praising his animals, though he had to report three lost at the Nile crossing at Abri:

the boats were so bad — one broke his neck, one got spiked, and one bruised his wind-pipe and couldn't eat or drink: all three good camels; but no others have given in, and we generally come along a good three miles an hour; but we always march by moon or in early morning. They would jack up at once in the sun.

The saga of the camels has taken us outside the narrative, but without them there could have been no narrative. The expedition itself could not begin to be seen as a story by Noel until it was virtually over. As he wrote to his father on 13 March 1885:

I am beginning to see what a tremendous undertaking it was to advance with a small force across a desert against unknown enemies. But at the time and through the fighting I had implicit confidence in the General and didn't think of the risk we were running.

The General was, of course, Lord Wolseley who several times walks on to the stage of Noel's narrative as he is encountered casually walking or riding about or acting as affable host at some dinner in the wilderness. It was Lord Wolseley's plan which organized the extraordinary thrust of some 7,000 troops by rail, Nile boat, camel and foot over 1,200 miles from Cairo to the outskirts of Khartoum and back again during the months of November 1884 to July 1885.

The force concentrated at Wadi Halfa by the end of November, but from then on the cataracts of the Nile meant progress had to be by land. Wolseley's idea was to go steadily up the course of the Nile and capture Berber, which lies above the fifth cataract before the Nile describes its great loop round the Baiyuk (or Jesira) Desert. It was assumed that Gordon would hold his own in Khartoum.

But Wolseley had always contemplated the possibility of having to make a dash across the desert from the region of Korti over to El Metemma where there were some of Gordon's steamers whose shallow draught and good speed could allow him to get more quickly into touch and encourage Gordon's troops with the sight of a few British redcoats. (Wolseley had some red coats sent out to Gakdul (pronounced Jakdool) near El Metemma, but they were lost or looted in the confusion.)

It was to make this drive across the desert that he had organized a Desert Column under Sir Herbert Stewart consisting of some 2,000 officers and men, mostly mounted on camels but including the 19th Hussars who had white Arab horses. The artillery contributed a half-battery (three guns), and Noel Du Boulay was one of its three officers, together with Norton and Lyall, joined later by Guthrie of the Royal Horse Artillery.

At Korti news came from Khartoum which made the dash across the desert necessary, while the further advance up the Nile continued. In the event the Desert Column encountered the Mahdi's troops and fought the victorious engagement of Abu Klea and the dubious one of El Metemma before ultimately withdrawing, the objective lost.

The subaltern's story is embodied in the series of letters home, begun when he was embarked at Assiut with guns and stores in the headquarters steamer *Behara*, bound for Wadi Haifa. This was on Monday 27 October 1884.

'We didn't start as we were told [last] Wednesday,' Noel wrote to his mother, 'but on Friday. On the Wednesday we played a cricket match, officers' teams, against the 19th Hussars and were beaten by a very few runs owing to bad fielding on our part. In the evening Napier and I dined with Ernest Floyer at the Club and adjourned to his house afterwards for a rubber.' This was Floyer the noted explorer and scholar, later Inspector of Egyptian Telegraphs and a distant cousin of Noel's mother.[4]

'On Thursday morning,' he continued, 'I was nearly killed doing range duty for "G" Battery [Royal Horse Artillery],' and he went on to describe in bantering fashion the effects of a rival unit's fire in the showers of stones thrown over him by each shell as he observed. Noel was, incidentally, one of the few members of the family with a developed though dry sense of humour, and was quite capable of sending the womenfolk at home his life-size drawings of large insects found in his quarters with the solemn assertion that they barked like dogs.

The business of war was to begin on Friday. Detailed as baggage officer for the embarkation, Noel went off the day before in Cairo for the last-minute buying of bootlaces, toothbrushes and pencils. In the morning the fatigue party marched to the station and spent all day loading up the train with 90 newly made camel saddles and other equipment. The 19th Hussars were doing the same with a baggage party under an officer and this was the beginning of the battery's long and close association with that cavalry regiment.

When loading was finished Noel and the Hussar subaltern went to dine in Cairo and got back half an hour before the train started. 'We slept pretty soundly, arriving the next day at Assiut at 10.30 in the most filthy state,' to be met by Colonel Pringle who gave them orders and asked them to dinner. 'The dust on this railway is something frightful.' Next morning was taken up washing, and after lunch the loading of the ships began.

This was done by native labour: the British officers and men had to draw rations for the main body coming up next day and get everything ready for them, but also to show the dockers where to put every box. 'The natives carried the most wonderful loads on board. They put a rope loosely round a box and get it lifted on to their backs; then put the loose rope round their foreheads and carry the load across a plank on to the barge.'

There were three steamers for this journey up to Wadi Halfa, the first towing two barges and the other two one each. The first steamer

---

4. For his obituary, see *Journal of the Royal Asiatic Society*, April 1904, pp 381–6.

carried officers and staff sergeants except the Battery Sergeant Major; the first two barges were filled with Hussar troopers, the third barge held gunners and the fourth took the party of Royal Marines going up to join the Camel Corps. The whole flotilla was under the command of Colonel Barrow of the Hussars, 'a very good little man, thoroughly practical and very pleasant'.

The men arrived on Sunday 26 October at 11 a.m., marched straight on board, and the convoy got under way at 12.30 midday.

> We are now steaming up the Nile in beautiful weather, a cool breeze blowing behind us and keeping all the smoke away from us ... All the officers are on the 'Behara', and very pleasant it is: good cabins, a good climate, novelty, no rolling of the ship, very fair food which we eat off tin plates, for of course we have got our war kit only.

At first there was a sameness about the scenery. The west bank was flat and mostly cultivated with sugar cane, the east bank consisted of high sand-cliffs with a narrow strip between them and the water, dotted with a few palms. In between the river was at least 1,500 yards broad and the ships wound about to keep in the channel. Boredom was relieved by shooting at birds. 'There has been a great fusillade all day from revolvers, pistols and carbines against the birds on the banks which has resulted in the death of two pigeons.'

The men were allowed briefly ashore at the evening halts; roll call was at 5.30 a.m., and off again at 6. One evening there was a concert at moorings from banjo, guitar and an Egyptian brass instrument. At other times the officers sat after dinner to listen to the men singing in their barge, one or two voices especially fine in the night air.

For the officers daytime was for work and planning. Only a small number of maps had been supplied, so everyone made copies for himself, of the routes they would traverse from Wadi Halfa to Dongola, Ambukol and on to Shendy on the Upper Nile above the cataracts and within striking distance of Khartoum. A few of Noel's maps and sketches survive, neat and economical in line; but even the slow riverboat was too quick to allow much sketching of the sort he executed later in his career. 'We pass everything too quickly and when we land it is generally getting dark, and our first duty is to get

7. An evening view of the Nile. Sketch by Noel Du Boulay.

as much exercise as possible.'

The officers were of course professionals and considered the work at every stage as a job to be done, with an eagerness for interest and action but without anything like jingoistic sentiment. Noel hoped to be ordered on to the desert march – 'a very hard job but worth something: it starts with about 50 miles without water, and there is another stretch like that in the middle. If the Mahdi chose to attack about noon on the second day he would probably be able to do what he liked with us ... I am half afraid they will only take the mounted infantry, Camel Corps and cavalry.'

Noel's hopes were realized, his fears not. Artillery was included and the Mahdi was not able to do as he liked.

On 6 November the convoy reached Aswan where there was about a week's halt to strain the patience but which was perhaps necessary for concentration and deployment. 'The 19th Hussars have gone on to Shellal opposite Philae, and the Marines are encamped next to us. Everybody seems to be here – 42nd, 46th, 56th Regiments and two or three divisions of the Camel Corps.'

It was made clear in orders that the desert march from Wadi Halfa would be made with just enough men to man the six guns and on the minimum number of fighting camels, 'so now we are practically part of the Camel Corps, which I can't say I am very proud of. However, it means going where they go, which is what we want.'

The halt was not agreeable. 'Cold at night, too many natives about, too many smells ... typhoid'. As the force went south the political temper of the inhabitants was naturally less certain, and there was neither leisure to see sights nor equipment for training, as the guns had gone on by train to Wadi Halfa. Noel missed seeing the temple of Karnak at Luxor because he was orderly officer, and he fidgeted at the lack of gun practice.

At least there were the men to look after. 'Our men are the <u>smart-est</u> lot here in appearance ... My servant is a treasure. Having proved himself an excellent valet, waiter and hospital nurse, he has now come out as a first-class cook and gives us the best-cooked dinners in Aswan except, I suppose, the General's.'

The gunners had been issued with cord pantaloons, puttees and blue woollen jerseys – 'helmets have been dyed brown but pugarees kept white'.

The usual army contradictions between action at the double and unaccountable delay were present at Aswan too. General Sir Redvers Buller came down on 11 November on a hastening excursion and made the local commanders jump about. 'He said we were to go "at once", but "at once" in the British Service is a very elastic phrase.' 'Our claims to go on are so very strong,' he added, 'as our camels and guns are both ahead of us ... They are sending up people from here now in sailing boats which they have to manage themselves, and an old Captain of the Boats at Eton has gone in charge of the first lot.' This is not the only comparison in the correspondence between the battleground and the games fields of school.

At last on 14 November they left Aswan and embarked at Philae on the SS *Garbieh*, more able than the previous steamers to negotiate the higher reaches of the Nile up to Wadi Halfa. With the Gunners were the Blues and Bays detachments of the Heavy Camel Corps under Lord Arthur Somerset, and together they steamed southward between precipitous rocks and into less cultivated land where they were no longer able to buy chickens, turkeys and eggs.

On 18 November Noel wrote to his father, 'We arrived at Korosko [Kurusku] last night at about 5, posted letters and invited the only three Englishmen in the place to dinner.' Penny postage obtained even in the Egyptian Sudan. It would have been enough to write 'Active Service' on the envelope to get it sent except, as Noel observed drily, 'that you would have to pay the postage. I shall have to do this when I run out of stamps.'

The three Englishmen are examples of the unflagging brotherly hospitality with which Victorian army life in general and these letters in particular were filled. The men were Pinching, a doctor who had just arrived, and two young officers, La Terriere, a Hussar attached to the Egyptian cavalry, and Rundle (General Sir Leslie Rundle (1856–1934)), a gunner, also attached to the Egyptian Army, who were both doing duty among the Bedouin. Perhaps they are better described as intelligence officers, though there was as yet no I. Corps. Rundle had been all over the place with Major Kitchener, whom Noel regarded as the only 'I' officer of any value in Egypt. The two young officers and 40 men had been reconnoitring the Berber road nearly as far as Abu Hamel, above the fourth cataract, but for lack of water Rundle had forged on with only three men, finding rainwater in the hills sometimes 20 miles away from the main road but often so bad that it made even the camels ill.

The three young men discussed strategy and after dinner went for a walk which Noel described sombrely and illustrated with sketches:

We went to the top of a steep hill (Ab Gurnah) just south of the village, from which we got a good view of the river to the north and of the road to Berber on the south – such a road – a regular valley of death. It is a narrow, sandy track running straight away to the south with precipitous rocky hills on each side and precipitous rocky hills everywhere as far as the eye can see, absolutely barren and waterless … Rundle says all the natives to the south are tremendously alarmed by the expedition. Just as the Mahdi is reported sometimes to be advancing with thirty or forty thousand men, so the English army with all its steamers and boats and camels rolling up the river is reported as being much greater than it really is to the natives down south. He says we must chastise the people who killed Stewart [officer killed earlier in a skirmish] and that very likely they will fight. They can out about 3000 men in the field and have got heaps of camels. After that he thinks we should be quite unopposed.

The scene was indeed alive with troops moving south: detachments of the regiments which made up the Camel Corps along the banks of the Nile, steamers and barges on the river moving into the more barren country round Wadi Halfa. But the Wadi was the end of comfortable travelling on the river. The second cataract was just upriver, and much of the force had now to form a line of march.

Noel described it as more or less tedious. The battery started on 2 December, praise ringing in its ears for the most sanitary camp, and with a full complement of fit officers and men. At first the order was single file over rocky ground which sometimes gave on to sandy plain surrounded by rocks which seemed to hold the heat like an oven. Occasionally a camel died, but the march was carefully planned to start by moonlight in the middle of the night and to press on at some 3mph until about 5.30 p.m.; shortly before dark, the camels were picketed down. On the way they stopped an hour for breakfast and half an hour for lunch. Later, towards Dongola, the marching became better, with open desert and good hard sand just outside the cultivation, where they were able to march on a good broad front.

At first they used Canadian *voyageurs* tents, ordered presumably by Lord Wolseley of Red River fame and supplied through a Canadian officer who was accompanying them; but soon they pitched the lighter French-made *tentes d'abri* which they thought wonderful until one night an hour before sunset a 'most frightful sandstorm came on and buried everything', forcing the column to wait till the next afternoon to start again.

Rations of tinned meat – 'bully beef' – are thirst-provoking, so they got fresh meat where they could and supplemented it by shooting pigeons, of which there were a great number.

On 6 December they suddenly debouched on to the river which had been near but unseen, and now they got 'the most delicious bath'.

'Bathing is dangerous but we stood on a rock in the middle of the cataract and had the most splendid wash.' It was a place to pause for a day and make up by a longer march later. 'I am sitting on a stretcher writing,' said Noel, 'listening to the reports of Lyall's gun who has gone to try and get some doves, and watching the Nile boats sailing up with 46th and 56th on board ... We have some palm trees to shelter under. I am a bad campaigner for my appetite is enormous. Lyall has just returned with a haversack full of doves – we shall have a tremendous dinner tonight.'

Cutting across a bit of desert in a day had saved forage in a barren district, but they now looked forward to a more fertile stretch. On 16 December they were opposite Dongola, the Mahdi's native village, but were not allowed to cross into it because there was said to be smallpox there. In fact they pressed on faster at this point partly in a spirit of rivalry, not to be passed by sections of the Heavy and Light Camel Corps, and partly to get well up in the queue to cross the Nile at Shebabat (Shibabit by the fourth cataract) which had been ordered as a jumping-off place for the drive to Korti, and thence across the Jesira Desert, to meet the Nile again below Khartoum after its great loop northwards.

Noel was pretty scathing about the staff work for ferrying the expedition across the Nile. 'The arrangements for crossing were a disgrace to the service,' the future staff officer confided to his father on Christmas Eve. 'If the staff had been up to anything they ought to have had several crossing-places and large rafts, or at any rate a lot more boats and convenient landing-stages made.'

'When we arrived opposite Shibabit we found a lot of Commissariat and Hospital Corps waiting on the bank to cross, no wind blowing and only six small broad-beamed sailing boats (holding four camels each) at work, – or rather, not at work. We were told we should have to wait four days. However, the next day a breeze got up and by helping <u>ourselves</u> we made the boats come across and get to work.' This meant constructing a makeshift wharf of sandbags and manhandling each animal into a boat by force, while other men waded into the water off the boats the other side and carried guns and stores up the steep bank. All the time they were at the mercy of a wind which rose and fell, so it was slow work, especially as the boatmen absolutely declined to start before 6.30 a.m. But next day the whole battery was across by 4.30 p.m., and so too were the Marines, their rivals of the moment. A little self-congratulation was in order. 'The crossing was a very good business, the men working like horses, lifting camels bodily into the boats if they were unwilling. We got over 280 camels in 12 or 15 hours, including guns and ammunition.'

Then it was a matter of marching on, day by day, ignorant of future plans. Rumours started: that all camels would carry baggage and all men would foot it across the desert; that an enemy of 14,000 awaited them. Yet the letters retain their optimism: no one left behind sick, camels doing well, and the fame of their swift progress going before them.

He wrote home to Winchester, 'We eat our Christmas dinner tomorrow at a place that has no name … I got your letters of 21 November at Shibabit … Now I must shave and bathe before the sun goes down.'

Four days later Noel continued with even courage, 'We had long march on Christmas Day to a place not marked on the map and dined off boiled lamb, excellent soup, rice and stewed dates and water-melon.' The next day they were at Korti – 'the only party who had marched in without leaving a single man behind sick'.

At Korti the strategy slowly became clearer. Even at the time it was described by Noel as 'the front', and though he knew no details the presence of the commander made it obviously a place of grouping and deployment.

> We are encamped in our tents … Yesterday I was surprised by an invitation to dine with Lord Wolseley again, and I did so – a different dinner to the one at Cairo: soup, beefsteak pudding, chicken, sardines and Cyprus wine to drink, – not much more than we got ourselves, but he has the advantage of chairs and a table and lots of light. Buller was there, and a very pleasant man he is at dinner, though some people dislike him much. A sailor called Tyler and myself were the only guests. Lord Wolseley was looking a bit seedy, with a cold and a bad hand.

8. Campsite at Korti. Sketch by Noel Du Boulay.

Buller apparently held forth about his having led the march 'as camels of the artillery dropped dead on the road for no apparent reason', and was listened to by Noel with silent reservations.

Naturally there was no discussion of plans at dinner in the presence of subalterns, and Noel's letter which was continued next day refers to comings and goings then little understood at regimental level: infantry going off in boats and being sketched and photographed, reconnaissance parties of Hussars also, and camels being dispatched to take stores and water to a dump and return in four days, escorted by Guards. In fact, Noel's colleagues Norton and Donaldson with 20 British and 20 Egyptians together with almost all the artillery camels formed part of a large convoy under Sir Herbert Stewart which on 30 December took provisions to Gakdul wells, about 100 miles on the desert track towards El Metemma. Of the Royal Artillery party Noel noted in his diary that 'they were the only party that delivered at Gakdul every box they had received at Korti'.

All that was clear at Korti was the imminence of a general advance. Noel was envious of his two brother lieutenants who were going with the stores party 'because there is just the chance of their looking on at a skirmish'. He ended that letter: 'Sir Herbert Stewart commands us as far as the fighting goes, and we couldn't be under a nicer man or a better soldier ... Breakfast is ready and mail goes during breakfast.'

This was 28 December 1884. In the series of Noel's letters a significant gap occurs here, and the next one home is dated from El Metemma on 22 January 1885 and starts, 'I believe this to be the 22nd, but we have been rather knocked out of our reckoning.'

It was, of course, the interval during which the actions of Abu Klea and El Metemma were fought, and thanks to Noel's capacity for balanced recollection their stories can be written from his slightly delayed letters, his concurrent diary and the subsequent more official report he put together in 1926.

What happened was the arrival at Korti of news of Gordon's urgent plight and the decision to send a task force – the Desert Column – straight across to attack and occupy El Metemma much further up the Nile. From there it was hoped to relieve Gordon by a river-borne expedition in his own steamers which had escaped down the Nile from Khartoum with native crews.

The Desert Column under Sir Herbert Stewart comprised in all some 120 officers, 1,900 British troops and 300 natives as drivers and interpreters, and it included only one-half battery of artillery: three guns with Lieutenants Du Boulay, Lyall and Donaldson. From Korti to El Metemma via Gakdul wells where the supply dump had been made was 176 miles; from El Metemma to Khartoum another 98 miles up the Nile.

The story may be taken up here from Noel's texts. On 5 January 1885 a lieutenant of Hussars arrived at 8 p.m. from Gakdul with the news that the supply column had reached the wells safely, that there was plenty of good water and that they had captured a convoy of dates and a local brigand called Alidoba. On 8 January the Desert Column itself marched off about 2 a.m., with the guns just in front of the Naval Brigade. Stopping for breakfast 'we made the acquaintance of Lord Charles Beresford, Pigott, de Lisle (whom I knew before) and Munro. We then marched on at 2 p.m. until dark.' In this way, in forced stretches, the column penetrated the desert until it too arrived at Gakdul wells about 10 a.m. on 12 January. It was a very long column and the march was not difficult except that they had to be careful of water, so it was a relief to get there.

> We suddenly turned due north and marched up a gorge and then through a narrow entrance into an open space surrounded with rocky, bare hills. Our camp was to be immediately on the left as we went in. Straight on opposite this entrance were the wells, consisting of two pools, one on the lower level to which the path led, and the other a beautiful deep trench in the rock up above and behind the first. A large, semicircular trough was made at the entrance to the lower pool, from which the camels could drink as water was pumped in. A pipe brought water from the upper pool for our drinking purposes, though at the end of our time there the demand for drinking water became so great that the men had to climb up to the top of the rock and let down their buckets into the pool and so fill the water-tanks. We had our first wash since Korti.

The Desert Column paused for only a couple of days, enough to refresh men and beasts, and then pushed on in more cautious formation. There had been few changes in personnel, though Lieutenant Guthrie, P.H.A., was now attached to the half-battery.

Contact with the enemy was now almost made. Marching through heavy drift-sand and then gingerly in the dark over a plain scored with ditches, the dawn of 16 January revealed the Abu Klea hills, harbouring the wells, blue in the distance.

> We breakfasted at the foot of the hill about noon, and were soon aware that the 19th Hussars had been in contact with the Arabs. Whilst at breakfast, Col. Burnaby [Hussars] was sent for by Sir Herbert Stewart and from that time acted as second-in-command. The 19th Hussars had come across the enemy early in the morning and had been pushing them back into the hills. The white ponies of the Hussars manoeuvring against the black ponies of the Arabs made a very pretty game to watch.

The game then became serious. It was established that the enemy were holding Abu Klea wells, about six miles away, in force, and intended to defend them. 'Our expectations, formed on board the Nile steamer with the help of the Intelligence Department maps, were about to be realized.'

All morning the British force of nearly 2,000 men advanced on a broad front with the three camel regiments leading, in a solid square formation. They halted in the afternoon at the foot of a small rocky rise which gave some protection to the parked camels.

> The General rode ahead to the hilltop on our left front with Col. Barrow, reconnoitred the enemy, and ordered the force to dismount on the right slope of a wadi [hollow] which ran in the direction of our march. The camels were tied down, still in the square formation. The main body of troops then had a first glimpse of the enemy as a party on the hill-top to the left front, whose spears were glittering in the evening sun, 'ran forward a few paces and brandished them at us'.

The British position that night was on a forward slope but in a hollow and just behind a sharp rise of a few feet which made a semi-circular parapet round the camels. The rear of the camel square was on higher ground, and it was from this rear that the enemy could be seen in the distance.

As soon as the camels were secured the Guards and Heavies began forming a wall on the high rise in front, piling up the black stones which lay about everywhere till the breastwork was about three feet high. Similar walls were made on the other faces, and the mimosa bushes in the wadi were cut to form *zeribas* (Sudanese: stockades), and a small redoubt of biscuit boxes surrounded by a *zeriba* was made at the right rear corner of the camel square (the highest point) to act as a hospital.

> Our three guns were run out to the right front corner of the defensive wall. It was very hot work moving about on the black polished rocks, and several of the Footguards fainted from the heat and want of water.
>
> The hill on our left was occupied by a party of the Sussex Regiment, but the hill some 2000 yards to our right was too far off to be held by

us, and in consequence, just as the sun set, a party of Arab riflemen established themselves at its top and opened fire upon us. We replied with one shell from No. 1 gun, which astonished the enemy and made him retreat hastily, though it probably went miles over his head. He very soon returned and opened fire again, however, and owing to the darkness there was no reply on our side.

I believe that the first blood shed was that of Gunner McMahon and Lieutenant Lyall who were standing on the opposite sides of No. 1 gun and were both of them scratched just below the nose by a bullet which struck the gun and apparently split in two.

Enemy fire was kept up all night. We had orders not to sleep too soundly but to be ready at any moment to repel an attack. No lights were to be used, not even pipes except in the hospital, which was very sound, for when one or two men lighted their pipes there was an immediate volley from the enemy.

No attack came during the night and in the darkness only one man was slightly wounded and three camels killed.

An hour before daylight we all stood to arms and listened to the curiously deceitful sound made by the tom-toms giving us the idea every now and then that the enemy was coming nearer and nearer, and then suddenly appearing to be far away again.

The next morning began an eventful and ghastly day. We returned some of the fire from the surrounding hills on our right, and at first light skirmishers from the Guards and Mounted Infantry were sent out and did good work in silencing the rifle fire from the enemy.

At 7 a.m. we had breakfast, and orders were then given for the formation of a square which was to advance and take the wells.

It was during these moments that our serious casualties began. Just before breakfast Sergeant G. Lee was fixing a fuse for No. 2 gun when the forefinger of his right hand was smashed by a bullet and he had to go to the hospital; his place was taken by Corporal W. Eaton who was later to be awarded the D.C.M. Immediately after breakfast Lieutenant Lyall was talking to me when he was hit by a bullet in the middle of the back and fell at my feet writhing in pain. Luckily for me there was no time to think about it. Lieutenant Guthrie, R.H.A., who was messing with us, took his place commanding No. 3 gun.

The business of getting the guns mobile on their camels to join the advancing square was carried out rapidly according to drill. I was much pleased to see the matter of fact way in which Corporal Eaton acted. His camel was shot dead just as the gun-carriage was placed on its back but without the smallest delay he took it off and put it on the next camel as though this were a normal occurrence.

The fire got sharper as the skirmishers were withdrawn to join the square. We took only our gun camels in the square and then at the order began to advance under a really nasty fire from the front, right flank and left front. Everyone was very steady and fortunately only a few men were hit. We moved slowly on for a mile or so, Colonel Burnaby directing us. I saw Major Dixon being carried away wounded, and Colonel Burnaby came to Colonel Barrow with a request for another horse as the one he had been riding was wounded.

Then we got the guns into action, dragging them with ropes and occasionally running them out and firing at bodies of the enemy. One shell we sent right back to our right rear at some horsemen: it seemed to have burst too far off but we learned afterwards that it went into and dispersed a large body of horsemen who were making for our zeriba with stores and wounded in the rear.

The enemy was now all round us, potting at us but occasionally being chased away by the skirmishers while his main force was formed up on our left front in regular companies with their flags.

Suddenly we saw them move and come down at us, charging the left-front corner of the square. Running out our three guns we turned them towards the enemy and loaded with case-shot. I was in charge of two and Guthrie who had taken Lyall's place in charge of the other one. I waited till the enemy was about 250 to 300 yards off and then fired, almost at the same time as Guthrie. We fired two or three rounds in this way at an enemy running towards us out of a shallow depression in the ground. The result was an almost clean sweep of those enemy who would have come on the front face of the square.

Unfortunately, a similar attack from the left broke the square's left side and at once the enemy was among us and we were fighting hand to hand.

These were Arabs fighting with spears and swords and not carrying shields. Arabs mounted and armed with Remington rifles were round about, but the mass charge was made up partly of desert Arabs and [partly] of some of the Mahdi's own men, dressed in the patchwork signifying holy poverty and wearing the string of 99 beads round the neck. Many were observably very young, 16 or 17.

After his guns had disposed of the frontal charge in the nick of time, Noel turned back to the square to bring along the ammunition camels and only then realized the formation was broken.

No-one thought of giving way. The wretched camels helped by forming a barrier between the enemy and the right flank of the square; but there was naturally a swift and bloody mêlée in the middle. The front and right face turned to fire at the enemy inwards, shooting some of their own men and camels in the process.

I came upon poor Guthrie on a stretcher. His gun was on the left and when the square was broken he and a few others were left alone with it and an Arab came for him. He knocked the Arab down but the Arab made a cut at him from his knees. A gunner, A. Smith, saw it and just managed to ward the blow with a handspike and then brained the Arab, but the blade had cut Guthrie thigh and severed the artery. He nearly bled to death but was tied up just in time, though he died, later. Smith was sent for by Sir Herbert Stewart that evening and wondered what crime he had committed, and we none of us knew that he had been recommended for the Victoria Cross until the announcement appeared in the Gazette.

I had my escape too: a man came at me, and though I wounded him with my revolver he was close by and had his spear into my left cheek close to my ear when I heard a kindly shot on my left and he fell dead, so that I had a scratch which just drew blood instead of a nasty wound.

In the confusion just as the enemy was running away Noel found himself close to Sir Herbert Stewart who was shouting something he could not hear for the din, so he asked him to say it again. '"I want them to have the musketry fire; give them the musketry fire!" So I passed on the command amongst the infantry all round us.' The second time he encountered the commander was when the square had formed up again and the cavalry who had gone on were seen signalling but there was no one to read it; 'so I offered my services which he accepted most gratefully. However, his chief signaller, Colonel Bonham, came up just after so I was not required.'

After a few minutes of fighting in the broken square the enemy turned and ran, leaving a ghastly scene of carnage. All those who had got into the square were killed. But the square too had suffered. The rear face had been routed and the entire Naval Brigade operating their Gardner gun was dead except for Lord Charles Beresford. Colonel Burnaby had been cut to pieces almost at once. According to Noel's estimate 'the square lost 9 officers and 66 men killed and about 42 wounded. Of the Arabs about 1500 were recorded killed here at Abu Klea and some 800 in the subsequent engagement at El Metemma.'

This enemy was obviously more primitively armed but was not in any way contemptible. Fired with zeal and loyalty, they too were capable of ordered movement, lying concealed, getting up as one man, wheeling and advancing. Reading Colonel Sir Charles Wilson's published journal alongside Noel's private account reinforces a picture of the extreme youth of many of the Arabs. Words spoken about their dead by English officers moreover seem to have been of pity and not of hatred.

In some manner the square was re-formed and moved on to the next hillock, leaving the guns to fire wherever they saw the enemy regrouping. 'We got back then into the square. Just before we went I saw a small-arms ammunition box on fire among the wounded on stretchers, so I did my best to pull it clear and got my hands burnt in the attempt' (this in a letter home). 'We afterwards had all boxes of ammunition we could not carry set fire to.'

After the guns had rejoined the square there was a long halt whilst the wounded were attended to. Water was issued to the hospital and there was enough left for each man in the force to have a small tumblerful. This was about 3.30 p.m. and the force had been at it since daybreak, so thirst was intense on the polished rocky ground.

The 19th Hussars then came up on the left and went on to the well from which they signalled back that there was a fair supply of water. Spirits rose and about 4 p.m. 'we toiled on with our guns in the square and encamped at the wells and drank and drank'.

That night the Desert Column bivouacked in square by the wells but without blankets or food beyond any biscuits carried in pockets. Most men spent part of the night stamping up and down to keep warm. The change of temperature in desert winter is very great. 'The next morning we were all on our legs before daybreak, and about 7.30 a.m. were gladdened by the sight of our camels coming in with food. There was a hard day's work cleaning guns and filling water-tanks, ready for a fresh start which was made about 4 p.m.'

Noel wrote sadly of Lyall, the first officer shot, whom he then believed wrongly to be dying. He had been carried from the *zeriba* to the wells on a stretcher 'in awful pain and conscious, but when I saw him he had been relieved by morphia ... He was left with the rest of the wounded and his servant at Abu Klea. His father is dead, his mother and family live at Hedley Park, Epsom.'

When a fort had been built for the wounded, garrisoned by the detachment of the Sussex Regiment, it was time to move on again towards the enemy.

We pushed on right through the night, a terribly hard march for 25 miles, mostly in the dark, no bugles to be sounded, no pipes to be lit. The camels were done up, the men short of sleep, and towards dawn the column had to pass through about two miles of mimosa scrub which was very disorganizing in the pitch dark. We were moving towards El Metemma, but bore away to our right.

At 7.30 a.m. on 19 January we halted on a gravel ridge from which we could see the tops of palm trees marking the course of the Nile about 3½ miles away. At the same time we could see considerable bodies of the enemy preparing to bar our way.

Our camels were parked in a solid square and a zeriba made all round them and a small defence-work built on a knoll close by. We formed line outside each square-face, turned the guns towards El Metemma, and awaited attack.

This came in the shape of a very hot fire from enemy riflemen who had got all round us, and to which we were practically unable to reply owing to the good cover the enemy had got.

It was at this time that Sir Herbert Stewart was fatally wounded and the command devolved on Sir Charles Wilson. There were a good many other casualties but the Gunners were luckily unscathed.

Noel wrote that this went on all morning and he was so tired that he went fast asleep for a time with the bullets flying all about him.

At last a resolution was made to go over to the attack. About 2.30 p.m. skirmishers went out, and the defensive knoll was improved and made into a gun position. A guard was set about the camels and the wounded, and the remainder formed into a fighting square to get to the river and establish itself there.

In this way the close combat moved away from the guns, which were to give supporting fire from the higher ground. Lieutenants Du Boulay and Norton in charge of the guns were able to see what went on. Wilson in his memoirs alluded to the accuracy of the artillery fire. For his part, Noel watched with amazement as the square advanced: 'it was a grand sight to see them move down steadily, occasionally firing a volley into the enemy's sharp-shooters'.

We could see the enemy masses advancing to attack them, first from the right, then from the left, and finally in great force from the front, and the square looked so very small ...

After a time the main force with flags and spearmen was seen going at the square. Then was the time for our guns, and we put a round or two into them of shrapnel which stopped them considerably; the square itself finished them off with a volley or two.

The first two attacks against the halted square were thus not pressed home. A third and frontal attack came on with great rapidity, and it was too risky to fire over the heads of the square at an uncertain range. Yet once more the square was absolutely steady and I believe no Arab came within a hundred yards of it. The attack was dispersed and we gave a great cheer. Then the square moved over a ridge and disappeared, just as daylight was failing.

Then we all turned to squaring ourselves up, building up a rampart, clearing camels away from round us, and issuing water. We were under Lord Charles Beresford and Colonel Barrow, 19th Hussars. [They] gave us out all the orders by word of mouth, and every man knew what was wanted.

That night we had an alarm. Everyone was up in a moment in his place without the slightest noise. Not a shot was fired. But it was some of the 19th Hussars' horses loose. Little Barrow was triumphant the next morning. He said it was the best show of discipline he had ever seen.

Shortly the square returned from the river and was received with loud cheers. In the afternoon the whole force moved down in peace, leaving a small post at El Gubat held by the Guards. We bivouacked by the Nile once more and gave the camels their drink after six days without water and very little food.

This position, established on 20 January, was about three miles upstream from El Metemma. The Desert Column was now faced by several situations: the need to attack the enemy in the neighbourhood, the problem of reaching General Gordon in Khartoum by his small steamers which had arrived, and the problem of defence against an enemy force said to be marching from Khartoum to attack, probably with artillery.

Each of these was described in his own personal but dispassionate way by Noel in his long letters home, written as occasion allowed and sent off when a mail went. To him first things came first, and that meant getting clean! 'My dear mother, we have got into a very dusty place here by the river, but it is a great thing to be by the river and to be able to wash. Two steamers left this morning for Khartum taking

Sir Charles Wilson and two companies of the Sussex Regiment.'

Nearer at hand he reported all quiet and hoped the enemy had been sufficiently hammered to keep him quiet despite his chance of crippling them. 'Lord C. Beresford put on his naval uniform and went down and shelled Shendy [village the other side of the Nile] this afternoon; it is a great nuisance for us having so little ammunition, as we have to think about every round we fire.'

The British troops could see the whole thing had now turned into a holding operation as they were too few now to do anything against the enemy, yet quietly confident against any attack. 'Our supplies are all right for the present; the commissariat have started baking and we get very good brown bread, and we have raided some fresh meat.' He noted the newspaper correspondents had begun to leave and thought them 'quite right'.

On Sunday, 25 January 1885 they had a church parade and Colonel Barrow read the service, and the time was taken up moving guns to and fro which Noel thought a waste of effort. 'We have been sadly in want of a Chief, and we all long for Buller's arrival.'

Throughout the letters there is a strong sense of the leadership, sometimes critical, always loyal, ready to give extreme confidence to the men of mark:

> Sir Charles Wilson commanded on Sir Herbert Stewart's being wounded, and therefore must have the credit of the actual march to the river from the zeriba, but I don't think the next morning's performance against El Metemma was very creditable. However, his business is Intelligence and I fancy he left the conduct of affairs more to the next senior, Boscawen. Now he has gone to Khartum, and thus Barrow becomes Second-in-command, which is a good thing as he is at any rate a soldier of experience.

News of the river expedition's failure to help Khartoum and of Gordon's death followed in the next few days, with sorrow expressed but not surprise. Noel's account of the steamer adventures was of course hearsay and not eyewitness like the rest of the story, but it does not differ in important respects from Wilson's own published report. According to Noel, Wilson himself did not know at once of

Gordon's death: he was telling people he thought it certain, 'though I can't see why he should believe it any more than any other native's reports,' Noel added sceptically, and continued, 'If it is true, what is to be the end of this expedition? That is the question which no-one here has the smallest notion of answering.' At some point the bottom half of the page, in a letter to his mother begun on 5 February 1885, was torn off.

They must have been wondering the same at home in Winchester. At any rate, in late January and early February some telegrams of reassurance were sent to Noel's father, the Reverend J.T.H. Du Boulay, at Southgate Hill by Sir Ralph Thompson at the War Office. This was 'Uncle Ralph Thompson', Mrs Du Boulay's brother-in-law, Permanent Secretary at the War Office. The world of Winchester reached out for its own.

It is well known that General Redvers Buller, given command of the Desert Column when news of Stewart's wounding reached Korti, decided to withdraw silently, and this was the beginning of the long march home. Although the story is no longer a build-up to battle, the play of comment on character and event holds as much historical fascination as the outward thrust.

Buller was one of the 'Wolseley Ring' – the group of officers liked and promoted by Lord Wolseley – and he certainly earned his reputation with juniors on this campaign. Writing from El Gubat, the village the British had fortified near El Metemma, Noel said:

> On 11 February we were rejoiced by the sight of General Buller. He came in with the 18th Royal Irish and a convoy. They had marched on foot from Korti, a performance for which that deserved the greatest credit. The arrival of Buller restored confidence to everyone. We were all getting to look upon ourselves as forgotten. There had been absolutely no official communication from HQ to us since we had left Korti, over a month, in spite of the fact that we had fought two or three battles and that at least one message from the Queen had come to Korti in time to send it on.

What Noel did not know was that Wolseley had been kept ignorant of the whereabouts and operations of the Desert Column for a full week before 28 January, evidently because Stewart's dispatch riders had been misled by guides.[5]

Buller's arrival at the Desert Column's outpost speeded everything up. Dispatches flowed, wounded were evacuated, lurking enemy among the mimosa bushes put to flight by Light Camel Corps and Mounted Infantry. Lyall was replaced in the Gunners' mess by Lieutenant J. Adye, aide-de-camp to Wolseley himself and strongly loyal to him, but who had asked to come as he was sick of Korti.

The march back was to be on foot for lack of camels, and it was begun by day, cover by the sailors and by the artillery, with their guns dug in. Buller, the Royal Irish and the Sussex also formed part of the rearguard. The enemy was on the hills round about and there was skirmishing and some exchange of artillery fire (illustrated by Noel with pen-and-ink sketch). He was dismissive of their threat: 'probably they are just waiting for our departure to have another loot of commissariat stores left behind'.

In fact the enemy was reinforced on 23 February while the retiring rearguard was reaching Abu Klea, and at this point Buller ordered withdrawal in the dark. Major French of the 19th Hussars (Lord Ypres) remained behind himself for half an hour after the rearguard in case the enemy should come on, but they did not, and after a 25-mile march the rearguard halted on 25 February for the officers to receive a reprimand from Buller for bad loading up of the remaining camels. He made a special exception in favour of the artillery: a fitting tribute to Corporal Law who had been to buy camels in Cairo with Noel and had given them good care ever since.[6]

This was effectively the end of the Desert Column as a special force. The Gunners' march continued from well to well: Abu Klea – Gakdul – Megaga – and by stages to Korti which took nearly a month, from 14 February to 11 March 1885, and was characterized by a mixture of discomfort, uncertainty and moments of physical enjoyment: 'some trying marches ... but everything done in such

---

5. Preston (ed), *In Relief of Gordon*, pp xxxvii, 121–7.
6. A corporal in the Royal Artillery is called 'bombardier' but both terms occur in the letters.

good order under Buller that one didn't mind it'. 'We are all wondering what is to be the end of this campaign and where we shall spend the summer. Telegrams sent from Korti represent the English press as being very bloodthirsty and full of revenge. Our feeling is that we don't mind going on and fighting a bit more, as long as we can clear out and get to some cool climate before the hot weather.'

One of the problems was personal cleanliness for a man who was concerned with it almost to the point of obsession. 'I feel very clean today after my wash yesterday evening, but my face is already beginning to get another coating of yellow dust over it. Gakdul was beginning to stink in the heat and was alive with flies.' 'Magaga is a nasty place; the water is such a long way off up a rocky ravine which is crowded all day long with camels.' From Korti he wrote, 'I have footed it most of the way from El Metemma and it has done me a lot of good.'

Unusually for one of his family, Noel was interested in food, but as a consequence of physical fitness – perhaps one could say his metabolic rate – rather than of any gourmet's palate:

> We mess entirely off commissariat products, but we don't live at all badly. Our dinner last night was soup (of preserved vegetables, meat and tongue) fried fillets [?] of beef, boiled rice, sugar and tea. Then we have tea or coffee and ship's biscuit at 5.30 a.m. Breakfast is of oatmeal porridge, bacon (when we can get it) and tea. Lunch today of soup, cold tongue and bully beef, tea and some chapatties made of flour issued in lieu of bread, for one of the baking ovens has fallen in ... We get a little limejuice issued daily which does instead of spirits, wine or beer, and very occasionally, by a careful look-out, I am able to expend a piastre or two on about a pint of goat's milk.

Alcohol never featured much in Noel's life, and, while in no way a censorious man, he had a sardonic word for friends who kept dropping in for a 'drink'.

The letters of these weeks show his mind roving among the characters and friends he met and who would be of interest at home, now that the urgencies of battle were past.

'Major Kitchener is the man whose acquaintance I have made in the last week. He is said to be the only man in the Intelligence Department out here who is any good.' This was, of course, the future Lord Kitchener, Consul-General in Egypt and a lot of other things. He occurs in Sir Charles Wilson's memoirs of the Nile expedition with a cryptic and not very friendly reference to being discovered by the colonel in a cave and ordered back to Korti, but one may equally suppose Kitchener took his 'I' duties seriously and carried out his own reconnaissances. But he was already a public figure and attracted Noel's admiration.

> He presided at a great ceremony in our camel lines two days ago. Mr. Kashm el Moussa who commanded the soldiers of Gordon's who came to El Gubat received a letter from the Khedive [nominal ruler of Egypt] and was promoted to the rank of Pasha [Turkish title given to high civil and military governors] for his loyalty to Gordon and the assistance he gave Sir Charles Wilson, and about six others were made Kaimakans and Bimbashis [Turkish ranks more or less equivalent to Colonel]; and then there was a great shaking and kissing of hands and congratulations all round. Mr. Sayad Effendi, our Egyptian officer, being the only man who could read Arabic fluently, had the honour of reading out the proclamation and did it very well.

Noel directed his straight glances at chaplains and doctors. Father Brindle was a 'most excellent' Roman Catholic chaplain who used to be at Abbasseyeh (Cairo barracks) and who marched up by river and road with the Royal Irish; but he thought less of the medical doctor attached to his battery who is 'not much of an addition to us, but a bad specimen of the Medical Staff Corps as they are now called'. As usual, his highest praise was for the 19th Hussars whom he found again at Megaga. 'We couldn't have pleasanter companions. At El Gubat when everybody else's face was long and dismal I used to go to the 19th's bivouac where I was sure to find them cheerful.' One is reminded of de Vigny's dictum that the first duty of an officer is gaiety, in the old and civilized sense. 'The 19th have been trying to catch some robbers but have failed,' he went on, 'and yesterday afternoon all our cattle were looted. But as they were sent out to graze under the charge of one old native it is not surprising. This is about the place that the robber chief, Ali Doba, was caught by Stewart's first convoy.'

At heart Noel was a regimental officer, friendly, caring about his men, disliking office-work and hating formal engagements and social occasions. He was in no way gauche and was in frequent demand for dinners, but much more interested in personalities than in staff matters, as his future letters show. More than once on the march back he encountered the commander-in-chief. '[At Korti] we were met by Lord Wolseley out for his morning ride', and 'I met Lord Wolseley walking about the same morning that we came in and he congratulated us on the job. I have got to dine with him tonight and my best coat is in the hands of the Battery tailor in consequence.'

But the narrative is more lively when the subject is Buller:

We are having Buller to command us here [he wrote in April from Dongola] and we have got a fine old camp commandant called Blundell who treats everyone alike, both Europeans and Natives, with the most perfect politeness – though I believe that he is beginning to find out that the Natives abuse his treatment of them by making all sorts of frivolous complaints which they know he will listen to most patiently ... By the bye, I nearly forgot my dinner with Buller and his excellent champagne. I got him on to the subject of Exmouth, and he then told us stories of Penrose and also of his days at Eton. He knows you [the letter was to his father who had connections with Exmouth in Devon] very well by name and knows Winchester very well of course from being quartered there in the 60th. His mess consists of himself, his A.D.C. FitzGerald, Colonel Lascelles and Captain Kekewich. The funny thing about them is that none of them smoke.

It would be a faulty omission not to convey the sense of 'old school' which pervades the letters. Nowadays this is understandably irritating to many people. In 1885 it was natural enough to write home to one's father, who was after all a respected housemaster in a famous school, and speak of old boys who seem to have been encountered at every turn. It was news, and if there was some pride it was of a cheering kind:

the Livingstone who was wounded at El Gubat was not the one in Morshead's house, – he belonged to the 42nd, too. The one in Morshead's distinguished himself I believe by putting one of the Yarrow steamboats together, which are the grand success of the river. The man of whom I as a Wykehamist am proud of is Fanshawe of the 19th Hussars.[7] The 19th were the only cavalry up and there were only a very small number of them [120]. However, as Buller said in his despatch about the retreat, each man did the work of ten, and Fanshawe was specially thanked by Sir Herbert Stewart and by Buller.

There were others as well. To recite them would be tedious unless a point is made about the affection implicit in the mention of names and games from the past: 'Craufurd[8] here with the Guards and lives in the next field to us [at Dongola]. He tells me that General Stewart got the telegram from Winchester and was more pleased with it than with any others which he had. He was told this by Colonel Boscawen who was in command at El Gubat and knew Craufurd to be a Wyke-hamist.'

If Noel himself wrote sometimes in similar vein it was wholly without a Newbolt-type school-athletic jingoism, but rather with an expression of longing for the security of his distant home: 'Cricket, I suppose, is in full swing at home. I wish I was there for it. The battle of Gubat was almost as exciting as Eton Match 1870, and I thought of it at the time, whilst at Abu Klea I had a sort of sensation of having been planted at football.'

And then it was a matter of getting home. Korti was pleasant enough after the squalor of the battlegrounds which already 'seems like a dream'. The town had improved since they had passed through it the other way, trees with new green about them, grass growing, and 'a regular Post Office where stamps <u>are</u> available and money-

7. Hew Dalrymple Fanshawe, a contemporary of Noel's, by 1904 Colonel of the 2nd Dragoon Guards and much decorated.
8. H.J. Craufurd (1855–1905), in Du Boulay's House at Winchester, 1868–72. Sir Herbert Stewart, mortally wounded while commanding the Desert Column, had entered Winchester in 1855 and had a distinguished military career. He was one of the 'Wolseley Ring'.

orders... and even a pillar-box, for the camp is large ... and Reuter's telegrams are posted up'.

But there was an unconcealed fear that any of them might be left to garrison duties in an Egyptian summer, and at such a time comments were not unreasonably laced with venom. 'The Mounted Infantry and ourselves are the only Corps that have come down [to Dongola] by camel. Everyone else has boated, including Lord Wolseley' and 'we were hardly surprised to hear that Lord Wolseley has gone on down'. But what would happen to them?

> The army up here is quite resigned to a summer on the Nile, but I am afraid there is very little zeal for an autumn campaign. The fall of Khartum removed the only reasonable object of an expedition, and no-one is at all keen to go toiling away again up the river with no possible benefit to be gained. The general feeling is that it will take us all our time to get down the river comfortably.

Meanwhile, one had to make the best of camp life. Norton, Noel's fellow lieutenant, 'bought a donkey yesterday, and we ride into the Bazaar in the evening, Norton on his donkey, I on my camel, and purchase odds and ends of things to make life more comfortable'. Nevertheless, 'Dongola is an uninteresting place and prices are very high, bargaining being almost impossible, for the people don't seem a bit anxious to sell their goods. The country people bring in milk, butter and eggs. Milk is about 9 pence a pint, eggs 3 for 2½ pence, butter about 2 shillings a pound. But they are all vastly inferior to the English varieties of the same.'

Noel did not observe that Dongola was the Mahdi's native village, which perhaps had something to do with its commercial coolness. Still, the British had to make the best of it. 'We have made an oven out of a biscuit-tin and have started roasting and making puddings which are novelties.'

This was in April 1885. In June Noel was still in Dongola but imminently expecting the rest of the Battery to join up again from the Sudan.

We have got four chairs and I think we shall be able to manage the required fifth, and we have laid in a stock of whisky and brandy, rigged up a table large enough to hold us all, and taken over three of the Guards officers' huts. You would be astonished to see how comfortable we have made ourselves; it will be unwonted hardship marching after it all. For the men we have pitched a lot of large tents and thatched the sunny sides with Dhurra stalks.

Despite heat, bugs, fires and other discomforts, there was an air of hope and expectancy, darkened by occasional doubts and disappointments as others left for the north and the Gunners still remained. In April they were 'living in a state of expectancy – hoping for orders to begin a downward movement. It will be dreadful if we are left at Aswan, Korosko or Wadi Halfa, but it will be better then being here, for communications are easier north of Wadi Halfa'. By early June,

we are all in high spirits: everyone is coming down the river at full speed, looking as fit as possible, most of them hurrying past in the wheelers and nuggers [Nile flat-bottomed boats], though some are staying here to bring up the rear, amongst whom I suppose we shall be; but we shall clear out of this by the 18th of this month if there is no hitch. It was dismal, however, seeing the Guards go off yesterday; they have been most excellent neighbours. The river looks more like the Thames, with boats and steamers and flags, some of them sticking on sandbanks and others going down with all sail set at a tremendous pace. General Dormer has just punted past our hut in a nugger in his shirt-sleeves looking completely happy ...

It is a blow to hear the 19th Hussars are only to stay a short time up the river and are then to be relieved. We shall be the only ones of the Desert Column left up ... familiarly known as the Agony Column here [contemporary slang for the Personal Announcements in *The Times* newspaper].

At last they were off, moving in late June by quick stages, marching with the camels in moonlight and early morning to avoid the heat, making a steady 3mph, bathing where possible in a cataract, 'the men distinctly fining down'. At Abri their spirits went down to zero, for they were told their halt was in consequence of the change of ministry at home, and that a new government would order new hostilities. But it was a false alarm, and they made on again for the rail-head at Ambigol near Wadi Halfa.

At Abri Noel dined with General Grenfell, 'who was here the night we arrived, and he at once asked about you [to his father]. He is a most popular man out here. I also went for a sail with him yesterday evening [2nd July] … General Grenfell is going to do what he can to have us relieved, for he thinks our claim is good enough.'

At Ambigol Noel's fears were realized that he would be left to march the unloaded camels on down, while stores and personnel took the train. 'I got really sick on that march,' he told his mother, 'and was bad for days: I don't know what was wrong with me but I felt done up and weak and could only just crawl on and off my camel.' He recovered quickly but it was during this bad period that he lost part of his field diary referred to above in the Preface.

Noel arrived at Wadi Halfa on 15 July, picketed down the camels and went aboard the *dahabia* (Nile sailing boat) where the rest of the Battery officers were already gathered, to be towed by steamer at a good pace to Shellal and thence by rail to Aswan, talking hopefully about the chances of leave and what General Grenfell might be able to do for them.

Typically of army life, relief came when hope had almost gone. At Aswan they were sent up to a fort on a hill, 'absolutely barren, a long way from everything, where nobody knows anything about us… an appalling place to live'.

But the series of letters ends here, and there are still two telegrams placed at the end of the old file of correspondence, the official paper yellowing but bearing clearly under the dates 22 and 27 July 1885 the terse, glad messages from Aswan and Cairo respectively, counter-stamped at Winchester: 'HOMEWARDS' and 'BREAK JOURNEY THURSDAY'.

'The English mail is late this week and will not arrive till tomorrow, always a nuisance as I like having something to "answer", though on this campaign I have generally had to sit down and write hard without any reference to letters received.' For us a century later it is good that Noel had to rack his brains for things to tell them at home. Father of course was always asking for exact descriptions. But either way we get lively detail: men and events, not airy reflections or mere chatter. All this makes for deeper regret that so many of his later letters must have been destroyed or lost. It is certain he went on writing, because he says so in what survives. But his years in the Far East, so full of incident and colour, are seen only in brief flashes; and when he was a middle-aged staff officer in the Great War there was less for him to say and less he was allowed to tell.

His watercolours and pencil sketches bring vivid immediacy to the written record and some inkling of lost years fully lived, but they supply only tantalizing clues. Yet there is indeed something to go on. The fragments kept by Noel himself signify their importance by their very preservation and can be made to tell their story. His printed lecture is meticulous and also touched with colour for the year 1894. These pieces challenge us to put the chronology together, not just as a historical exercise but to bring back something of the practical and modest man caught up in the great events of a hundred years ago.

In 1885 Noel came home to England and was present at some Gunners' social event on the polo ground at Aldershot, for which his personal programme survives. In 1888 he was gazetted captain, and in 1889 qualified as a staff officer. This meant he passed the stiff course required for senior promotion. Graduates of the Army Staff Colleges, at Camberley in Surrey or Quetta in India, were signified in the official lists by the magic initials 'p.s.c.' after their names and ranks. Noel's course was in England, as the Quetta College began only in 1906; he made a pencil sketch of the Lydd countryside down near Romney Marsh where there were artillery ranges and a gunner depot ('lyddite' was an early high explosive), and he dated the little drawing September 1890. The next move was to China.

Noel himself supplied a few details for the *Winchester College Register, 1836–1906* including his appointment as staff captain Royal Artillery in Hong Kong in 1891. A letter also tells us he travelled out in 1890 via Malta 'where I found our trumpeter, Wilson, as a mess-waiter, and married'.

Hong Kong was enjoyable. He was a member of the Royal Engineers mess for a time, and had a room overlooking the harbour, alive with shipping on the brilliant water.

Details of his routine and even of episodes during these years are shadowy. There was a trip, either duty or leave, in summer 1892 to Vancouver, the Rockies of British Columbia and the Yosemite National Park of America some 200 miles east of San Francisco. He travelled by rail, stayed in hotels and as ever filled his sketchbook with scenes, but without indication whether or not he was alone. On both the outward and return journeys he sailed via Japan where his views of the Fujiyama district, the Hakone tea-house by a lake and the Inland Sea are particularly delicate.

Back in Hong Kong he had time to observe the familiar figures of daily life in unhurried vignettes: the Sikh and Chinese policemen, the bricklayer's labourer in conical hat with his load precariously balanced on scales across his shoulders, the Cantonese boatman in his 'slipper' craft.

There was also some kind of assignment in North China, judging from the Safe Conduct dated 8 June 1893 from the British Consul in Tientsin for Captain Du Boulay 'about to travel in Siberia', but the questions this raises are not answerable.

In 1894 he was back in England, presumably on home leave, and here his own words can take up the story because two years later he gave a lecture, which was printed, on the China–Japanese war he was sent to observe.

In summer 1894 Japan attacked China through Korea and seized the Chinese Port Arthur which lies at the southern tip of Manchuria. This was followed by a successful assault on mainland China which would have been exploited by a thrust to Peking if a peace settlement had not been made.

The history of Japanese expansionism is not part of this story but it is the setting. The British government, which already had amicable relations with the Japanese Navy, decided to send military observers to each side of this war, and Noel was chosen as attaché to the headquarters of the Japanese Army in the field. He received an official telegram in September 1894 in England asking whether he would accept this special service, and was glad to do so, just as the Japanese High Command was obviously pleased to receive a witness from friendly Britain.

One may surmise that Noel was an obvious choice as a level-headed officer with experience in the Far East, and one whose powers of observation were known through his draughtsmanship as well as his ordinary artillery training.

Anyhow, he set off carrying camera and sketchbooks, to be welcomed by hosts who allowed him freely to record his observations and offered him both official and personal friendship.

In September 1894 there was no time to be lost if Noel was not to miss the war altogether, for the Japanese had already concentrated at Seoul in Korea and were driving the Chinese out, closing on Port Arthur on the tip of China across the Korea Bay.

Noel travelled with Surgeon-Colonel Taylor who had been appointed with him as observer on the Japanese side, and Captain Cavendish of the Argyll and Sutherland Highlanders who was to go to the Chinese side. They all went together as quickly as possible from England across Canada and the Pacific as far as Yokohama in Japan, where Cavendish went his separate way to Peking.

Noel and his colleague travelled down to Tokyo where they met an American, Lieutenant O'Brien, and all three took a train down to Hiroshima on 7 November accompanied by a Japanese officer and two interpreters.

Hiroshima was the base of Japanese operations against China and was virtually the seat of government during the war. It was the western railway terminus and isolated enough to keep Japanese preparations to a certain extent secret.

The three Western officers were lodged in a hotel for a few days at Hiroshima. Japanese courtesy completed their comfort by supplying tables and chairs to allow them to eat and write Western fashion, sitting upright. On their side the Westerners observed courtesy by removing their Wellington military boots whenever they went indoors, but staying in uniform all day and putting their boots on again whenever, as frequently happened, they had to go out to pay their respects to all the Japanese generals and heads of department. The repeated need to get booted and strapped up with the aid of a Japanese girl and emerge in front of a dense and curious crowd became a trial to them.

On 13 November, however, they went down to the port of embarkation at Ujina, three miles away, and went aboard a Japanese transport. This steamer, probably the SS *Yokohama* whose troop deck was sketched by Noel, took them by way of the Piong Yang inlet in western Korea to Talienwan, where they arrived on 18 November.

The Westerners were attached to the headquarters of the Japanese Second Army under Marshal Oyama who had been war minister and in 1905 was to command the whole Japanese Army in Manchuria against the Russians. He became quite a friend, as will be seen, and his photograph is among Noel's papers. For personal transport ashore a horse was given to Noel by General Kodama of the Imperial Headquarters. By this time the Japanese were in possession of Talienwan and other places on the Korean isthmus and were all ready to assault Port Arthur itself.

The road was crammed with supply columns and siege artillery. Struggling along after dark without their baggage they found Marshal Oyama, the commander-in-chief, in 'an apartment eight feet square and dirty beyond description'. After paying respects they went off to their own billet in the little village of Donjoshi where the old schoolmaster made them reasonably comfortable.

Port Arthur was defended by a series of Chinese forts built into surrounding villages, and the idea was for them to be pounded by Japanese artillery and then assaulted by infantry. Japanese strength was of several divisions. The battle was fought on 21 November 1894. Both sides loosed off a great deal of high explosive in shells and, on the Chinese side, in a huge land-mine, but the total effect of all this in casualties seems to have been inconsiderable. Victory was won by disciplined and savagely executed infantry attack. At some points the Chinese were wise enough to bolt. But in one fortified township, Wogozan, the Japanese attacking battalion encountered the heads of four of their own comrades hanging by the lower lips from some small trees by the roadside, and in that town no quarter at all was given to the defenders who were shot without discrimination.

Port Arthur itself fell on 22 November, and Noel was astonished at the mixture of weapons and ammunition, some new but most obsolete and even antique, with which the Chinese had been provided. Noel came across one dead Chinese surrounded by the latest rifle ammunition but holding an ancient musket.

There was little now for the Western observers to do until the war was carried across the strait to Wei-hai-wei on mainland China. The British fleet arrived after three days with food which Noel and his companions badly needed, and they then went back a few miles to Kinchou where Oyama had established his headquarters. The inhabitants were busy selling eggs, fish and chickens to their conquerors by a bargaining process: the Japanese could not speak the language but could be understood by signs and sometimes by writing, 'as many of the Chinese characters and Japanese characters are the same'.

The newspaper correspondents had now left but Christmas was to be celebrated by Noel, Taylor, O'Brien, two Frenchmen and Japanese guests including Oyama himself. 'We sat down, a party of 10, in a room nine feet six inches square. The band was very kindly sent to play for us, and towards midnight we got the Marshal to join hands with us round the table and sing "Auld Lang Syne".' Noel's Christmas card home to Winchester was, however, a sketch of Kinchou Bay, icy and desolate.

The Japanese had yet to push the war on against China on the mainland as well as to deal with the Chinese forces north of Port Arthur and the Yalu River.

Noel himself went with the Japanese Headquarters from Talienwan to watch the landing at Yungcheng on the Shantung promontory made by forces from 20 ships between 20 and 23 January 1895. His pencil sketches show barges full of troops towed by steam-launches towards the sandy beach. A modern mind will find them chillingly familiar.

The Royal Navy was also present to watch and Noel, who had got the permission of Marshal Oyama for a flag lieutenant to accompany the headquarter party ashore, felt himself irritatingly upstaged by the navy's success in sending a full report of the action home before he himself could do so.

The campaign to clear the entire region round Wei-hai-wei was fought in the bitterly cold weather and driving snow of late January and early February 1895. Headquarters moved close up to the fighting, lodging in Chinese houses 'generally better built than those near Port Arthur but even more filthy' which Noel and company swept out and were able to garnish with clean straw.

At one place (Onsento) there were hot springs and Noel was fascinated to see Japanese troops make holes in the dry sandy bed of the river and sit in the hot wells thus formed while the outside thermometer stood at about 0° F. and the stream flowing close by was thickly crusted with ice.

Noel's reports, formal and informal, offer a forceful lesson in the mingling of friendship and barbarism in all armies. Cruelty and atrocity freeze us and the next moment killers appear bathing, laughing and bargaining among survivors. There is no other moral than to seek peace.

The details of hard fighting with the Chinese by land and sea may be left aside here. On 12 February the Chinese gave in and sent out a gunboat flying the white flag to surrender to the Japanese Admiral Ting. By the end of February nearly all the Japanese troops had returned to the Port Arthur area. They were ready to advance against Peking but negotiations brought the war to an end. Noel spent the time touring the northern battlefields and even sailed to a point off the north-east coast of Korea where he was able to paint Gensan from seaward. When he left Port Arthur after the treaty had been ratified in 1895, he did so with Japanese Army Headquarters while the band on shore included in its parting repertoire 'Auld Lang Syne' and, improbably, 'The girl I left behind me'.

Noel's position and personality combined to make him friends in the Japanese Army. Special among these was Colonel Shiba Gorō, commander of the 15th Artillery Regiment (Guards Division), and sometime Japanese military attaché in London. At what stage they first met is unclear, and the warm friendship between these two stocky, affable gunner commanders is known only through four letters (and his photograph) from Shiba which Noel treasured all his life.

The four letters were written long after the China–Japan war of 1894–95, namely, in 1903, 1904, 1905 and 1906 respectively, but they throw some light on the five-year period after Noel had left Port Arthur for which no evidence survives.

Between the time of his assignment to the Japanese war and its end, there would have been no time for Noel to have visited Japan at leisure, but he evidently did so later on. Shiba wrote in 1903, 'they have made me a full Colonel lately and I am still commanding the 15th Artillery Regiment. We all got the new quick-firing guns of 7.5 cm.

9. Colonel Shiba Gorō (1860–1945) of the Japanese Imperial Army. Military attaché, Boxer Rebellion, 1900.

this year. I am going to fire practice at the place I took you many years ago at the foot of Fuji.'

Whatever Japanese experience Noel had after 1895 he obviously returned to England where he was able to entertain Shiba who had come as Japanese military attaché in London before 1905; Shiba refers to a visit they had enjoyed together to Nelson's flagship *Victory*.

Shiba and Du Boulay were thus two of a pair, regimental officers of medium seniority and military attachés in each other's countries. Shiba indeed had received the C.B. about 1902 from King Edward VII and was very proud of it. As a diplomat as well as combatant soldier he was acquainted with very exalted officers in the Japanese War Office. He conveyed Noel's congratulations and good wishes to 'your old friends in the Japanese Army', naming Colonel Iditti (Ijichi), another gunner colonel who had been military attaché in France after 1894, as well as the great Oyama, Kodama and others. Shiba's letters also refer to British Army officers who seem to have been successors to Noel as military attachés or visitors to Japan, like Captain Vincent (who learned Japanese) and a Colonel Churchill. This is interesting against the received view that Britain took little interest in the Japanese Army (unlike the Navy) before 1894.[9] So perhaps Noel was a pioneer in the good military relationship between Britain and Japan.

While Shiba was maintaining his friendship with Noel by letter, Russia was replacing the defeated China as Japan's main enemy. Shiba himself wrote of the Russians not as a politician but as a serving soldier, which makes his views all the more immediate.

In 1903 'the Russians are withdrawing gradually from Manchuria but very slowly', he told Noel. In January 1904 he saw war looming:

I don't know whether we will be quiet still many more months. Now the situation is very gloomy and dark; the war seems to be unavoidable between Russia and Japan. At first both did surely not want the war, Russia meant only to threat[en] Japan, but she came too much ahead and now it is rather awkward for her to give

9. I am grateful to Professor Richard Sims, School of Oriental and African Studies, University of London, for some identifications of Japanese officers among Noel's photographs and for his comments.

in. Japan also seemed too humble, so that let Russia to come too close and now she can't withdraw safely ... We have been making preparations ... waiting every day the order of mobilisation. Perhaps before you get this letter some thing may be began [sic]. In that case I have to go first and may be unable to write you often ... G. Shiba.

How right he was! On 8 February 1904 Japan attacked the Russian Fleet at Port Arthur and went on to seize Mukden in Manchuria and annihilate the Russian Baltic Fleet.

A year later (1905) Shiba brought Noel up to date with personal news, wishing Noel had been still in Japan but admitting the dangers and hardships, greater than those of the former war.

'I am still living,' he wrote in mock surprise; 'our foes are much braver and fight far better than Chinamen but we hope to be able to come to the end'; and a year later again, in 1906, 'I am still in Manchuria, living in a miserable mud hut seventy miles north of Mukden. It is pretty cold – thirty degrees under zero.' He wrote too of his hope for leave in Japan and of his government's wish for him to go again to London as attaché, 'but I am now pretty old and thinking what I will do. In the case I will accept this offer I will have the pleasure to see you again in your country.' The reunion seems not to have happened. But the friendship endured in Noel's mind if his retention of photographs and letters signifies anything.

It is curious to think of a Japanese of such education and English understanding being detained at the fighting front, while an equivalent English officer was seemingly employed more appropriately. Yet Shiba was asked if he would *like* to go again to England, just as Noel was asked if he would *accept* his tours of special service. We are a long way from the authoritarian postings of a world where gentleman officers had disappeared under the sea of state functionaries.

We have run ahead of the story to meet Colonel Shiba and underline Noel's continuing familiarity with Japan and north China, but it is time to go back and explain his new employment in 1900.

China was deeply shocked by her defeat at the hands of Japan and was a scene of ruinous disunity.[10] The European nations intervened

---

10. For a modern general account, see *The Cambridge History of China* vol. 11

10. Military attachés with the Japanese during the Sino-Japanese
War, 1904. Seated front left: Noel Du Boulay.

in 1895 supposedly to guarantee Chinese territorial integrity against
Japanese demands, but in reality to scramble for commercial conces-
sions and profit of various kinds. The burden of defeat was felt not
only by the ruling Manchu dynasty but by the whole spectrum of the
Chinese population, from official and educated classes down to simple
people. They had come to hate foreigners and the Christianity with
which they were associated after half a century of humiliations. The
old Ch'ing Summer Palace in Peking had been burned by Lord Elgin
in an Anglo-French expedition in 1860, and the new Palace which
enters this narrative was only built (by the Empress) after 1885. This
was the setting for complex struggles amongst Chinese themselves,
for and against reform, and – more immediately to our story – for the
so-called Boxer disturbances which culminated in 1900.

'Boxer' was the English rendering of the Chinese phrase for 'righ-

(1980), ed John K. Fairbank and Kwang-Ching Lin.

teous and harmonious fists', expressing hostility to foreigners which had old roots in Chinese history and now flared again across northern China in the killing of a certain number of foreigners and many Chinese Christians. The Dowager Empress, now aged 60, fled from Peking, taking the Emperor with her – a young man of 24 who owed her his position.

In Peking foreign legations were besieged, and they called for the protection of troops from their own countries, so that in the first days of June 1900 assorted detachments of foreign soldiers arrived in north China.

Oddly enough, the task the British considered they faced as leaders of the China Expeditionary Force was not the defeat of the Boxers, which had been accomplished by 14 August when Peking was seized, but the restoration of order and the protection of the Chinese capital where the Chinese court had left its imperial treasures unguarded.

The besieged legations had been relieved by an allied force of 8,000 Japanese, 4,800 Russians, 3,000 British, 2,100 Americans, 800 French, 58 Austrians and 53 Italians. Every nation was shouting for indemnity, the Germans especially hostile, the Russians more conciliatory to the Chinese but getting the biggest share of compensation and going on to occupy Manchuria.

These circumstances, briefly outlined, explain the Europeans' anxious concern with each other as well as the growing hostility of Japan to her neighbour Russia which Colonel Shiba's letters have already reflected.

The British were friendly with Japan, and they took the lead in organizing the China Expeditionary Force. Its chief of staff was Major General E.G. Barron. In this way it fell to the Europeans in general, the British in particular and Noel in person to protect the heart of the Chinese Empire – the Summer Palace in Peking – until order could be sufficiently restored and the court could return. This occupied the year 1900–01.

Before ever Peking had been relieved, General Barron wrote to give Noel some orders. By now a major, Noel was known as a Far Eastern expert on the spot with friendships formed with the numerous and influential Japanese and familiarity gained with the Chinese scene, especially in the north of that vast country where he had witnessed war and where the Chinese themselves had risen in revolt.

In a way history was repeating itself on a small scale as Noel was once more sent, as in the Egyptian Sudan of 1884–85, to enter a hostile country on a military rescue mission. On both occasions he was commanded in action in the old-fashioned way of friendly personal orders from officers greatly superior to himself in rank. On this occasion the mission was presumably a success.

Writing on board the SS *Zibaighla*, as from the headquarters of the China Expeditionary Force, General Barron addressed Major Noel Du Boulay on 13 July 1900:

> My dear Du Boulay, – I am very glad the Chief has accepted our recommendation and appointed you a Special Services officer with this force. Sir Alfred considers your services can best be utilized in North China, and I am therefore now writing to direct you to join the headquarters of this Force wherever it may be by the earliest opportunity. The sooner you can join us the better. We may have to attach you to the Japanese contingent, but it is impossible to form any definite plans or give specific orders till we know what we have to do. Perhaps at Hong Kong we may learn enough to enable me to give you more specific orders. If so, I will add a line to this. Meanwhile, Yours sincerely, MG. Barron.

The situation was cloudy for another couple of months. Then on 2 October 1900 Noel's task was defined for him in orders issued from the China Expeditionary Force at Peking, appointing him Officer Commanding detachment guarding the Summer Palace. They read as follows:

> 1. You will at once proceed to the Summer Palace and there take possession in co-operation with any of the allies who may wish to join in the occupation thereof.
>
> 2. Mr. Cockburn on behalf of the British Minister will accompany the detachment and you will be guided by him in all matters of a political nature but you must remember that as regards military

measures you are entirely responsible.

3. Captain Norie will accompany the detachment and is charged with the duty of taking stock of the contents of the Palace. If he finds they have been wantonly damaged or flagrantly plundered he will record the fact in writing, and if any of the allies collaborate with us he will obtain their attestation to the facts recorded by him.

4. You will issue the strictest orders against wanton damage or unauthorized pillage, and in this matter you will endeavour to obtain the co-operation of our allies.

5. Endeavour to get into signalling communication with Peking.

The task was difficult because it was many sided. It was in the first place a military command over a force composed of widely different nationalities and races,[11] on whose discipline the success or failure of British policy depended. The Chinese court's treasures had to be preserved during its absence. Secondly, this involved policing the neighbourhood in order to keep brigands at bay, whether Chinese robbers or non-Chinese interlopers with or without colourable claims on the treasures, and to keep the local peace, so far as possible acting in friendly accord with local Chinese authorities. Thirdly, came good relationships with fellow officers of allied forces. All this is sharply reflected in Noel's official reports and in his private correspondence.

For a British major to guard the treasures of the imperial family with motley allies and against evilly disposed men was an awesome task, the more so as it had wide-ranging political implications. Noel set about it in his unfussed way. Two documents show two different sides of the man. The first is his formal report to the chief of staff, written on 7 October 1900, less than a week after his receipt of orders. His pencilled draft among his papers reads:

---

11. Among Noel's papers is a bundle of 78 photographs taken at this time in Peking by himself showing officers and men of the various allied contingents as well as of Chinese soldiers and police. By far the most variegated was the British contingent, composed of many Indian and Burmese units. It may be noted that these were not welcome in South Africa where the Boer War was taking place.

To: Chief of the Staff
Summer Palace, 7th Oct. 1900

1. In accordance with your orders of 2nd October 1900 I occupied
the Summer Palace on the 3rd inst. at about 1.15 p.m. with a party
consisting of 12 sowars 1st B.L. [mounted troopers, 1st Bengal
Lancers], 60 men under 2 officers R.W.F. [Royal Welch Fusiliers],
and 60 men under 1 British officer 26th Bo.I. [Bombay Infantry].
A party of 100 Italian sailors arrived at 3.30 p.m. to assist in the
occupation.

2. On the road out we passed a small party of Russians engaged in
removing their telegraph wires.

3. I went through the greater part of the Palace, as soon as I arrived,
with Capt. Norie and Mr. Cockburn.

4. The main buildings are as follows:

   1. The Reception room and side rooms near the entrance

   2. A Reception room between No. 1 and the lake

   3. The Dowager Empress's apartments

   4. The Emperor's apartments

   5. The Theatre the Entrance

   6. The small theatre (or similar building) West of No. 4.

5. We found all these buildings, as well as other less important ones,
completely swept of small ornaments, hundreds of small stands
being left which presumably had each held a small object such as a
vase or piece of jade. In many cases small screens, clocks, artificial
flowers etc. had been damaged by the removal of inlaid pieces of
jade, etc. In all the rooms, I think without exception, were boxes in
which were roughly packed a number of articles such as porcelain
vases and bronzes. These were in many cases packed together in
the same boxes, and as a consequence much of the porcelain was
broken.

6. The Dowager Empress's sleeping apartment was in utter

confusion and had been completely ransacked; and apart from the clean sweep of everything portable there were more signs of wanton damage in the two theatres and in the corner building close to the water, west of No. 6, than in the other buildings.

7. Almost all the buildings were closed and sealed with a Russian seal.

8. There were a few Chinamen in the Palace who stated that they had been sent in that day, to take charge, by the man to whom the Russians had handed over the Palace.

9. The British troops occupied buildings at the Entrance, and others on the east side of the lake; the Italians occupied No. 2 on the 3rd, and moved into No. 3 on the 4th instant, and I then withdrew the British police from No. 3 asking the Italian officer in command to prevent all wanton damage as far as he possibly could.

10. As there was difficulty on the 4th instant in efficiently policing the whole of the Palace, I gave orders that all the porcelains etc. left in the various buildings should he collected together; and the Italians began collecting in No. 3, whilst we collected in No. 1.

11. Since our joint occupation some of the clocks to be found in many of the rooms have been wantonly damaged, and I regret that I did not become aware that this was happening until too late. A more serious matter is that one panel of the screen behind the throne has been damaged either wilfully or by gross carelessness, and I sincerely wish I could discover how it happened. Beyond this, I think, there has been no damage done since our occupation though the rooms look very bare in consequence of the removal of the ornaments.

Summer Palace	N.W.H. Du Boulay, Major
7th Oct. 1900	Commanding at Summer Palace

So much for the official report sent to the expedition's headquarters in Peking.

But Noel continued no less than in the desert to write family letters, and, luckily, one survives to make a human contrast with the report, for on 4 November 1900 he wrote as he would always have done to wish a happy birthday to his elder brother Hubert, a medical practitioner in England. From the Summer Palace he said:

My dear Hubert – Many happy returns of your birthday ... You have I hope seen letters from me, and are aware that I am a sort of Governor of the Summer Palace with a detachment of British and Italian troops under my command. I should much like to get rid of the latter: they worry the natives in the villages round, are always trying to pull the buildings in the Palace to pieces, and are very unsanitary is their habits: but when we came out here a month ago it was, I suppose, thought right to ask the other allies if they would co-operate with us; though that again, I fancy, arose from a desire to make nasty remarks to the Russians and to have someone on our side in the matter. The Russians have of course behaved with very bad faith over and over again, and came in here originally contrary to their agreement with the other allies, who were most of them successively annoyed – especially as the Russians thus secured some very fine loot.

We have got a party of Sappers over here now, engaged in removing some electric light engines which they hope to be able to utilize for light locomotives on the railway. The railway is being repaired from this end by the Japs and ourselves and from the other end by the Germans and Russians (at least I think that is the arrangement) but at this end there is no rolling stock whatever except some wheels and axles, and they cannot therefore run the smallest construction train to assist in the work.

We had a visit from the Field Marshal, Count von Waldersee, some days ago. He himself and all his staff speak English very well, so we had no difficulty in the matter of conversation. He was very 'affable' and pressed me to come to lunch or dinner whenever I felt inclined. But I go into Peking very seldom. Last time I lunched with Sir E. Satow whom of course I knew very well in Japan. He was to have come out here last night to dine and sleep, but postponed his visit for a few days. The ministers are all at work at negotiations, but I suppose nothing definite will be settled for weeks or months.

The villages round here are gradually settling down to peaceful pursuits – they have been dreadfully harried, and when we first came out here they all used to take to their heels as soon as we were seen approaching. Now we are on very good terms with those close to us, whilst the more distant ones, who have not been harried, only seem to be afraid of our capturing their mules and ponies. The inhabitants are chiefly Bannermen, i.e., members of the old Manchurian army, and not therefore the best of peasants, and they have been doing a good deal in the way of looting one another.

Reuter's telegrams have at last been started in Peking, and as I have subscribed to them I got them today for the first time. We also today have started fish for dinner. There are plenty of fish in the lake but we had no means of catching them; however, we have now found two Chinamen with long four-pronged spears who understand the job. As far as I can tell I shall have to remain out here for the winter, but plans are so liable to be upset that one never knows. Yours ever, Noel H. Du Boulay.

It is a great pity that Noel's other letters from this period are lost. But he himself kept a few key documents among his own most personal possessions, presumably as a reminder of interesting times and specimens of the type of work with which he was faced.

The keeping of local order was an important duty. A nearby village sent Noel a petition written in Chinese by 13 leading men, which was translated by someone in Noel's office:

Graciously appoint soldiers to manage the affairs of quietly holding the place around Men Tou. Now there are bandits, Wen Hua Chang, Wu Li Tang, Ho Hsui Feng etc. [who] collect many men to assume (?) the private security office of the German interpreters, forging printed letters in each village, unscrupulously to enforce subscriptions, planning to defraud (or blackmail) people to do all kinds of illegal doings.

We proclaim in this village [that] we are establishing a Pacification of the People office. These brigands desire to gather together many people to destroy (?) the office, to pluck out their enemy's flag; truly [they?] belong to those who despise the law, so ordinary people will meet with great harm if some kind of method of curing this iniquity [is not found?].

So then we beg the great ones graciously quickly [to] appoint soldiers to deal with this, that officials and people will be for ever grateful.

This incident, or one like it, must have occurred soon after Noel had assumed command, for on 11 November 1900 he reported crisply to the chief of staff:

I have carefully inquired into the accompanying complaint. The man Li was taken prisoner by a party of the 7th Rajputs under Captain Parr, acting I believe under your instructions, on 20 October. But the chief men in Haidien state that his abduction has not affected the village generally in any way whatever, that no insurance or ransom has been demanded by anyone, and that the villagers have no fear of a house-to-house search being made by us. They think that the complaint or petition must have been written by a friend or relation of the man Li; but they themselves do not understand why he was made a prisoner as, so far as they knew, he was a peaceable resident. He belongs, however, to a class above them, and they know little of his dealings outside Haidien.

I inquired whether any of Li's relations were now in Haidien, but was told there were none.

As regards the complaint that Indian troops had 'harassed them to a still greater extent' and 'proceeded to ravish' the women, the villagers state there is no truth whatever in it.

I may add that we are on very good terms with the people of the village, and that a small civil police force has been established there, the members of which wear a uniform bearing the Union Jack on the left breast.
N.W.H. Du Boulay, Major R.A. Commanding at Summer Palace.

No more is heard of these particular complaints. But peacekeeping action continued, and on 24 January 1901 an official of the Chinese regent in Peking, Prince Chang, wrote to Noel:

Dear Major Du Boulay, – The seven prisoners that were captured and sent here we have received through the British Legation and put in jail. The Prince Ching directed me to thank you for your kindness.

As lately the Prince received two petitions from the natives of the Summer Palace district, I showed them to Mr. Jamieson [British Legation]; he wanted me to send them to you, therefore I wrote out their general meaning and now forward them to you and hope you will be kind enough to look them over and decide how to act.

Yours truly, T.J. Chang.

In the bundle of papers are a few Chinese letters containing confessions of robbers, but the judicial function was not Noel's. His work was clearly defined as the keeping of peace and order. In that connection there is a specimen of a local police identity card and authority, handwritten on British government paper: 'Kow, residing in Haidien, is authorized by me to maintain order in the village of Haidien', signed by Noel Du Boulay and stamped by 'Her Britannic Majesty's Legation, Peking'.

Turning from the problems of peacekeeping in the district, we become aware that a different kind of tact was needed in dealing with important allies. It so happens that Noel preserved four communications he received, respectively from an American, German, Russian and French sender. In a way they seem so appropriate to the nationalities concerned that the reader finds himself wondering if they were kept as souvenirs as a sort of private joke. Still they have some historical interest in their own right.

On 8 October 1900 the British Legation requested Noel to allow His Excellency Mr Congar, American Minister, and his party to see the art treasures collected in the throne room and let them view the rest of the Palace, and the request was accompanied by the visiting card of Mr Edwin C. Congar, Envoy Extraordinary and Minister Plenipotentiary of the United States of America.

About the same time there arrived a long and formal letter in German from General von Hoepfner requesting the return of a vase bearing the German Emperor's likeness, which he knew to be still in the Summer Palace, and also if possible a rococo clock, both being presents from the German to the Chinese Emperor. As these were believed to be in the Italian portion of the Palace it was thought they might perhaps be obtained through the Ministers. The British Staff

EQ asked Major Du Boulay to comply if practicable with General von Hoepfner's wishes.

The third letter has its amusing side in the light of the Russians' alleged past dealings with the Summer Palace, coming as it does from high diplomatic level:

> My Chief and Mme. de Giers are organizing a pic-nic to the Summer Palace to-day and send out their boys before-hand to arrange the tiffin. Will you kindly indicate them or allow them to choose a suitable place to prepare all that is necessary?
>
> Yours sincerely, B. Kroupensky.

This is accompanied by a paper written roughly in pencilled Russian, perhaps a copy of the official request from which the translation was made in the Russian Legation.

Finally the French with Gallic wit addressed

> The Physician to English Forces, Summer Palace, – I would be much obliged if you could supply me with a little citrate of magnesia to purge three of my soldiers who have eaten too much.
>
> Yours sincerely E.S. Mariez, Captain.

> [*À Monsieur le Médecin des troupes anglaises, Palais d'Été – Je vous serais bien obligé si vous pouvez me donner un peu de cedrat de magnesie pour purger trois de mes soldats, qui ont mangé trop. Votre Dévoué E.S. Mariez, Capitaine.*]

Such were the joys. Whatever the mutual suspicion between their governments there was camaraderie among the military officers on the spot. They smile from the group photographs at Noel behind the lens, and they exchanged portrait shots, signed sometimes with nick-names.

Noel's dislike of the Italian troops did not result in their removal, and the first hint of the foreign withdrawal came from the Italian side when on 8 July 1901 General Stephen Gaselee, commander of the British contingent of the China Expeditionary Force, wrote to Noel: 'My dear Du Boulay, – Col. Garioni informs me that he expects to withdraw his troops from the Summer Palace before long.

I am suggesting 1 August or other convenient date for a simultaneous withdrawal of both our detachments and handing over to the Chinese officials. I hope you will have everything ready on our part.' General Gaselee went on to explain how everything must he done with great formality, with all receipts taken and handed to the British minister. Noel himself was to remain till last.

In the previous few days he had received a mysterious letter from a British official to say that a Chinese agent – 'bright and intelligent' – would visit him on 6 July 'to talk over the future arrangements you referred to on Friday evening', and would be accompanied by a British interpreter. This must refer to the handing over of the Palace and authority to the Chinese.

It was all done in best order. Noel's final report was a model of precision and gives the facts well enough:

> I have the honour to report that I handed over the British part of the Summer Palace yesterday to the Chinese official Shih Hsü, President of the Board of Ceremonies and Comptroller of the Imperial Household, who was accompanied by Hu Yü Fen, Assistant to Prince Ching on the Commission for the Restoration of Order.

> Mr C.A. Campbell, acting Chinese Secretary of the British Legation, was present, and made all the arrangements with the Chinese.

> With the assistance of Mr Backhouse I have prepared a list of the articles of value left in the Palace, and this we handed to Shih Hsü who, after checking it, formally accepted it as correct. Copies are in the possession of the British Minister, who will forward one to the Chinese Foreign Office.

> A strong company of Chinese infantry belonging to the force at Ching Ho was drawn up outside the gate of the Palace and presented arms as we marched away at 2 p.m.

> I would wish to record that during the time I have been at the Summer Palace, namely, from 3rd. October 1900 to 16 March 1901, and from 15 June to 14 September 1901, I have not had a single complaint from the Chinese living in the neighbourhood against any soldier, British or Native, of the Garrison, and in only two cases have there been complaints against followers.

In the draft report from which this is taken a sentence at the end was crossed out by the writer: 'The garrison has been small but it has been very frequently changed, and upwards of 1000 men have been ...'

Exactly which troops formed the British or other detachments in the Palace is uncertain, but a note of 17 August 1901 mentions stores required for British troops on duty there and names them as the 16th Bengal Lancers, the 7th Rajputs and the Royal Welch Fusiliers. All these feature in Noel's large collection of photographs.

The imperial treasures of porcelain, now presumably those in Taiwan, were indeed listed in Noel's hand, ink written but much emended in pencil, covering some 30 foolscap sheets and giving amateurish descriptions of the pieces, dynasty by dynasty, from the fifteenth century onwards. It was an unlikely piece of staff work for a Gunner Major.

Soon after this Noel left the Far East. He was at Portsmouth during 1904–06, but his letters are not extant until the family copy-extracts begin in 1908. That year saw him take up command of the artillery garrison in Mauritius in the Indian Ocean, where he remained until autumn 1911.

Perhaps what follows will seem like an anti-climax after the Desert Column and the colour of Peking. Questions about him tumble over one another in the mind. Was he passed over for earlier promotion? A rapid ascent might have been guessed for an efficient young officer liked by the great Lord Wolseley and others. Yet his confidential work in Japan and China gave him responsibilities we know only partly. In a later letter he admits too to having refused one staff appointment after another.

Behind the career pattern there is another Noel, no less interesting than more dashing figures. Like his brother Jim, to be met in the next chapter, he was trusted. The confidence given by others was greater than the confidence these men had in themselves. In a way they feared important social functions more than bullets. On the other hand, the career continues to display a character of genial worth, and also to illustrate a service of empire not much noticed in the conventionally glamorous or denigrating accounts.

Noel sailed for Mauritius in the SS *Guelph* and had arrived at the port of Beira, Mozambique, by 5 September 1908, when he wrote home to say he had managed to get briefly to Pretoria and had also admired the beauty of Lourenço Marques with its harbour and red sandy cliff. He took a lot of trouble to get a glimpse of his sister Mary in the Transvaal, though she said slightly ungracefully that he'd come ashore for the sake of lawn tennis. But they met gladly, and that was typical of the family.

By 23 September Noel was in Mauritius to take up his command as colonel of artillery, and he wrote back at once to his brother Ralph with birthday wishes and thanks for the typewritten copies of family letters.

His comments on Mauritius need a word about background. The island had been taken by the British from the French in 1810, during the Napoleonic Wars, and was used as a base for guarding the sea routes from Suez, the Persian Gulf, South Africa, Ceylon and India. Its permanent inhabitants were descendants of Indians and Africans brought in to work on the sugar-cane plantations. They spoke a kind of French and lived in poor conditions mainly in the coastal capital of Port Louis and also in other small towns and villages.

History apart, it was not the kind of place to appeal to a British officer obsessed with personal cleanliness and fitness. But then, few foreign postings in those days could have been to places where the British could find both love and shower-baths.

I am at present living in a so-called Hotel at a place called Curepipe, 1800 feet above sea-level, but I hope in a day or two to go into quarters near our Mess, as the artillery have just moved up today from Port Louis for the hot weather … The objection to Port Louis in my mind is its dirt. How a place which has been nominally under British rule for almost 100 years has continued to be so dirty and untidy and dilapidated I cannot understand; but I suppose the Governor [12] has to act according to the wishes of his legislative

12. The Governor, George Smith, later Sir George and Governor of Nyasaland (Malawi). He and Noel became good friends.

council, and if local gossip is true there is a great deal of corruption amongst the elected legislators, – but local gossip may be libellous.

Two weeks later he told his sister Bee in Winchester:

> I believe Mauritius is about five times the size of the Isle of Wight … I have been moving about a bit by train, horse and motor-car … I had to dine with the Governor the other day and was fortunate in getting a lift to his house in a motor, for he lives in an out-of-the-way place. I have been dining out much too often but hope I have come to a halt in that respect … I have bought a Raleigh bicycle to convey me to dinner-parties. I also have a Government horse useful for transport purposes, but the whole country is so rocky that one can't get the proper enjoyment of riding.

In this way Noel's simple lifestyle emerges from the letters, surprising to anyone who imagines a regimental commander in a crown colony under King Edward VII to have lived amid waving ostrich plumes and fine carriages. On the contrary, what he longed for and got was the tenure of a small house with a garden which would supply his rooms with roses. But that would be only for a quiet base. On duty he had to be everywhere.

There was plague round the native artillery barracks at Port Louis, 'a dreadfully insanitary place', but up at Curepipe good lawn tennis and some cricket. News was of ships' arrivals and departures, of gun-practice with wooden dummies and live ammunition, and of his own injured knee which took away chances of games and was to trouble him for some time. It did not stop Noel from reconnoitring the country and doing his job. Gun-practice was a good and sufficient excuse to be let off the levee for the King's birthday. On that day there were races organized by the Turf Club 'or possibly the Jockey Club which is a deadly rival … I looked on for a short time and then took a little walking exercise instead. I had an idea of learning some French here, but hitherto have had no part of a day which I could keep for the purpose.'

The question arises whether Noel's dislike of anything in the nature of 'society' life was occasioned by lack of private means or by family temperament. Probably it was both. His pay did not go far,

11. Cricket team in Mauritius.

and the young subaltern whom senior officers had once liked to invite never turned into a public man with figure and desire to impress the *beau monde*. 'That comic little man', a shipboard lady acquaintance once called the colonel, not without affection. Another time Mary, whose tongue was as keen as her eye, burst out with exasperation at Du Boulay reticence and shyness of parties and engagements, all the worse she thought because once there Du Boulays seemed to acquit themselves with verve. Yet it would be vain to suppose a unique family curse. Perhaps for Englishmen a natural enjoyment of social-izing is the rarer quality. In this memoir it is interesting only as a way of drawing character and of understanding these Winchester-bred mentalities which again and again insisted that enjoyment was not work and that work was what justified pay. 'I am an idler just now [November 1908] – all work seems to have come to an end for the present, so I have been getting through [social] calls.'

But work when it came could be welcome if it was regimental, not boring office stuff, like the board of inquiry he had to conduct into riots which had occurred on the island. To Noel the sharp point of interest was work that bore on the characters of men: the way natives cut grass so short with scythes, not the civilities of tennis on the lawn; the fresh drafts of men for artillery and infantry, not abstract rights and wrongs worked out on paper. 'I have just dressed my syce up in a dark-blue native costume with brass buttons and a khaki pugga-ree and kumerbund [head and waist bands] and he is quite proud of himself.' The phrases recall those long before when he described his gunners' battle dress as they rode southward from Wadi Halfa into action.

Undoubtedly Mauritius was rather boring. It was not unknown for officers in transit to refuse shore leave there in sheer dislike of the place. Noel's thoughts were already dwelling on some place in or near Winchester to spend leaves and ultimately retirement, the more urgently as the army of those days placed lieutenant colonels who had served a certain time on half-pay retirement until or unless room could he found to promote them. In 1908 Noel was 47, and the army was not expanding.

There was leave from January to June in 1909, to have the knee treated, and back to work round the Cape, bored with his first-class co-passengers except for a traveller in Nottingham lace who seemed to be able to describe how something worked. Back in Mauritius 'the trippers from South Africa have gone', he observed sourly, 'complain-ing they wouldn't give kaffirs the accommodation ... They are mostly well-to-do people who live in the lap of luxury in Johannesburg [and] possibly a little roughing it did them no harm.'

The island had its episodes of colour and animation. 'Saturday is the great day of Mauritius. All the ladies of whatever colour or shade come to the races in their best clothes, and they say the Indians dress themselves up magnificently. It is a very pretty course, rather like the one at Hong Kong, but the racing indifferent. There are very few horses in the island and they have to reappear constantly.'

Noel as a soldier was clubbable, not the snarling and solitary type of commanding officer, and at this point he proposed to move from his private quarters into barracks at Curepipe to help keep the mess going, 'for besides myself there are only 3 bachelors, all subalterns'. He was sad to see that General Creagh, who with Mrs Creagh was kind and affable to him, was giving up his command after only two years, but thought he was right to do so. Interestingly, General Creagh like Noel was something of an artist. 'The General has given me two sketches – water-colours – that he has done here, but the walls of my room are coloured a bright blue so it is no good framing and hanging them'. Mrs Creagh was sailing home first, and the General was glad to stay in Noel's mess.

Acquaintances were hardly numerous on Mauritius, but even there echoes of Winchester and home sounded faintly. An invitation came to call on a Mrs or Miss Tessier at her cottage – 'her little island home' – to hear her thanks at having been 'a grateful humble guest of your kind parents at Southgate Hill, Winchester at Christmas-tide more than thirty years ago'. She had heard of Noel's presence through a lady missionary.

There were dinner parties too for married officers – a test for the new cook – and farewell smoking concerts in barracks for those going home, one for the sergeants and one for the Royal Artillery generally, including the children. 'The latter gave us much amusement. I had to make speeches at both concerts, which was a serious undertaking.' 'I have for the moment fallen into an era of speech-making,' he added two weeks later, '... now I have got two more, one in presenting medals to men and one to say good-bye to the General.'

Beneath these routines the note of boredom began to sound more insistently. 'There is really nothing to write about here,' he told his brother Ralph in March 1910. 'In Mauritius there is always the feeling of being left behind by the rest of the world.' So Noel began to wish he were himself 'time-expired', not like his sister Mary in South Africa who dreaded the uselessness of all her life, nor even like his brother Jim at the seat of power in India who longed for relief from the burdens of work – or said he did; but because he felt there had been great days, on the Nile, in Manchuria and Peking and who knows what secret journeys in Siberia, but that they were done.

Relief came in autumn 1911. After the military exercises, devised by himself, after the weeks of inquiry into riots with tedious examination of witnesses, after inspections, policing, the dreaded coronation celebrations of 1911 and the endless dinner parties when he briskly agreed to his experienced servants the menus he did not understand – after all this the day of sailing came.

He spoke in a last letter from Mauritius of his flower-garden and the fine rose in his sitting-room, and then he was on the ship bound first for Africa where he hoped to meet the family members who were there, and then for England and home.

England at Christmas time 1911 might seem to us a calm and magic point before the holocaust we know was coming. To Noel it meant a staff job and the imminent transfer to half-pay. A letter from a friend still in Mauritius says, 'I am glad to hear you like Dover, but I heard you were going to be Commandant at Shoebury. Did you refuse it?'

Whatever the future, the year 1912 saw him living in Dover Castle and able a little to play the uncle – another role at which he was excellent – to a young French artillery lieutenant, son of a Far Eastern colleague, Colonel de Cazenove. The French boy was entertained by Grandfather Du Boulay at Shawford and Winchester and went on to see Noel at Dover, staying at Ringwould Rectory nearby.

The last moments of peace passed without dramatic statement in the correspondence, for the Great War had begun when Noel wrote again, and by that time, September 1914, it was almost as if another man were writing.

Another man? Another age certainly, of limited utterance about the movements and deaths of men on a scale which were terrible to a Victorian gunner.

For one thing there was the censorship, the first in a military correspondence of 30 years' duration. But beyond that was a sort of new busyness of a staff officer, in which dullness and excitement are blended and yet are of no account in themselves beside the overall determination that had now to be applied to the enveloping conflict.

All this is seen in Noel's first letter to survive from wartime France, written to his mother:

> This is the first moment I have had to write a line, and there is not much I can say. We have been doing a lot of marching … I was making a round in a motor-car yesterday and came across Johnny Evans [13] with the 2nd Army Group HQ, looking well, but said he had no clothes but what he stood up in … met Fred Parker and Tom Du Boulay soon after I landed. I was watching the [blank] Regiment passing a few days ago and suddenly saw the postman at Shawford smiling at me. [His mother was of course living in the house grandfather had built at Shawford, near Winchester, for his retirement.]

> We are mopping up a good many German prisoners as we go and our servants in rear are often capturing stray Uhlans who are probably unaware of what is going on and are foolish enough to show themselves and even to open fire. Our guns are firing as I write and the retreating Germans must be having a bad time … This would be a very pleasant country if there were no war. The inhabitants are most kind but I am afraid they are mostly ruined, and there are very few remaining in the villages.

In these early months of the Great War there was still some mobility and a sense of space and identity about the countryside. Noel referred to a comfortable house where he lived and did his office work and from which he could see Allied aeroplanes in the sky with German shells bursting round them without apparent effect.

Of course it was not peaceful and the Allies were in retreat not advance. He wrote on 25 September 1914 after visiting 'the front' to say with a professional gunner's interest that

> at one of the first fights when we were retreating the Germans got some guns fairly close up to us during the night and at daybreak opened fire on a cavalry and horse-artillery bivouac, killing and wounding men and horses and scattering the latter. Our guns were

---

13. A.J. Evans, son of Noel's sister Isabel, Kent cricketer, and publicized escaper from prisoner-of-war camps (*The Escaping Club*, etc).

practically in the enemy's hands, but not long after our cavalry had not only recovered our guns but captured those of the enemy. Considering that we were retreating it wasn't bad work to capture guns and send them down country to the base. It is 24 September and there was a white frost this morning.

During this first autumn of the war Noel was about 53 and a staff colonel with the 3rd Army Corps of the British Expeditionary Force. In army jargon he was an A.Q.M.G. (Assistant Quartermaster General), which is to say he looked after supplies. Fortunately for him it was not a young man's job, though he didn't see it that way. In any case, he disliked being indoors, as he always had, and was happiest walking, riding or even driving about. He wrote of his search for a good horse, and snatched hours when stationary to go after partridge and pheasant with borrowed guns. But mostly he wrote home of his routine's tedium.

Father wants to know something of an A.Q.M.G.'s duties [he replied with evident delight to one of the old man's insatiably curious letters]. I have to deal with the bringing up of food and ammunition from the rear, movements by rail, and billetting, and various other odd jobs. I have had a good many very anxious times when supply columns (that is, lorries bringing up food and forage for different portions of the force) have not turned up and I have had to go off at a moment's notice at night to try and find them. But hitherto I am glad to say I have always been lucky and have pitched on them in time to get them up, sometimes 5, 10 or 15 miles away, once 25 miles away. Sometimes the French railways get blocked, and the train bringing supplies to the station from which they are taken in the lorries is late, and that also adds to the anxiety as to whether the troops will be fed or have to go hungry. In ordinary normal times there would be supplies for a day or two with the troops, but we have had many abnormal times when we were living from hand to mouth and when it was almost impossible to get the necessary food in the country. Everyone has fed well hitherto, but they little realize what narrow escapes they have had sometimes from going without food for a day.

Conditions unhappily within everyone's experience are referred to: the mud, the bombs, the dead village folk, women and children.

Occasionally a moment of farce breaks in, seized on by Noel with his taste for the ridiculous. He wrote of the arrival in his office of a great consignment of mouth organs for the troops which at once reminded him of a Chinese war maxim a thousand years old: 'fill the camp of the enemy with voluptuous music in order to soften his heart'. Of course the reality was not ludicrous, as he might have reflected back to the soldiers' voices and strumming in the night air on the Nile before Abu Klea 29 years before, or for that matter have heard some tune of home from a dug-out a few miles up the road.

But mostly it was tedium. 'I have to do a dreadful lot of sums now, – for example, if half an ounce of tea extra is to be allowed for men in the trenches and the men in the trenches are a certain proportion of the whole number, how many pounds of tea will be required for a week and what if any extra transport will be required to carry it' – all this without benefit of calculator – 'and will the men drink it when they get it?' which, if incalculable, was a very Noel-like question, directed to human beings beyond the columns of figures.

By the early summer of 1915, movement, tactical interest, hopes of an early end, even the rags of gaiety had gone. A brief letter spoke of the German use of poison gas and he found it in his heart to hope the Allies would not have to retaliate.

'I accomplish 35 years service today,' he wrote to his sister Bee on 19 May 1915, 'and the last six months seem to have been half of the whole time. The early part of the war, up to the time when we left the Aisne, seems to have occurred years ago.'

Even in the huge melting-pot of men in France old friends were sometimes strangely encountered before disappearing again and they form in the letters a kind of tapestry thread through the years. In the Rifle Brigade trenches he came across comrades of long ago, and to him their rank was nothing beside their persons for whom he felt friendship: 'my old servant Holloway,' he wrote home, 'also [I met] Brig.-Gen. Hotham, – he was my Captain in Malta and Egypt in '83 and '84 and I think I met in '85 but not since. He was very little changed'.

By November 1915 Noel would have given anything to be out of the office altogether. 'I refused so many Staff appointments in peace-time that it is a hard fate to be tied to one in war-time.'

This comes at the end of the surviving correspondence. Undated notes by Uncle Ralph show that in early 1916 Noel had 'taken up his command at Portsmouth', living in the George Hotel, High Street, with a house and garden at his disposal, but he was not occupying it since he had to move about constantly, doing very little office work. What he did he could not or would not say, adding vaguely, 'everything is so different in war-time'.

About this time he was gazetted as promoted to the (now obsolete) rank of brigadier general, and decided to move into the Gun House, Portsmouth.

There I must leave the Victorian gunner. It was still a good 15 years before he emerged into my consciousness as a favourite uncle, a stocky figure who took trouble to meet us at holiday times and produce several half-crowns he pretended just to have found. A little later he was a relaxed and thoughtful host to adolescent nephews in his two rented rooms at the Bridge Hotel, Shawford, Hampshire, and he died soon after the Second World War. The nursing home told us he was shouting out fire-orders at the time.

12. Sir James Du Boulay, KCIE (1868–1945) in 1911.

CHAPTER 3

Viceroy's Secretary: James

After the soldier came the 'civilian', though in the caste-like hierarchy of the British in India they used the word in a most special sense. To the reference books he became Sir James Du Boulay, K.C.I.E., C.S.I.; to nephews of course 'Uncle Jim', and to this memoir Jim, and grant that he may excuse the liberty.

If he was the most public man of all the brothers, he had, like them, a private heart. Nor, despite his air of authority moving with age into cragginess, was he ever a conceited man. He entered Balliol College as a Commoner in 1885 and passed into the Indian Civil Service in 1887, thus becoming a 'civilian', but said later he would never have been capable of winning a scholarship to New College, which, as a good Wykehamist, he would dearly have loved to do. His early years in India were spent in the Bombay Administration to the Governor, Lord Northcote, in 1903, and Political Secretary to the government about 1908.

By the time the series of surviving letters begins in December 1908 he had already been married seven years to Freda Elais Butts Howell. The marriage to Aunt Freda was clearly one of mutual understanding and happiness, and through all their anxieties, external or self-generated, their letters display a deep regard for each other. The letters complement each other too in a striking way, to show their India through two pairs of eyes, each pair able to see the political dance against the background of event and colour.

Returning to India from leave at Christmas time 1908, Jim wrote from Aden to his mother, 'please note that independent accounts of Freda's health will gratify me', and in the same letter he told his mother he had liked meeting her cousin Vernon, 'and though both he and I are rather reserved and poor conversationalists we seemed to understand one another'. The two remarks exactly hit off two of Jim's dominant traits: anxious care for his wife and family and the silent Wykehamist reserve which was a by-word in the family.

Other dominant characteristics emerge quickly from the early letters. There is the love of natural surroundings which made jungle, forest and mountain sources of refreshment and best enjoyed without a rifle; also the sense of family which made it more than natural, almost compulsive, to seek out and meet brothers and sisters wherever possible when journeys intersected across seas and continents, and then perhaps to sit a short while without much talk before parting again for months or years.

'I did not go to bed till all hours last night,' he wrote on the voyage out. 'I got a friend to point out the various constellations. I wanted to get a sight of the Southern Cross, for we are a good deal south of Bombay here at Aden, but he doesn't rise till early morning ... I was disappointed not to see Phil at Port Said.'

So Jim sailed on without a reunion with his youngest brother, then aged 28 and just beginning his life's work in Egypt.

Jim arrived in Bombay at the New Year 1909 and was rapidly caught up in the arduous work of Political Secretary to the Provincial Government; but its routine was savagely interrupted by the death of Lady Clarke, wife of the Governor, Sir George Clarke.[1] His letter home is a reminder, if such were needed, of the mortality in India which struck down so many in the prime of life, sparing the great no more than the poor:

> You will have read of the disasters that have overtaken our poor Governor. There seemed to have been a fate against him. At the funeral there was a crowd of natives, many of them running across the graveyard in order to see more. Then they had some new-fangled dodge for letting the coffin down and the thing went wrong, and

---

1. Sir George Clarke (1848–1933), Governor of Bombay 1907–13, created Baron Sydenham on his retirement.

the coffin went down with a crash, and a sob went round. Then he decided to rush away to Aden, and on the first boat he selected an officer died of enteric the night before, on the second there were three cases of smallpox, and an officer who had served on the third committed suicide in Bombay the day before they sailed ...

I very much hope he will come back, not for any personal reasons, for I hardly know him sufficiently well, but rather for public reason. I think he came out with very mistaken notions on many points, but he is the ablest Governor we have had within the memory of man, – a far abler man than any recent Viceroy, save perhaps Lord Curzon, whose ability was marred by great faults. He has learnt a great deal and has secured a position of influence with the natives which is itself a most valuable asset.

I go on slaving at my job and see in the vista of the future a never-ending succession of big questions ... I cannot help thinking that I am in for this job for a much longer spell than I anticipated, as everyone seems to think that the man for whom I am acting will not come back to it.

It is a great joy to have Freda, and I think there has been pleasure to her in finding how glad people were to have her back.

He was only half right about his prospects. Jim's life was indeed set fair in the Bombay Presidency (Provincial Government) which he always loved, and the letters of 1909–10 are a duet of Jim and Freda to the family at home, describing in some detail the circumstances of a high official's daily round. He could not know that in 1910 he would be plucked out of Bombay and set down on a higher pinnacle in the Government of India. But this is to anticipate.

The early letters, then, come from Government House in Bombay, from Poona, and from the hill-station of Mahableshwar, 75 miles away from Poona. Each had its 'season', but it was in this last place that Jim and Freda seemed happiest, and he describes it well:

Mahableshwar is a plateau up among the Western Ghats 75 miles from Poona and perhaps 90 as the crow flies from Bombay. It is 4000 feet high and though it is quite hot there in April and May, you get into an evergreen scrub jungle, with red sandstone roads which are comforting to the eye, and you get away from the turmoil and crowds and the dust and the relaxing climate of Bombay. One of the greatest charms about the place is that you can get away into real country walks within ten minutes of leaving your bungalow, and some of the bungalows are right in the jungle.

'We have a charming bungalow,' Freda confirmed, 'and are sharing it with the new member of [Government] Council who is easygoing and lets me do exactly what I like.' By this Freda meant she had *carte blanche* about decorating the house and about entertaining. On the one she had strong views, on the other they had the obligations of society. She liked to bring in jungle flowers instead of the pink and magenta phlox which was the gardener's pride and joy. On every possible occasion she superintended the decoration and good order of all rooms, wherever she was. Then there were carriage-less people to be taken for drives, for 'we have a large and comfortable victoria and pair, and up here the horses never get enough work'.

To ride and to play golf were occasional recreations, but entertaining was an unremitting duty. The housekeeping was superintended by an evidently trustworthy butler, but though Mahableshwar was quiet in summer 1909, it was necessary to put on a dinner a week. 'We have the house full of people who have come up for a few days cool.' To her brother-in-law Ralph, Freda wrote, 'I never get accustomed to the craze people in India have for being amused. If only they could be content to dine at home life would be so much more tolerable.'

Looking back, this sounds strange. I clearly remember Aunt Freda had a strong personality. With her upright carriage, hair that went white early and splendidly, and rather severe blue eyes, she seemed to play the *grande dame* effortlessly, to entertain with ease and apparent enjoyment and to go out and meet the world from which her husband and his family appeared so often to recoil. Yet she was never without affection and love for husband and the children whose absence in England she minded and whose arrival and life in India with her she enjoyed with maternal terror: 'I miss the children terribly, but am thankful they are at home, for anxiety about children in this country is endless.'

As to Jim, he liked his new job as Political Secretary though said it was harder work than the Private Secretaryship to the Governor. Today's slang would dub him a 'workaholic'. He was at his desk all hours, and, like so many of his type, was always announcing how hard he worked and what a burden it was to be driven by an obsessive conscience that told him he must earn his pay. He liked also to think of his own indispensability.

In Freda's words, 'cases pour in by post, and he always seems to leave the room full of large files. He gets rather depressed about it, but I am told by others his work is excellent. Friends tell me he "looks much older [he was now 41] and takes life much too seriously and is much too conscientious", but these are faults I can never break him of; he never rides now, but I hope he will get out for one day a week hunting in Poona.'

From Jim's pen to his mother we hear of 'a pricking conscience' at writing home so little, 'no days off and no relief from the relentless torrent of knotty questions to be unravelled by my inexperienced fingers'. As if that were not enough, Jim about this time became a Volunteer (we should nowadays say a 'Territorial' soldier), drilling and shooting with a dozen others. He was a bad shot and often missed the target altogether.

The highlight of 1909 was the visit to Bombay by the Viceroy of India, Lord Minto. At that time the Government of British India was based in Calcutta, but the Viceroy, as we shall see, toured constantly and paid official visits to the governors and lieutenant-governors of the various provinces and districts as well as courtesy calls on the Indian princes.

Later Jim would experience all this from the viceregal side, but on 15 October 1909 he wrote as chief executive of the Bombay Presidency, 'the Viceroy is coming next month and I have to spend weary and useless hours in examining and correcting programmes for his official arrival and for the arrival and reception of various Chiefs [meaning Princes] who count their guns [salutes] and watch their ceremonies with lynx eyes'.

The visit itself was described by Freda who relished detail and saw the proceedings all the more closely because the sad death of Lady Clarke meant she was called on to play the role of hostess for the Governor:

> We got to Bombay and came straight up here [Government House] to find we had only half-an-hour before dinner, but mercifully my ayah is a treasure and I was ready when the gong rang. Only Sir James Wolfe Murray, his daughter, Lady Sutherland, and the bishop of Southwark and his family were here.

> Early on Sunday morning Captain Greig came round and simply begged me to stay on and help over the Viceroy's visit. He said that the last time the Mintos were treated so badly by the Curzons that H.E. was particularly anxious that they should be comfortable and happy here this time, and having no lady here he fears it would not be right. My heart sank within me. I quite trusted that Jim who hates staying here even in the quietest time would sternly refuse; but I trusted in a broken reed, for with the tiresome Du Boulay conscientiousness he said if we <u>could</u> help the lonely Governor we ought to; and then came such a pathetic note to me from Sir G[eorge Clarke] that I said all right – I would.

> Monday and Tuesday I toiled at the rooms. The furniture did not arrive from Poona till Tuesday afternoon, and the whole party arrived at 8.20 a.m. on Wednesday. There is nothing pretty in the house now. I got hold of multitudes of plants and ferns and hung them in baskets, and odds and ends of my own, and contributed to make the Mintos' rooms as pretty as I could. In India you must see to everything yourself: you cannot trust servants. I gave out all the paper and envelopes etc. for all the rooms of the Staff and went round at the last minute at quarter to 9 p.m. to see all was right and found they had put <u>every one</u> wrong. So that of course meant stepping round all over again, accompanied by an army of servants upon whose guilty heads I poured abuse for their stupidity.

> Jim, poor dear, in the meantime was frightfully busy with his Chief's visits and all the police affairs – he is head of that department as well as the political – and the bombs at Ahmedabad of course meant a lot of extra anxiety and worry.

This place is arranged as though we were going to be besieged: 62 policemen in the grounds, two companies of soldiers on guard, quantities of native and English detectives and some of the bodyguard, while there are boats rowing round the whole place on the 3 sides of the grounds which overlook the sea. My room and the verandahs round Lady Eileen Elliot's and Lady Antrim's who are in the same block with me have sentries all day and all night, and as the heat is intense and I am obliged to open all the windows and doors there is nothing the sentries can't tell you about the details of my toilette. However, it can't be helped.

Well, Jim set off stiff in full dress on Wednesday and met them at the station. It was a public arrival so the station was simply blocked with officers in every service, consuls and dozens of [illegible]. Poor Sir G. had got fever the day before and was looking and feeling a wreck, and seemed quite dazed and totally incapable of introducing anyone, and Sir Basil Scott, the Chief Justice who was supposed to introduce people to Lady M[into] did nothing at all, so Jim simply took the law into his own hands and introduced all the Europeans as well as his own chiefs: he never forgets a name or a face; and I was told afterwards by several who were there that his performance was quite wonderful.

They came up as a procession of three state carriages with outriders, the bodyguard and a company of Inniskillings. I met them at the steps and took them all to their rooms. They are all so nice and friendly and delighted with everything, so I do trust the visit will be a success.

The Bombay Government has come to such loggerheads with the Government of India lately that it is politically most important that everything so far as we can do it should go well here.

Last night was the big night: 120 at dinner and 1200 to a reception after, as well as an investiture before dinner. I was very tired last night, and getting a rest in one of the verandahs before Their Excellencies came up, when a High Court judge came running up to me, despair on his face, to say, 'Mrs. Du Boulay, what shall I do? My knee-breeches have split!' I simply roared with laughter and rushed off for a needle and black cotton, meeting the A.D.C.-in-Waiting on the way to fetch Sir George. (He had to come up first and go round to shake hands with the 120, and then the Viceroy's party is fetched and a procession formed, and the same proceeding goes on with them, only the (lady) guests curtsey instead of bowing.)

The beautiful velvet breeches had 'gone' right up the seam in front. I hastily cobbled together the rent sides and got it done just in time, but it was too funny.

Well, the Viceroy arrived, and when the curtseying was over he and she walked up the lovely gold carpet to a dais, and the Chiefs who had got honours were led up one by one to receive the ribbons and orders, and then we went off to dinner, which was in a huge tent in the garden, as the rooms in the house were wanted for the reception afterwards.

A very funny incident occurred. We sat down and there was a long pause. No soup came. Then the house-servants rushed in and went up to Captain Greig and said something very excitedly. Captain Greig got up and went out, and in a few minutes the soup came in and the dinner went on. It afterwards transpired that the sentries had strict orders of course not to let anyone pass except the diners, and when the servants appeared at the other entrance with the soup they were met with fixed bayonets and dogged determination not to let them through. The house-steward in despair said he would fetch the Military Secretary. 'I don't care if you fetch the Major-General,' answered Tommy, 'them's my orders.' However, Captain Greig got hold of the officer in command and the soup went in.

I told the Viceroy afterwards and he was delighted. My labours did not end at dinner. When we got to the first entrée the lady in front of me began to faint. Her partner, a helpless official, dragged her out and then came to me. I found her rather bad and took her off to my rooms where I dosed her with sal volatile, and she lay still until she had recovered, which was not till the dinner was over. Jim saw me go out, thought I was ill, and sent an anxious note, but I was all right and went in to the reception afterwards.

Yesterday the Begum of Junagall gave a purdah party. Mrs. Claude Hill whose husband is what is called agent to the Viceroy in Kashmir where Junagall is, and I being the Political Secretary's wife, had to receive Her Excellency and introduce people to her.

We had not got to bed till 12.30 the night before, and Jim got up at 8.30 to meet Rachel Du Boulay[2] who came out by the City Line and was going up to Quetta. We thought she would go straight on, but she had to wait till today and travel with friends. It is 5 days in the train. So Jim brought her up here to breakfast, and then I took her off to the Jenkins to stay. She came to the purdah party and enjoyed it I think very much.

Today is a quiet day and they all leave together after dinner tonight. We are all to be photographed before lunch, always a trial, and apparently a necessity when people come here to stay.

The poor Governor has been ill all the time and looks wretched. Jim is very well and does not seem at all too tired with all his work. We go to our own house as soon as we can get away from here. It is a great relief to have had no bombs here so far. The Mintos were so plucky about the two that were thrown at them at Ahmedabad. We shall be happier when the train leaves Bombay tonight, before anything else happens.

In the lives of Jim and Freda provincial Bombay was the first act of a single play which would culminate in the Viceroy of India's residences and camps; yet Bombay held for both of them the remembrances of friends and a social circle never to he displaced in their affections. Freda's letters add an apparently light-hearted air to the life, but in fact they do more than merely entertain, for they underline the personal quality of government, easily concealed perhaps in complicated countries, but quite open in the little society of exalted expatriates set over the Indian millions. Beside ceremonial and luxury were loneliness, anxieties and fear, which could be allayed by affection as well as ordinary courage. The correspondence will have something to say about these personal requirements in due course, and they were evident even on the morrow of the Viceroy's visit

---

2. Second cousin of Grandfather Du Boulay, she was then aged 21; in 1912 she married Captain William Haire Forster, Royal Irish Fusiliers.

when Jim and Freda were invited to keep the Governor company on the anniversary of Lady Clarke's death. 'He has a little staggered us by begging us to come up and stay with him … We had so looked forward to a little time alone and so I hedged and said I would ask Jim, etc., but he [Clarke] always puts it on the ground of being a help to him which makes it so difficult to refuse.'

A more public and serious problem was that of sedition or, as our contemporary world would phrase it, terrorism. Almost farcically present at the Governor's banquet, the problem occupied Jim daily as Political Secretary, just as it was to do in the Viceroy's service.

In March 1910 Jim was complaining characteristically to his brother Ralph in London:

the work has been appalling ever since Christmas. Poor Jackson's murder led to the working up of a very big criminal case and to the passing of a press law which in itself means a lot of additional work … The press law has already had a very good effect, but we shall have to go on working it quietly and steadily, seeing that it does not become a dead letter; and at the same time we shall have to keep a sharp look-out for sedition secretly printed and preached. We shall very likely have more outrages down here as in other parts of India, but though one may have a very rude shock at any moment and is constantly anxious, the prospect is brighter for the moment in this Presidency than it has been for some time past.

The prosecution of Jackson's murderer and his confederates has cost an enormous amount of time and labour, but the case is over now and we shall have the decision on Tuesday. My own opinion is that four of the seven accused will be sentenced to death. They are all boys, and though they must hang there is very little satisfaction to be got out of the process, and it is impossible to escape the reflection that it is the Editors in the scurrilous native press who really ought to swing. In almost every one of these cases, if the accused are pressed to explain their attitude, they will say it is due to the tyranny of the Government or of its officers; if they are asked if they have ever experienced it themselves they will say no, but they have read about it in the papers. It is these same papers that we are getting hold of, but the mischief has been done as far as the rising generation is concerned, and we can hardly hope for much result for another ten years.

A curious fact which I have only recently realized is that the beginning of this poison was being distilled at least 30 years ago, and one of the essays written by a Maratti scholar in the late 'seventies has been a regular mine of simile and metaphor, rhetoric and invective to the latter-day press man. All this sedition adds a very real interest to life: it is twenty times more interesting than all the rest of the kaboodle, [though] one gets occasional excitement over large questions of police administration or when one has to deal with a peculiarly bad case of gross misrule in a native state.

Last rains I had a case that one could hardly believe to be true, of a man who under his mother's tutelage had removed two obstacles to his accession to the throne and procured the death by poison of 6 or 7 other people who had proved objectionable. The Minister who showed it all up was a British officer, and his loyalty and honesty cost him the life of one of his children who [was] undoubtedly poisoned under the orders of the Chief, while he himself went in peril for years. The police officer who finally worked the case up knew that he did it at the utmost risk to himself, and [he] died by poison just as it neared a conclusion. Finally the British officer who reported the whole thing to the Government has undoubtedly been conspired against not once but several times.

That indeed is the important fact in the midst of all these rumours: they are always hatching murder somewhere or other; but no egg of that sort produces a chicken unless it has within it that essential element – one man who will risk his neck. They talk and froth and foam and they search about for likely instruments and use every sort of means to work them up to the proper state of feeling, and yet with this teeming population they can only find a brave man here and there after careful search.

Within the next few months Lord Minto's tour of duty as Viceroy came to an end, the government in London chose Lord Hardinge of Penshurst as his successor and the authorities lighted upon Jim as the new Viceroy's Private Secretary. He and the Military Secretary

(P.S.V. and M.S.V.) were the two officials closest to the Viceroy and occupied the undefined area between prescribed official functions and personal friends and advisers.

The Viceroy travelled out from England to assume his functions, and his Private Secretary understandably went with him, so that in Jim's case there was a period of home leave before he sailed with his master in November 1910 on the SS *Persia*. Arriving at Aden on 16 November Jim was able to make a first comment in a letter to Ralph:

> I have had rather an interesting voyage. We have on board 8 of the 15 Calcutta High Court Judges, some of whom I knew before and other men I was glad to meet; also the new member of the Viceroy's Council, one Clark who is a junior member of the Home Civil Service. He is only 32 and his appointment gave rise to a great deal of criticism in India, but he gives me the impression of being an exceedingly able fellow, and more important still a very good one.
>
> There have been rocks too – people past whom one has to clear one's course with great circumspection and exceeding rapidity lest one come to shipwreck. One of these has written a book. She has forced through me a copy on Lord H[ardinge] and has ever since pestered me with demands for an interview with him. I have tried to combine politeness with the firmest possible refusal, but I dread the appearance of her next book almost as much as I dread re-visiting the dentist whom I refused to put up for the Mahableshwar Club. Another is the wife of a member of Council who seems to want to pump me, and asked me questions which it was impossible to answer without some suspicion of a snub.
>
> It is extraordinary how everyone with an enthusiasm desires to pour it out upon the P.S.V., and I listen diligently to disquisitions upon the Sikh religion, the state of Bengal, the problem of the Indian student in England, the financial position of the Bombay City Improvement Trust ... all interesting, but it means that I have but little time to myself.

If these thoughts sound arrogant it has to be remembered that Jim, sailing out with a new and heavily responsible position, was without his wife to talk to and was confiding in a private letter to

13. James Du Boulay (front left) with the Viceroy, Lord Hardinge (centre), his daughter and Lady Hardinge.

a brother close to him in age and temperament. And to complain of life's problems was natural enough when cooped up on board ship for weeks with the incoming Viceroy and passengers who were doubtless random members of the public with business in India and the means to travel first class. In the circumstances Jim's sarcasm seems mild and his letter the work of the character which comes through his whole career: extreme discretion, mastery of the work and an innate loathing of being a public man. He could not easily switch on *bonhomie* and was never wreathed in smiles, yet he was courteous to everyone.

Sometimes he put assessments of his Viceroy into his private letters; more often he wrote self-assessments, and they are very different in tone: the first soberly cautious but written with genuine admiration, the second ruthlessly honest with a tendency to self-deprecation which borders at moments on inverted boasting. 'I like my Chief immensely. He strikes me as able and cautious and sympathetic and tactful, with plenty of strength of character, and unless things go very much awry both he and Lady H. should be most successful.'

After a month in office in Calcutta Hardinge continued to impress his Private Secretary:

> H.E. is determined to take plenty of exercise for which I praise him. He has a quick instinct for doing the right thing. It was the Viceroy's Cup on Tuesday and I had to go in the procession ... The senior steward is crippled by a stroke [and] H.E. readily fell in with the suggestion ... that it would be nice if he would go and say a few words to him. Later on, when his horse won ... H.E. picked up the enormous mug and himself carried it up to the rostrum to present it to the steward.

Working for a Viceroy in early twentieth-century India was unlike any job in England because it combined politics rather like a prime minister's office and a royal court where every gesture was noted; and the whole thing was set amidst a vast and diverse population at once more reverential and more dangerously critical than the British public.

Jim tried to indicate the difference he found between his earlier work in the Bombay administration and his present post in the Government of India:

> The Viceroy has a Council of seven members, each of whom is in charge of his own departments, and each of whom has secretaries, deputy secretaries and under-secretaries chosen from among the ablest men in India. In this galaxy of talent my single person can only exercise a small influence, and among them all the private secretary who has no very well defined place is what circumstances choose to make him. I have hit upon a Viceroy of absolutely first-class ability, and my scope does not therefore extend beyond any reasonable limits.
>
> It is however very curious to note the difference of scale between Bombay and the Government of India. Down there my friend Jenkins, who was [Secretary and] a member of Council, was practically omniscient, and if he really made up his mind was able to get his way about most things. Up here [the P.S.] is often confronted

> with large questions of which his past experience gives him little
> personal knowledge, and he has to fight his battles with colleagues
> more than half of them not civilians [i.e. members of the I.C.S.] at
> all, and none of them from his own province. The waves of politics of
> local Governments seldom extend beyond the borders of India, but
> at headquarters you never know when the ripples may not affect the
> House of Commons and at times even the chancelleries of Europe.

From this point Jim went on candidly to confess, 'I find myself unsuited for life in Government House, and it will be a great joy to have Freda back and be able to start a *ménage* of our own.'

Jim was a private man who seems to have unfolded in the security of his own family. The underlying diffidence which appeared like severity was a secret of his integrity. In 1914 a newspaper cutting kept by Freda defended Hardinge and his staff at a difficult time against various political criticisms, and went on, 'Sir James Du Boulay [as he had become] is a straight and taciturn official. In our dealings with him we know where we are. He is loyal to his Chief and has a patriotic sense of duty which he extends to the Europeans and Indians alike. Sir James may be strict and unbending but he is pure gold. No humbug or sham finds a place in his official code.'

When it was all over and Hardinge was back in England writing his official memoirs he said much the same thing, adding that James had been a safety-valve for his own irritability under strain and that the family had been delightful companions, especially in the years of sadness after Lady Hardinge's death in 1914.[3]

These are formal tributes. Freda was more outgoing and less inhibited, and the Hardinges liked her for it, and she in her turn spoke her thoughts sometimes with an artless honesty that make the Hardinges seem less royal and more human. After a weekend near Simla in summer 1911 she wrote to her father-in-law:

> the Viceroy was in great form and he is certainly the most interesting
> man I have ever met. He has such unique chances of knowing all
> the great people and being in the most epoch-making times of the

---

3. Lord Hardinge of Penshurst, *My Indian Years, 1910–16* (London, 1948), p 143.

century. He is, as Jim thinks, extraordinarily indiscreet in what
he says. Lady H. is very sweet and kind, and neither [has] one bit
of side, and they are only proud of their relations who have done
something to help the world.

The life upon which Lord Hardinge embarked when he became
Viceroy in 1910, and into which Jim was necessarily drawn, may be
illustrated from three different angles.

There were the great political events and problems, among which
stand out King George V's Durbar in Delhi in 1911, the move of
India's central government from Calcutta to Delhi and the continuous
and stressful problem of terrorism. Secondly, there was the social life
and supposed relaxation up in the hills during the hot season, and this
chiefly involves the family at Simla. Thirdly, there was the viceregal
practice of touring India and in the course of formal engagements
taking viceregal recreation in various forms of hunting, not unlike
the progresses of a medieval European king who showed himself to
his subjects and did them justice and hunted year by year.

A minor problem which occurred near the beginning of Hardinge's
viceroyalty which is colourful and indeed ludicrous enough to recount
was the visit to India of the Crown Prince of Prussia, the Kaiser's son
Wilhelm – 'Little Willy' to history. Jim had no time for him either
literally or figuratively. 'That young gentleman arrived here in state
the other day and was taken down to Barrackpore for the week-end.'
Barrackpore was the country residence of the Viceroy when the capital was in Calcutta. But the Prince did not fall in with the programme
assigned for him to visit Darjeeling and then go on to the Far East.
He preferred to amuse himself in the pleasant accommodation of
Barrackpore where the Viceroy took the trouble to stay for a week as
personal host. The P.S. showed his usual mixture of sharp observation and avoiding action:

> He is a smart-looking young fellow and has a curious way of shaking
> hands which he shares with all the Continental royalties, grasping you
> firmly and staring you straight in the face for a quite embarrassingly
> long period. He is full of spirits and evidently intends to get as much
> enjoyment out of life as he can. The other day he played truant from

14. Visit of Crown Prince Wilhelm of Prussia, 1905. Seated from left: Sir H. Stewart, Mrs Kernealy, J.B. Wood, Mrs Mackenzie, German visitor, H.E. Viscount Hardinge, the Crown Prince, Lady Hardinge, H.E. The Aga Khan, Miss Sandford, James Du Boulay, Mrs Wood, Hon. H. Fraser, ADC. Standing from left: five German visitors, Hon. H. Forester, Col. Kernealy, Col. Dicks, visitor, Capt. Pelham Burn, Capt. Jelf, Capt. Mackenzie (comptroller), Col. Maxwell.

Lucknow. He evaded his staff and got away in a motor-car, broke down, rowed across the Ganges and took train, and had to wire some excuse to a large meeting of nobility assembled to entertain him.

Jim added the story was confidential and thought the Kaiser, 'his august father', would 'give him beans' when the young man got home. For his own part Jim took the trouble to avoid Barrackpore and to see as little as possible of his Imperial Highness.

The Viceroy in his memoirs was both more and less discreet. He said the Crown Prince had escaped to meet a notorious lady, and also said that the Kaiser, by way of thanks, sent a portrait of himself which was at once put away in an attic and never hung. But this was written after Germany and Britain had become enemies. According to Jim's letter at the time, the portrait was 'magnificent and dominates the room where it is placed'.

Almost from the start Hardinge's viceroyalty was dominated by the decision to hold a Durbar or court audience, for which the new King-Emperor, George V, should come out from Britain and preside, receiving homage and bestowing honours. In February 1911 Jim wrote about the Viceroy's hard and worrying work over the preparations, and to say that though his own task in general was to save the Viceroy from being worried by small matters, there luckily was a special committee for the Durbar, and the executive officer was his opposite number, the Military Secretary.

The Durbar was to be at Delhi, where the new seat of the British Government of India was to be fixed. As yet it was but a city of tents, contractors' apparatus and dust. The story of the Durbar in December 1911 was told by Freda in a long diary-letter home, remarkable not just for its incidental detail but for being written while she was concealing her grief at the loss of her little son.

Freda left Simla with their two little girls on 28 November. Special and luxurious trains were organized to take children to Calcutta and the government wives to the Durbar city of Delhi. Finding the children's train ready at Kalka, 'I put the little girls to bed with a basin of soup each and bread for their suppers'. The wives' train got to the newly built station at Delhi at 9 a.m. where the husbands had been waiting for two hours. Jim and Freda drove off in a motor-car, not an everyday sight in 1911, and Freda remarked that there were 16 in the camp apart from the King's special ones.

The drive took them through miles of camps assigned to the various provinces and states until they got to their own, which was sited next to the Viceroy's. 'We have a large drawing-room, bedroom, bathrooms and two official tents ... The tents are in a semi-circle and to the right of us is the dining-tent where all the staff has meals, and to the left of us are the Viceroy's and then the King's tents. All the tents are hung with coloured plain muslins except Their Majesties' which are silk.'

Freda interrupted her narrative for a moment to note she had been called away to hang pictures in Their Majesties' rooms, which looked inside like a large house. In front was an enormous plot of green grass with a bed of ferns and a flagstaff.

While the Viceroy went to Bombay to meet the King and Queen and Jim stayed behind to cope with his work, Freda and Lady Hardinge drove round Delhi on roads crammed with carriages and bodyguards. Later there were volumes of petitions to read through for the Vicereine, and enquiries to answer from bewildered functionaries. 'Lord Charles Montagu wanted to know the way to the Indore camp. He had only to go to the Inquiry Office which has two special men in charge to find out, but ...'

In the afternoon there was

a rehearsal of the Investiture ceremony in the big hall, which is the largest Shamiana [ceremonial marquee] I have ever seen and is placed between the Viceroy's and the King's tents. Sir Henry MacMahon[4] is the Master of Ceremonies and is such a delightful creature. I hear that he and Jim are the only two men in Delhi who are still seen to smile and have not lost their tempers. They both expect to be 'broken' as the saying is when the King goes, for they have just had a

---

4. Sir Henry MacMahon, Resident in Baluchistan, Secretary of the Foreign Department on the Viceroy's Executive Council; appointed by London as High Commissioner in Egypt to succeed Kitchener in August 1914.

Marconigram from the Indian Ocean to say that the King wants a lot of detail altered, and they have had to do it without consulting the Viceroy who won't allow <u>anything</u> to be done without his consent, and this is amusing them both immensely. He comes in here every evening and laughs over everything which is very refreshing in this place where friction abounds.

We dined with Lady H. which I always prefer doing, for it means a smaller party, [and] Her Excellency asked me if I would receive the Queen in her tents the day she arrives, for Lady H. and all the others will be behind in carriages. It means I shall not see the arrival, but as I am totally indifferent to the whole thing I shall not mind that ... I said I thought the Queen would wonder what or who I was and she said, 'Oh no, she talked a lot about you', so I suppose she too has a royal memory.

The next few days were taken up with rehearsals and drives, ending up with the dress rehearsal for the arrival, at which the Viceroy was present in his own role and Jim had to personate the King in an old uniform which to Freda's horror had not been properly altered. 'However, his dear face is all that matters, and I have borrowed Mr. Jenkins's uniform which fits him beautifully.'

During this interlude the Durbar tent with all its hangings and silver fittings was burnt to the ground, evidently from glowing tobacco ash, and had to be swiftly replaced.

The next afternoon Freda took her *ayah* (maid/nursemaid) in a car while she called on the wives of the ruling chiefs, which gave her the chance of seeing all the lines and roads of tents 'and the swarm of gorgeous people and carriages'.

On the morning of the royal arrival the camp was awoken about 4 a.m. by band and bugles. The troops formed up to line the streets and await the King's procession.

The crying trouble was that the King and Queen would not go on elephants and at the last moment the procession was made to close in near the King, so that he was lost in the Viceroy and his escort. Consequently he was not recognized and was scarcely cheered at all. The Queen passed next in a carriage. She always looks well for she is so fat and fair you can't mistake her.

I just waited to see Jim and then we motored to the Ridge where we dropped Viscountess Hardinge, Miss Sanford and Lord Allington and I came straight back to camp.

Here the guards of honour were beginning to form up and I tidied myself up and went to the Queen's tent. I waited for three-quarters of an hour and then the advance soldiers came; the procession had broken off and it was now only the C. in C. in India, the King's Household and the Viceroy's staff.

Then came the Queen with the Duchess of Devonshire and Lord Crewe. I had been told to wait at her tent but the carriage went on to the big Investiture Shamiana next it, which was wrong. However, there was nothing for it but to pick up my skirts and slip out, and I got there in time to help the Queen out. She shook hands and said, 'I am so glad to see you again, Mrs. Du Boulay'. I told her the carriage had been brought too far but she said, 'Never mind, I'll wait here till the King comes.'

Introductions, settling in and luncheon followed, and many interviews between the King and Indian princes, which required the Viceroy to return their visits in full dress and with an enormous escort. The Queen was performing similar courtesies with Indian ladies, shaking hands and making quite a good speech.

Freda's description continued over the next few days to dwell upon elaborate ceremonial punctuated with tart criticisms such as of the band which drowned the choir in the church service. But more interest attaches to private contacts:

At lunch [on Sunday, 10 December] I was rather shattered by Sir Derek Keppel coming up and saying that the King wanted Jim and me to come and dine quietly in their private room. I suppose I looked as blank as I felt, for he laughed and said, 'You don't look as though you wanted to come!' I said, no, I didn't; I would be quite happy to clean their rooms for them, and then he said it was only a small dinner, just the King and Queen, the Duke of Teck, the Hardinges and Lord Allington (the Vicereine's father), eight of

15. The Delhi Durbar, 12 December 1911.

16. The Delhi Durbar, 12 December 1911. View of the central platform with the King-Emperor.

us, and I was to sit next the King. I went and told Jim and he was instantly reduced to the depths of depression, for he simply hates what he calls wasting time which means anything which keeps him from finishing his masses of work.

The dinner evidently passed off with ease and was followed by informal conversation largely between the King and Jim and the Queen and Freda about minor matters such as the Prince of Wales's chances of coming to India when older and the discomforts of Bombay; but perhaps true to form Queen Mary required Freda to buy a large number of Indian toys for her.

Beyond all this rather breathless account from Freda's pen are a few touches which illuminate character:

> Just as I was thinking of going to bed Mrs. John Mackenzie came rushing in and saying, 'I do congratulate you, and everyone is so delighted, dear Lady Du Boulay', and it then came out that a camp Foreign Office Gazette had published the list of Honours which included Jim's KCIE [Knight Commander of the Indian Empire, the second of the two orders of chivalry pertaining to British India].

When Jim came in at that moment Freda asked him how long he had known, to which he replied shortly, 'about six months'.

The Durbar itself was on Wednesday, 12 December. The medievalism of Indian life was here at its most intense, since it consisted of Indian princes paying homage and the King and Queen showing themselves in coronation robes. The King announced the hitherto secret decision to make Delhi the headquarters of the Indian government before he left the dais.

The Investiture itself was held the next evening, and here again there was a minor mishap to enliven the tedium of ceremonial and bring a quiver of life to the caparisoned performers. As Jim knelt to be dubbed knight there was a loud blast on a whistle and cries of 'Fire':

> I rose and Lord Allington[5] who was next me said, 'It's all right. Sit down'. But an awful smell of burning penetrated the tent, the

5. Lord Allington of Crichel, father of Winifred Sturt, the Viceroy's wife.

Most Secret

Copy No 2

Lord Stamfordham.

India Office,

Whitehall, S.W.

Draft of the King Emperor's Announcement :—
Delhi and Bengal.

We are pleased to announce to Our People that on
the advice of Our Ministers tendered after consultation
with Our Governor General in Council We have decided
upon the transfer of the seat of the Government of India
from Calcutta to the ancient Capital Delhi, and, simul-
taneously and as a consequence of that transfer, the
creation at as early a date as possible of a
Governorship for the Presidency of Bengal, of a new
Lieutenant Governorship in Council administering the areas
of Behar Chota Nagpur and Orissa, and of a
Chief Commissionership of Assam, with such administrative
changes and redistribution of boundaries as Our
Governor General in Council with the approval of Our
Secretary of State for India in Council may in due
course determine. It is Our earnest desire that
these changes may conduce to the better administration
of India and the greater prosperity and happiness
of Our beloved People.

17. Draft of King George V's speech at the Durbar.

electric light flickered wildly and the noise outside continued. Jim, not having moved a muscle, finished his bows, backed out and came back to his seat, whereupon the man in charge of the tents came straight up and whispered to him and he left ... The Queen's eyes got bigger and bigger and her colour higher and higher but she sat still; the Duchess of Devonshire got up but sat down again when she was told to.

In fact, the burnt tent was some hundreds of yards away, but the risks to the Investiture crowd of 4,000 was obvious and the lack of panic fairly remarkable. Later the Queen told Freda she had been terrified but the King never even knew what was happening!

To Jim the removal from Calcutta to Delhi and the reorganizing of India's government presented itself as 'a terrific rush of work' even without the drudgery which fell on the Secretariat rather than the Private Secretary. Whatever the great political arguments on either side, Jim was personally in favour of the move. There were natural regrets. 'Delhi may be cooler and cleaner and not so noisy but we shall have to live in tents or tumbledown houses; we shall lose the charm of Tollygunge with its beautiful golf-links; and we at Government House shall lose all the charms of Barrackpore, where I am writing now ... a beautiful park on the banks of the Hoogly 15 miles up-river from Calcutta ... I go in every morning by launch to my work', adding that that gave him an hour and a quarter of peaceful journey during which he could work.

On the morrow of the Durbar, with the King, to Jim's enormous relief, away from Indian shores again, he reflected on the native enthusiasm shown on the occasion, especially by the Bengalis,

> but with such emotional people one cannot count on this or any other emotion lasting very long ... That is one of the reasons why it is such an excellent thing for the Government of India to leave Calcutta. The grumbles are taken far too seriously both out here and in England: a vast outcry from the sentimental 'Indian' members of Parliament ... Government out here is worried to death by the Secretary of State [for India, in England], and the result is deplorable and often ignorant interference by the Central Government,

and paralysis of the spirit of self-reliance on the part of the local Government.

Commercial interests and local sentiment in Bengal were outraged by the plan to move the Government of India from Calcutta to Delhi, and the Viceroy had been accused of high-handedness and secretiveness in the matter, though it did not originate with him. Certainly he and his Private Secretary were in favour. Freda recalled in her feminine way the very first news of the British government's decision. 'It is so curious for me to remember the first day H.E. got a letter about the change,' she wrote home about April 1912. 'I think it was in early June or May 1911. He brought it straight over to Jim, and I can see Jim now reading it with an unmoved face in the garden where we were sitting, with H.E. talking to me with Tiny's arm round his neck.' [6]

By November 1912 they were able on tour to have a look at the Delhi site:

> We spent a day or two at Delhi, and it was remarkable to see what a change in the face of the country had been introduced by the temporary buildings which had been erected since the Durbar. The new city will be some 5 miles away, and a party of us went out with the Viceroy to look. The first thing will be to choose a spot for Government House, before the lay-out of the rest of the place can be chosen. The whole scheme hangs together and nothing can be finally settled until the experts return in December.

In December when they went back to Delhi Freda and family were evidently there too, and Jim wrote that the Circuit House had been converted into a Viceregal Lodge 'and they have hired a house at the gates for us. The rest are all in tents.' The house was insisted on by Freda, and she was later thankful she had done so, when the rains were flooding the tents. Even Jim's office was at first in a tent, one of a long double row extending a quarter of a mile down one of the approaches to Government House, to which he bicycled daily.

---

6. James's and Freda's two little girls were called Gwen and Wilmot, but Wilmot was always known as Tiny.

Underneath the routine of work in India with its highlights of splendour and its years of toil lay the fear of terrorism. The word 'terrorism' seems not to have been used: acts of violence in protest against alien rule or against injustice, real or imagined, were not in the India of that day incorporated into a comprehensive political philosophy or party programme. By the British at any rate they were referred to as 'outrages', 'conspiracies' and manifestation of 'sedition' by 'the extremists'. This is the vocabulary of Jim when writing about political murders.

The moving force was nascent nationalism, not simply a response to racial discrimination, though the two cannot be easily separated. Jim in his deepest heart was a law-and-order man, not a politician and not a racialist by conviction like a South African. This is not to say that he was incapable of apparent racial arrogance. He wrote once in 1912 of a certain Englishman who was running a 'public school' for the Brahmin of Kashmir who, he said in a moment's extraordinary bitterness, 'despises truthfulness and labour and courage'. This is a very 'public-school' remark, in the bad, old-fashioned sense, and suggests how closely allied the British brand of racialism was with class-consciousness, and, indeed, all the more damaging for that. But Jim escaped the worst sort of confrontation with race and class simply because his life was set in the highest echelons of government. He did not mix because he could not step out of his world. This was very different, as we shall see, from the lives and attitudes of his sister and brother in the Transvaal; and when Jim spoke up strongly for the rights of Indians, we may as well remember that he was speaking from the security of high position.

'We are bound to keep the Indian end up to the best of our ability,' he wrote home in January 1914, 'and the fat will be in the fire if we do not get them a little juster treatment. Meantime, I got the Colonial view to the tune of 3 sheets from Dick this morning, and it is quite clear he doesn't think an Indian ought to have any rights at all. The British Empire seems between the devil and the deep blue sea.' Mary too had written that Indians were not wanted in South Africa, that they 'confused' the colour problem and that Lord Hardinge should not have made a speech in favour of Sikh immigration into Canada.

In India itself the immediate problem was political violence, not interior debate about the brotherhood of men. The most dramatic assassination attempt was against the Viceroy himself at his state entry into Delhi on 23 December 1912. Jim wrote to his father six days later:

> I was on one of the two elephants immediately in front of the Viceroy, and our orders were to be 30 yards ahead, but we may have been a little more, when the explosion occurred. I thought it came from my right, and MacMahon who was with me suggested that it was some silly fellow with a throw-down cracker. Anyway, I did not look round at once, and when I did I saw that the Viceroy's elephant was advancing as before and there was nothing peculiar to notice except that the Viceroy had not got his helmet on and seemed unconscious of the fact. That puzzled me. Next I noticed that one of the attendants from behind was clambering round the howdah. He stopped on the elephant below Lady Hardinge and I could see he was saying something to her; then he let himself down and jumped off and disappeared. I then noticed that the State umbrella which was still up behind the Viceroy was rather battered. All this time the elephant seemed to be advancing. Then at last the Viceroy reached back, found his helmet and put it on, and immediately afterwards he stopped the elephant, the reason being that both he and Lady H. had realized that there was a dead man behind them in the howdah. Maxwell, Military Secretary, and Roberts the doctor then got off their elephants and I saw Roberts examining the Viceroy's back, from which I realized he bad been hurt. Next, Lady H. got off the elephant, which by now was kneeling, and then a number of firemen and elephant attendants ran up with ladders, and it was then that I realized that there was probably a dead man in the howdah behind. So it turned out. The Viceroy had actually advanced 155 yards from where the bomb was thrown out, and it must have been a gruesome sight for the spectators to see that poor Jamadar blown to a wreck lying backwards out of the howdah on the elephant's back. It was about then that I got down, i.e., just as they recovered the dead man, and almost at the same time the Viceroy fainted. I ascertained that he wished the function to proceed and went and spoke to Sir

Guy Fleetwood Wilson [Finance Member of Council] about it. I then got back and assisted to move the Viceroy off the elephant. He had recovered consciousness, and after he was put into a motor-car he again told me that he wanted Sir Guy to read his speech. They went off in two motor-cars: the Viceroy with the doctor and Military Secretary in one, Lady H. and an A.D.C. and her daughter [Diamond] in the other, and we went on with the procession and ceremony and the return procession.

One could not help feeling that they might have another man waiting somewhere with another bomb in case the first one failed, but nothing of that sort happened, and everyone behaved with great composure.

Since then I have had to deal with over 2000 letters and telegrams of sympathy and indignation, and the feeling of India has never in my time been so deeply stirred, though I have little doubt there are still the remains of the bomb conspiracy, and there are considerable sections among certain classes of the population who will regard the incident with approval and applause, though they will be careful not to say so, and will on the contrary send telegrams of horror. The Viceroy is doing well.

During the procession Freda was at their house in Delhi nursing a bad leg and looking after the baby Michael. She sent Nanny and the two girls to see the sight and lay on the verandah waiting for Jim to come home. The telephone rang. It was Mr Cotes, the Reuter's agent, who said,

'How is Lady Hardinge?' I said, 'I don't know. Is she ill? I haven't been to the show.' He gave a sort of gasp and I heard him murmur something and then say, 'Oh, it's all right, never mind.' I never feel happy in India till I see Jim safely back from these processions … I seized an umbrella and rushed off to the house [Government House?]: it's about 10 minutes walk … Colonel Maxwell was at the door. I asked if Her Ex. was ill, and he said, 'You know there was a bomb thrown?' I asked who was hurt, and he said, 'The Viceroy – we hope slightly – one servant badly, and one was blown nearly to pieces. Lady H. was not touched.' I asked him if Jim was all right,

as I knew his elephant with Sir Henry was immediately behind [sic].
He reassured me and was telling me how it happened when just then
Major Forbes in shirt-sleeves came out and said Lady H. wanted me.
I went into her bedroom and met Colonel Roberts coming out who
said, 'The Viceroy's are only superficial wounds in his neck and back
but down his thigh they took out 3 or 4 nails which were embedded
in his flesh, and they may cause trouble.' Lady H. was lying on the
sofa with a strained face talking hard. She said they were received
so well when suddenly there was this awful noise and she knew they
had thrown something. 'I said to the Viceroy, "are you hurt?" and
he said "I don't think so but go on, don't let them stop." He never
looked round and we went on, but the umbrella from behind had
fallen and I looked and saw an awful sight, and I said, "there is a
dead man and we can't go on", and then I put my hand behind [the
Viceroy's] back, for I saw a hole in his coat and there was blood
coming out, and then he gave a sort of convulsive shudder and I felt
he must be mortally wounded and this convulsive shudder was the
end. I waved to Maxwell who was on the elephant in front and he
stopped, and then the Viceroy fainted, and they got him down.'

I stopped her talking as I felt it was bad for her. She asked for the
Maharajah of Gwalior. He came in for a moment and I slipped out.

Outside Colonel Maxwell told me more. When they lifted H.E.
down he regained consciousness for a moment and said 'Give my
speech to MacMahon [sic] and go on with the procession', and then
they got him into a motor. Jim helped to get H.E. down and then got
on his elephant and the procession went on, but you can imagine the
blank which fell on the whole thing.

The eyewitness account at Government House ends there and
Freda went on in a naturally rather wild way to speak of the sedition
no one in England will believe exists, which was as bad as ever, and
of her own (unnamed) suspicions about the perpetrators. She added
comments on Jim shouting at some natives who had brought him a
present, 'and sure enough I saw a lovely carpet spread out – just what
I am wanting, but of course it was refused. I think he is about the only
man I know who does refuse things.'

In ten days the Viceroy was recovering well despite a large tunnel wound from back to shoulder. The impassivity of Jim's account is continued in the correspondence. There is a grim satisfaction that a convalescent Viceroy meant less work for himself, but husbandly anxiety for Freda who was anyhow strained by headaches, pain in her leg and having to keep house on what she felt was a restricted income.

Neither Jim or Freda seemed ever able to get away for a holiday. The Viceroy would neither consider Jim's applying for a better-paid job in the Indian Civil Service nor countenance his going on leave; indeed, he said in 1913 that he could not understand how Jim could want leave.

Yet throughout their official relationship and the stressful work which went with it, there flourished between the two families a clear friendship which through the children emerged as a kind of warmth. This is best explained against the background of Simla.

Climate and custom had given the Government of India a routine over the years. From December to March it functioned at the seat of government, first Calcutta, then Delhi. In the hot season, April to August, the viceregal court normally moved up to the hill station of Simla from where the Himalayas could be seen. The autumn was generally spent on tour, which enabled the Viceroy and his staff to see much of India, and be seen. There were some variations in this pattern. For example, the North West Frontier could be visited during April, and hunting holidays taken then in parts of northern India. But though wives and young families lived as far as possible at the centre of government and at Simla – which also became a curious kind of capital when the Viceroy was there – they did not normally travel the length and breadth of India, so that Simla was rather specially for them another home.

After Jim became Private Secretary to the Viceroy, Freda came out from leave in England to join him, bringing the two girls, Gwen and Wilmot (Tiny) and little Jamie. In April 1911 she wrote that they had arrived and settled in, and that the house in Calcutta was small but charming, while the one at Simla, called 'Observatory House', was perfect. The children enjoyed everything, little Jamie running about in gauze vest and flannel knickers.

They were united on the beauty of Simla and its environs. 'I am sure we shall be well here, which is half the battle. We are perched up with the Viceregal Lodge on a hill and look far away both sides to snows in the distance ... purple hills and dark valleys.'

Freda continued with a description of all the household organiza-tion needed. 'I have engaged a governess who comes for two hours daily', also cook and gardener. 'I expect [the cook] loots me right and left but he is so beautifully clean and cooks so well I hope I shan't find him out.'

Freda was a positive-minded decorator and her teasing of Jim for his vagueness sometimes had a slight edge. 'The house gets slowly on but Jim is in for a bad time when he comes. He never told me that everything new was wanted ... The colours already in the house are impossible ... He gave me all the wrong measurements for the draw-ing- room curtains.'

Jim on his side was deeply pleased to have his family, and could see that Simla was beautiful though flawed by what went on there. He told his old father how much he would have liked the place, anyhow till the rains began 'when there is nothing to do but live in the mist, dine and dance', and 'as dinner and dancing have few attractions for me I don't look forward to the rains. From you I have inherited a great love of the sun.'

He described how Simla was built on ridges, chopped up to make levels for hundreds of houses and scores of tennis courts, with polo on a plain three miles down a steep path. There were innumerable tennis parties. The well being of his family and his sense of being liked made Jim 'ecstatically happy in his work' – strong words for him.

The social life was a fly in Jim's ointment. Too often it meant being kept up late with consequent difficulty in getting up in the morning, and therefore no time for exercise in the afternoon. The climate, though beautiful in holiday time, was 'not always suitable for the extremely hard game the world plays here in the matter of dining out [which] is really crushing. Carriages are not allowed in Simla and we have to be drawn by coolies in rickshaws and it constantly means three-quarters of an hour's journey so that you are lucky if you get to bed before midnight. At the same time I feel that it is a good thing to go out a good deal and meet people and exchange ideas.'

Not surprisingly, Freda took to the social life more enthusiastically than her husband, though quite clear-sighted about its dangers and able to cope in a strong-minded way. The Hardinges liked her and she was much in demand. For instance, one Tuesday there was a Harrow dinner (the Viceroy's old school) to which Jim could not go (intentionally or otherwise) and Freda dined upstairs at Viceregal Lodge with Lady Hardinge and the other wives and went down afterwards to join in the singing of Harrow songs and so to dancing. There was also hospital work, European and Indian, into which she threw herself, and also the secretaryship of the YWCA. 'Out here one must help', as she put it.

As well as his Private Secretary (PSV) the Viceroy had a Military Secretary (MSV) who amongst other things supervised the viceregal estates and establishment finances. At the time this was Colonel Maxwell, VC, like Freda a strong character, and in summer 1911 she made a covert reference to some mild clash of wills. Jim's comment was, 'My dear, I hope you won't get too fond of power!' 'However,' wrote Freda, 'I feel that sooner or later we shall fall out, so I don't pride myself on the victory. Life here is so difficult, and I find the only possible way of living at all is never to go out to anything alone. Everything one says is repeated and added to and talked about till it is unrecognized, and the intrigues which go on would fill a book. However, we stand quite clear of it, and I think Jim is a <u>tremendous</u> success, both socially and at his work.' She ended her letter of this, her first summer at Simla, with the phrase, 'At the back of all is the sickening sense of disaster, for anarchy is rife and one dreads the King's visit and the whole time in Calcutta unspeakably', and she went on to explain to her sister-in law Bee at home how extremists intended to massacre all the Europeans as they had murdered Mr Ashe for sentencing a man to prison for sedition, adding for good measure that Ashe's poor sister had died of hydrophobia.

This was before the assassination attempt at Delhi, but Freda in her heart hated India and her abiding dread was not misplaced. Bombs were a hazard people in government might stoically expect, but illness (as all classes under the sun have at times realized) was indiscriminating. As soon after Freda's arrival as September 1911 an appalling blow was struck. It is told in the words written to Grandmother Du Boulay in Winchester by the matron of Marlborough House Nursing Home in Simla:

> Mrs. Du Boulay has asked me to write to you as she couldn't do so herself this mail. I am afraid I have very sad news for you, but you will have heard long ere this that dear little Jamie died very suddenly yesterday afternoon. He had had double pneumonia and I had been nursing him at night for a week. He was doing perfectly well, his temperature, pulse and respiration had gone down practically to normal and we all thought he was safely over it – and suddenly at 2 o'clock in the afternoon he got convulsions and died in about an hour ...

The rest is phrases of sadness and sympathy, and 'we are hoping to persuade them to go out into the country to the Viceroy's country house for a short time'. In fact they did so. Jim wrote to his mother a week later with gruff matter-of-factness:

> I have little to say this week. The funeral was on the 14th. The Viceroy and Lady Hardinge and a few intimate friends only were there. The cemetery is a series of narrow terraces made in the almost precipitous sides of the hill and surrounded by fir trees. On Friday I took the whole family out to The Retreat, the Viceroy's little cottage about 7 miles away in the peace and quiet of the mountains and forests. I have to come in the miles to work every day ... Nothing could express the kindness of the Hardinges whose guests we are out here, and Lady H.'s affectionate and wise sympathy have done more than anything else I think to support poor Freda.

The Durbar was on the horizon but a month after Jamie's death Jim was writing that despite Freda's great grief there was no question of her giving up her assigned role as lady-in-waiting during the Queen's visit. Of this the letters say little but family tradition records the firm but not unkind advice of another lady-in-waiting that in

India the loss of a child was something to be expected, and so too a mother's duty to mask grief and carry on.

If Jim appeared the less hurt, that was his role. His inmost being belonged to his family and four months after Jamie's death a letter to his mother spoke of the fullness of happiness he felt at Gwen and Tiny and 'their shouts of joy', even while they were distracting his train of thought about difficult cases.

The next summer the children (then nine and six) were taken for a treat to the horse show at Annandale, and their mother described how Tiny went off with her favourite General Slogget, deserted him and was found on the front seat by the jumps between the C-in-C India and the Viceroy, hand in hand with the former and arm round the other, while they talked affairs of state over her head.

The question of home leave was as thorny a one as that of the promotion which the Viceroy would not let Jim apply for. Lady Hardinge herself wanted to go home, and perhaps had the greater need. But Freda was disappointed and as much irritated as flattered by Lord Hardinge's earnest begging that she would stay and act as hostess for him in Lady H.'s absence.

It is easy to form pictures of viceregal selfishness, but impossible to judge. The two families remained close. Lady Hardinge returned to England and later died there. Freda stayed in India and flourished. In autumn 1912 Michael was born to Freda and Jim and the Viceroy asked to be godfather; the Hardinges would have liked the boy christened Charles, but the parents disliked the name and compromised on Michael Hardinge.

Home leave was not of course just a question of personal refreshment but of children's upbringing. Tiny especially had long been a problem in her habit of eating anything she saw, a bad habit in India, and as the girls grew to be seven and ten they were sometimes said to be in need of discipline such as an English school would give them.

At the sports day of 1913 Gwen confided to a friendly newspaper man that 'mother talks a great deal but Daddy is naturally silent', and the same week amidst the glitter of levee, drawing room and horse show at Simla Tiny observed of the immensely tall commandant of the bodyguard, 'I like Captain Keighley far better than his wife but of course I shan't tell him so.'

Perhaps Gwen spoke truer than she knew when she analysed the difference between her mother and father, the one outgoing, sociable, talkative, the other somewhat withdrawn and caring only for the dispatch of business. Yet they shared much and were happy enough to tease each other. Freda in her own way grew to dread Simla. In March 1913, with constant headaches and a leg infected since Michael's birth, she wrote, 'I dread the next Simla season <u>inexpressibly</u>', and in August was fearing also the next winter when Jim would have to go on tour with the Viceroy: 'such horrors have happened to me the last two autumns [Jamie's death and a carriage accident] that I feel sometimes I simply cannot stay here alone for another one. Jim can never understand nerves in any form.'

But the social round went on, as much part of government as Jim's files and interviews. 'I had hoped to have a quiet and cheap month, especially the latter,' wrote Freda in April 1914 to her mother-in-law, 'but it is quite impossible. I had such a nice dinner-party last night which I got up to amuse and distract Sir Henry MacMahon who is doing these negotiations with China and Thibet and which alas are not running smoothly ... I tell Jim there is really no <u>need</u> for him to come back to the house at all, his assistant ... is far more polite and attentive to his guests than he is.' But the discord was resolved in the next sentence: 'People always say this is the most homelike house in India. I think the children make it so.'

In this year or two before the Great War, with the Viceroy still shaken from his wounding and the tempo of diplomacy quickening, Freda seemed to live on a high ridge between the confidence given her by important people and the longing to be out of it. 'I hope the autumn of 1914 will see Jim at home, and then I trust never to set foot in India again.' But in the next breath she was rejoicing in the prospect of being hostess to H.A.L. Fisher and Ramsay MacDonald (Tiny's measles drove them away). Politicians spoke freely to her. 'The people who are negotiating a tripartite convention with Thibet and China have told her most of the course of the negotiations in confidence,' said a slightly scandalized Jim.

They both needed an occasional holiday and shared a love of the vast solitudes available: 'Freda and I have been having a break. I threatened the Viceroy with dire results if he did not give me a few days' holiday, so he let me go from the 12th to the 19th [September 1913].' The letter was written on their journey with hill-ponies along the Tibet road, riding and walking, with a little shooting, amidst great mountains clad in fir with their lower slopes sometimes green with cultivation and the open ground carpeted with flowers.

The life of a Viceroy required journeys over great stretches of India. The object was not mainly recreation, though 'entertainment' in the forms of shooting and hunting were often arranged for the viceregal party, but to see and be seen, by chiefs and Indian princes especially, and beyond them by subjects of the British monarch whom the Viceroy represented. The journeys were made in the Viceroy's special train and timed to avoid the hottest weather. There were also more private excursions for shooting or hunting, and Jim's letters dated from 'Viceroy's Camp' show that Lord Hardinge favoured Dehra Dun, within easy reach by rail of Simla, and here they were often to be found before the Simla season opened.

When he became PSV late in 1910, Jim found himself working at Calcutta between eight and 11 hours a day, with an hour or two for exercise and much of his other spare time spent in formal dressing and dining. Occasional weekends shooting duck or jackal were possible, but more complete breaks came when the Viceroy took his whole entourage. During an Easter holiday at the end of April 1911 Jim sent home a typical account of one of these:

I am writing this from a delightful camp on the banks of the Ganges about 20 miles from Dehra Dun and 5 from Hardwar, where the river after passing out of the Himalayas and through the adjoining valley (Dun) goes through another low range of hills called the Sivaliks. Lord Hardinge is here with Military Secretary, self, and one A.D.C. besides the Forest Officer who is running our camp. Lady Hardinge is in another camp about 10 miles away with 2 A.D.C.s and Miss Sandford and 2 of the Bodyguard officers, and there has been considerable rivalry between the two camps as to which would get the best sport. As a matter of fact, things have been fairly equal, – each party has got two tigers, both of them falling to the Bodyguard adjutant and both of ours to Colonel Maxwell (MSV). I have not had a shot yet, but each party has got several cheetah.

In his first experience of a big-game camp Jim was impressed with the delightful intelligence of the accompanying 28 elephants and the way in which at a word of command they would put the mahout and other riders on their backs with great gentleness by means of their trunks. They were used for all to get about, beating through the jungle in line ahead. At one tiger shoot,

we started off by rowing across the river, then got on to the elephants and marched 5½ miles to the bottom slopes of the Himalayas where a tiger had killed the night before. As we were moving to our places the mahouts suddenly called our attention to a crackling noise in the jungle which they said was wild elephant, and we looked with some concern at the rather fragile trees we had to sit upon and the very low seats they had given us ... The jungle was densely thick and I thought there was very little chance of their being able to get the tiger come out straight at the guns. Maxwell saw the elephant about 40 yards away and said he never sat so still in his life (we are not allowed to shoot them here – penalty 500 rupees) and at last the tiger showed herself in the jungle in front of him. He fired at what he could see and hit her in the stomach and sent her back into the beat. Then they reversed the line of beaters and changed the position of two of us. Our Forest Officer always goes with the beat on a pad elephant, – the beaters were also mounted on elephants – and presently we heard a shot. Apparently the tigress charged the line of elephants and put two of them to flight, but the Forest Officer, Rebech, came on his own staunch animal, saw the beast just ready for another spring, and hit her in the neck and that was the end of her.

Then we ate a joyous lunch and came down the river to the camp on a weird contraption consisting of cots tied across the inflated skins of nilghai, steered by two men each on another skin and propelled by their legs.

There is a sameness about tiger shooting and by the end of Hardinge's time Jim confessed he was bored by seeing viceregal tigers shot. Not that he was any sort of early objector to blood sports. He was an ordinary man of peace who never tired of the natural beauties of jungle and mountain, revelling in 'the quiet green where interviewers are hardly known', but at moments of personal risk and success not above triumphing in the violent drama of the hunt.

His own 'first tiger' fell to him the next year at Dehra Dun, where they had again gone for a holiday with some shooting for panther and stag as well as tiger. The first week was fairly blank. The Viceroy shot a huge python, Jim shot a small stag for the pot, but when the whole distinguished party turned to fishing they managed only one small trout.

In the second week there was daily news of tiger but 'with one exception he had already slipped out of the jungle when we began beating. On the one day we found him at home he came out between the Viceroy and me with his hair all on end like a runaway railway train through elephant grass that stood higher than a man's head. The Viceroy and I had each two snap-shots at him but none of our bullets took effect … I certainly cannot undertake to hit a tiger with a rifle going at that pace.' Another blank, it seemed. But on the Monday at Dehra Dun there was a telegram to say a tiger had killed, so they all motored at once to the jungle base miles away, transferred to horses and elephants for the last four miles and took their places where the buffalo bait had been laid:

> Just before 4 I saw a tigress coming through the long grass about 15 yards away. I had a steady shot and she turned and went back at a fast trot and disappeared. I was very down on my luck, as I thought I had missed, but when the beat was over we found a lot of blood and after following her up by the blood for about 60 yards on elephants we found her lying dead in a dry ditch. It is my first tiger.

Since the party was full of important people, such as Captain

Astor as well as the Viceroy and his Commandant of Bodyguard, it might be thought sporting of them to let the Private Secretary, not a natural shot, have the success. Matters were quite different when shooting as guests of an Indian prince, and when the party went to Gwalior in April 1914 Jim simply took days off, leaving the Viceroy to bag 13 out of 21 tigers in two weeks. What he most enjoyed on that occasion was one day on the platform when he saw a tigress asleep near the buffalo she had killed, hearing the beaters, 'sit up like a dog and as they came near suddenly slink off with great rapidity'.

Even native states could differ in their degree of formality. In Gwalior the Indian officials and courtiers ate with the Viceroy's party and on the last night even larked about with some of the staff. In Rewa, on the other hand, they never set eyes on the Maharajah and his courtiers except out shooting, and then there was strict protocol about who should shoot, irrespective of positioning: the Viceroy first, the PS not at all.

Hunting the wild boar with spears was a very different game, less expensive, less aristocratic, and yielding game which could be eaten (by non-Muslims). In Jim's own words from February 1914:

> I had morning's pig-sticking [in Jodhpar] of which I must tell you. First of all, the elements of the game are that the pig lives in jungle where they are sometimes fed so as to collect them. The party is divided up into heats of four each, and as boars come out, each heat takes its turn.

> When we got to our meet, they put me up on an A1 little polo pony, about the best beast I have ever had between my legs, as handy as a cat and with a snaffle mouth. The only crab was that when I did not let him go at full gallop his progress was more like that of a black buck than a horse, and it was as much as I could do to keep my seat.

> At the beginning we put up an enormous fighting boar, who charged on one of our party before we had begun the business. However, other pig came out and I found myself launched in pursuit of an average boar. He jinked, and while I was pulling up and desperately maintaining my seat through the black-buck motion, the other fellows who wanted me to get first spear shouted out, 'Here he is';

so I had to compose myself as best I could and start again.

This happened 3 or 4 times, and when I did eventually poke that pig with my spear I was so exhausted that I was all over my horse's head, my spear anywhere, and underneath, threatening vengeance with savage grunts, the pig. However, I was lucky enough to get off without my horse being cut. Then we went back for our old friend. One or two men on camels went to look for him. He charged out at the camels, and it was the funniest thing imaginable to see the camels executing *pas seuls* that would have done credit to a ballet girl.

This time there was no question of giving me precedence, and we all did our best. As luck would have it, the pig jinked away from the first man, and I was able to nip in with my handy pony, and as he turned to charge my spear found his ribs. He went on for about 20 yards and then began to stagger, then turned round and fell dead. I had reached his heart and got him in one, and was as pleased as a two-year-old when one of the old hands behind shouted 'Good spear!' He was a fine boar measuring 32¾ inches at the wither, – not bad, as the record is 36, so perhaps an old man [he was 46] and poor rider like myself may be excused for feeling pleased.

It was a sport which wives in those days sometimes followed as non-combatants. Freda certainly did, with a vitality at least as great as her husband's, adding her graphic description of the beaters in line on their riding camels with scarlet rugs (just like those in nineteenth-century Egypt), surrounded by other drivers and beaters on foot who whacked the tall grass above their heads, looking down frequently to avoid the deep holes and pits in the ground below. 'Suddenly you see the heat of 4 lower their spears and dash forward into the jungle.'

The tour was an annual activity for which the Viceroy's rather antiquated special train, drawn by two locomotives, was normally used. The visits Jim happened to write about in his letters provide some vivid examples.

At the end of March 1911 there was a visit to the Punjab, one of the most sensitive and historically important of India's regions. 'I am writing this in the train,' he told his mother; 'we have now finished with a Calcutta season longer by a month than usual and more strenuous than usual because of the novelty of the work. (He has just become PSV). 'After Delhi we move to Lahore where the Viceroy will visit his grandfather's battlefield and hold a durbar of Punjab chiefs ... The train is so heavy it will want four engines to pull it up the rather steep inclines to Quetta ... Then to Karachi where I shall meet people I know.'

It was not a tourist's holiday. On the way Jim had to collect material for the Viceroy's 15 to 20 speeches. But the reward was in the occasions where cultures hitherto unknown to him could be met, and the historic past encountered in living men. From the Punjab he reported home:

> We have just finished a most interesting visit to the battlefields of Mookbi and Ferozeshah, – battles you must almost remember being fought [Grandfather was born in 1832] – and then to Lahore, capital of the Punjab. The interest of the battlefields was heightened by a group of old Sikh veterans who had medals for many fights under the British flag, and also by the presence there of a battery which actually took part in the fights and now happens to be stationed close by at Ferozepore. At Lahore a durbar was held in the Reception Hall of Ranjit Singh with a most curious agglomeration of human units from Bengali Babus to wild Baluchis from the frontier almost hidden in their shaggy beards, and from the representative of the last of the Moguls to the chief of Kapurthala, who is far more at home in a Parisian drawing-room than at a durbar. I had a long interview with the last of the Moguls, and he told me he was the senior member of the late royal family of Delhi, and that there were 960 members of the family still alive ... The Viceroy made him Ph.D. at Lahore and had to reply tactfully successively to deputations of Sikhs, Hindus and Muslims. There was a parade of about 600 retired officers of the Indian army, one of whom had fought side by side with John Nicholson [hero of the Mutiny].

In October they were in Hyderabad, the largest of the Indian principalities where neither doctorates of philosophy nor memories of great campaigns were as prominent to the observer as the enormous wealth of the prince. 'I think the Viceroy has a very happy knack of securing the confidence and affection of those for whom he lays himself out. I am quite sure he won them from the young Nizam, who promises well but has many temptations to fight through.' In gentle words like these Jim indicated the delicate tasks which confronted British rulers in India within living memory, some in the political situation itself, to guide young independent rulers with care and respect, others in trying to lessen the effects of personal frailties like addiction to alcohol.

From Hyderabad sprawled over the centre of India it was three wearisome days in the train back to Delhi, where they had to spend hours moving about the city of tents and dust under the baking sun, marvelling at the progress made in the previous six months. Ploughed fields had become a busy railway terminus and a dozen wayside stations had sprung up in rural land.

In 1912, the Royal Durbar over, it was the turn of the North West Frontier. Then as now it seemed a mysterious country, not only for an unconquerability which draws admiration but for a sense of being at one of the world's ends. The mood caught even the official Jim:

> We have seen the Malahaud, and the hill up which our Military Secretary [Colonel Maxwell] charged with the Guides in 1895 at the time of the relief of Chitral, and where a few years later the small garrison, practically without fortifications, were suddenly attacked by 20,000 fanatics and did not drive them off until they had killed 4000. We have been up the Khyber [Pass] in the neighbourhood of which every Regiment in the Army must at one time or another have left some of its bones. We have climbed a high hill and looked down on the plains and mountains of Afghanistan, and made out Afghan cantonments through our glasses – and have seen the sweep of the snowy hills from the Safed Kola to the Hindu Kush, through Kafirisky to Chitral and the everlasting Himalayas. We have seen forts and outposts where officers and their wives can hardly go more than a few hundred yards without an escort, though the valley below is smiling with crops ... We have been in cantonments where large bodies of troops are collected, but where the sentries at night are protected by walls, lest they be suddenly come at for their rifles; and we have ridden about with an escort of wild-looking men

armed with every conceivable type of rifle, some of whom have undoubtedly been fighting against us within the last 15 years.

It is not until you come here that you realize what an enormous area is covered by these frontier tribes; the habitation may be sparse, but when they concentrate they are anything but despicable foes; when you have them at a disadvantage they melt away, and contrariwise when they have you at a disadvantage they multiply exceedingly; and they are very difficult to punish. And yet somehow or other we exercise a very considerable control over them which is only broken down from time to time.

My companion through most of these journeyings has been Sir Henry MacMahon, than whom I do not suppose there is in India any greater expert on Frontier questions. He is now Foreign Secretary [i.e. on the Viceroy's Council] and has put in almost all his service in various parts of the Frontier, besides demarcating the boundary between British and Persian and Afghan territory, visiting Cabul and taking the present Amir round India.

Rajputana, the great complex of native states south of the Punjab but still in north-west India, provided startling contrasts both to the Frontier provinces and within its own confines. Jim spoke in October 1913 of the good open-air life in Bikaner after what he considered the inanities of Simla, and spoke of the Maharajah as 'perhaps the most accomplished and progressive Chief in India', while of Kapurthala he fancied that the prince preferred Paris to India, confessing his abode too much for his own puritanical English taste: 'we found a Renaissance palace so decorated that I told Freda I had to pass through the rooms with averted eyes!'

In the autumn of 1913 the Viceroy made an extensive tour lasting over 7½ weeks through central and southern India. In Jim's letters home the undercurrent of anxiety is a little stronger. The threat of assassination lay over the Viceroy like a shadow, the riots at Cawnpore raised acute debates between the Viceroy and his Private Secretary, and the strain told. In September he was begging Freda earnestly not to go away on leave.

Yet there were always new scenes for him to describe, and if to human anxieties there are no geographical solutions, there are at least highlights of distraction. One such was the *keddah* or stockading of wild elephants with the view of taming them, which he saw in the great south-western state of Mysore:

> I am writing this from an enormous camp pitched in the heart of the Mysore Forest, where keddah operations are going on ... We were on one side of a river about 150 yards wide, and on the other side we could see a herd of about 30 elephants close down to the water's edge, with one huge tusker among them. The beaters who had been round them for some time gradually came on from behind. The elephants became restless, and after long hesitation entered the water. Then the beaters came rushing up to the water's edge and made a tremendous din. It was beginning to get dark and they had torches ... The elephants came over to our side and stampeded along the edge of the river below the steep bank [where we were]. We all joined the din and followed along above the elephants till they came to the entrance to the passage which led to their keddah or stockade. They were turned in here by the stockading and men shouting.
>
> In they all went, except one young tusker who came back to prospect ... only to be met by a man on one of the big tame elephants who had just reached this side of the river. He hesitated, put up his ears and tail as if he were going to charge but at the last moment thought better of it and followed the rest into the keddah.
>
> Next day in this strong stockade 15 or 20 yards in diameter practically the whole day was spent roping the big tusker. First some seven or eight men went in on tame elephants, armed with very light spears, dodging and prodding among the smaller elephants. They gradually isolated the tusker, and then half-a-dozen men got in, and from under the tame elephants managed to put great ropes with slip-knots round his legs, and then four great ropes round his neck. All this took hours.
>
> When all was ready they opened the gate to drag him out. For a long time he would not move and stood with his toes dug in like some huge Sphinx; and then suddenly made tremendous struggles which seemed to sway all the other elephants and shook the stockade. Finally he was dragged out ...

They took him down to the river and there, as he sulked, they made the biggest of the tame elephants go for him and knock him over ... and so the procession marched down through the river, occasionally delayed by Herculean struggles when the tusker seemed to drag about the tame elephants like dogs.

But ... finally he was ensconced in a small stockade just big enough to let him lie down.

Next morning we went to look at him. He had knocked every part of his cage which he could reach into matchwood, and stood there, a picture of Giant Despair, with intervals of terrible rage [when he] butted with savage and prolonged determination at a bit of the stockade still standing, and knocked it down.

There was a calf there hardly a year old that was quite friendly; and there was a two-year-old that was as savage as a mad dog ... and all around were the smaller cows being dragged about in the most casual manner by the big tame elephants, as if they were so many naughty puppies.

Today I went down again, and they were all tied up to trees, and you had to pick your way carefully between them keeping out of reach, for there was not one there that would not have willingly killed ...

But the whole thing leaves me rather sad. The majority of the cows and younger elephants will become quite tame and lead a decently happy life; but two or three were killed in the squash into the keddah and I think the old tusker will probably die of a broken heart.

This was written on 12 November 1913. By the end of the month they had moved further south, nearly abandoning Trichinopoly and points south because of flooding. 'But as the same bit was abandoned by Lord Minto [the previous Viceroy] on grounds of health, I pressed that it should not he given up if any possible means of carrying it out could be devised. So they made up a scratch train, in the absence of our Special, and we carried it through.' They were able to see the causeway and viaduct and the Palk Strait between India and Ceylon where the six-monthly race of waters is caused by wind.

From the tip of India they travelled up to Madras on the eastern coast where Jim seemed happy, revelling in the atmosphere 'more like that I was so long accustomed to in Bombay', liking the Governor and his wife (Lord and Lady Pentland) and meeting old acquaintances. 'Among others I had a flirtation with the bishop's wife. She had known me as "Jim" and reminded me that I had pulled her hair and admitted that she had preferred that to not being noticed. Her name was Isabel Duncan and these incidents occurred at Heddington when I was 10 and she was 8.[7] She was rather indignant that I had forgotten them but I played up as well as I could.'

It is hardly a discovery that the whole world grew more sombre in 1914. The outbreak of the Great War affected people in ways which are now almost impossible to imagine, but even at the time there were marked differences in response from these brothers and sisters in my father's family. Noel, as already seen, disappeared in his letters into a matter-of-fact professionalism, expressing few feelings save quiet praise for courageous acts and civilized hopes that horrors would not be aggravated. At the junior end of the family, yet to be encountered, Dick was bellicose against the Teutonic threat yet anxious at the same time not to leave his farm and wife undefended on the South African veldt. Philip became a soldier as soon as he could without fuss. The fever to join up and be part of the great patriotic duty affected Jim in India more acutely than most others. He wanted to fight and desired that everybody else should fight too, all friends and all relations, and that Indian troops should fight side by side with the British Army and not be shunted off into garrisons. If a latter-day cynic might note the keenest eagerness for battle in those the farthest from its likelihood, Jim's attitude was also in all fairness a testimony to his liberalism, for he clearly stood on the side of Indians as equals of Europeans in the army debates that had been raging.

There was too a nobility in desiring to give up 'the most interest-

---

7. Heddington, Wiltshire, in England's west country where all the family were at home. Here Jim's grandfather had been rector (d. 1836) and after him Jim's Uncle Frank was rector (1853–98). The event noted above occurred in 1878 when the Du Boulay family was evidently making one of its many stays.

ing post in India', as Freda put it, and to enlist as an ordinary soldier in any regiment that wanted him. In September 1914 Freda wrote, 'Jim is dumb with misery at not going [he was then 46]. He is a Lieutenant-Colonel in Volunteers and might go later ... I asked the Viceroy to let him go last night at dinner. He said, "Certainly not, and if he attempts it I shall have him manacled. He's got to stay here and defend you and me."'

The war which heightened Indian aspirations to independence found Jim deeply anxious about the civil peace while at the same time sympathetic from his heart towards those aspirations. He was indignant that Lloyd George should have compared the Kaiser to Mahomet, which the Muslims were quick to see as insulting. He was fearful of the effect Turkey's hostility might have too upon Muslim Indians. In the event the Viceroy's government guaranteed immunity from molestation of all Muslim holy places, and telegrams of loyalty poured in.

Interestingly it was at this rather late moment that a direct telephone line first established between Delhi and Simla enabled Jim and Freda to speak to each other regularly (November 1914).

Historians of that age will know (what the living have forgotten) that patriotism was often expressed more stridently by women than by men. The age of the suffragettes who fought for votes for women was certainly a time when women volunteered for every service in which their world would accept them. Yet it seems that those of more conservative temper were unsurpassed in egging on their menfolk to sacrifice in the armed forces. 'I tell Mike,' Freda wrote to her mother about her three-year-old son who had been born to replace the dead Jamie, 'he is to be either a soldier or a sailor and he nods his head and says "soger"... So I hope it is impressed upon him.' It was, for he lived to become a colonel in the Gordon Highlanders, though the absolute obedience to his nurse in which Freda rejoiced may perhaps have exacted a sad retribution in later life.

But people suffered without complaint at that particular time. Lady Hardinge had died on leave in England and their elder son died of wounds, but the Viceroy continued in his sworn office and accepted its prolongation till 1916. Jim accompanied him on a tour to the Persian Gulf and to Basra, newly captured from the Turks, and wrote (24 January 1915) of his chief's high courage.

Strange by today's standards, the Persian Gulf seemed to Jim sunk in a desolate sleep, and was indeed sunk in a real one in the case of a wireless station within sight of their ship where their messages were ignored though picked up as far away as Ceylon!

One good thing was the presence of the Viceroy's second son, Alec, who had been allowed to return and keep his father company after his double bereavement, 'and the Viceroy is I think as happy as he is ever likely to be again, with interesting work before him and congenial society'.

'Interesting work' and 'congenial society': such priceless benefits prevented the wartime letters at the end of Jim's surviving correspondence from becoming merely doom-laden or propagandist. In fact, they form an amalgam of political insight and amusing incident.

From Simla in April 1916 he outlined to his brother Ralph in London the major Indian problems of the moment: '(a) the conspiracy among returned emigrants in the Punjab (b) the Amir [of Afghanistan] (c) the Tribes on the Frontier [8] and (d) the position in Mesopotamia'.

'So far all well, but our margin of safety is cut very fine, and we cannot have a defeat in any direction without very grave danger ... In the Punjab we have nipped every development in the bud, but things might have gone badly if we had not had a splendid fellow at the head of affairs there in Sir Michael O'Dwyer.' It was a grim tale, though, of four executions after the bomb outrage in Lahore, and of the great number of the accused (82) in the Punjab conspiracy trial – 'the ramifications so many that it will be several months before it comes to an end'.

If the north and north-west were menacing, there was friendliness amounting to light relief from the far more northern kingdom of Nepal:

---

8. There were seven attacks on the North West Frontier during 1915 over which the Amir had no control (Hardinge, *My Indian Years*, pp 131–2).

I had a queer visit the other day (22 April 1915) from a little young man on a prancing steed, dressed in loose mauve breeches with a peculiar sepia coloured topi. He was General Babar Shuinshen Jung Bahadur, who is the son of the Nepalese Prime Minister, the real ruler of Nepal. He is up here to advise Government about Nepalese troops, a considerable body of which have been sent down to India to take the place of some of the Gurkha troops sent to the front. He was most friendly, – almost affectionate. Exactly 100 years ago we were fighting the Gurkhas in these very hills [Jim was writing from Simla], and he mentioned the fact with much unction the other day to someone, adding, 'this is pleasanter'.

By coincidence Jim was at the time taking part in Volunteer exercises and mock battles with a Gurkha detachment which seem to have carried realism to the point of hazard.

As Lord Hardinge's extended tour of duty as Viceroy moved to its end, Jim seemed hard put to dispel a gloom and harshness of view. His personal disappointment at the necessary postponement of his home leave to England was understandable, but bitter words were added in his letters about strikers in England and the 'labouring classes' who were making a good thing out of the war. (This was quite the reverse of Noel's liberal views of well-paid munitions workers whom he thought entirely entitled to buy the fur coats for which snobbish people mocked them.) Even the monsoon depressed Jim in 1915, against his better nature: 'I try to comfort myself with the reflection that it is "the gracious rain from heaven" which makes all the difference to the cultivators.'

A small incident betrays an inner kindness. At Simla the bandmaster was a German, and though he had been there many years he was the target of much ill feeling in 1915. His wife was in Germany when war broke out but she succeeded in making her way with her children back to India, experiencing enmity both in Germany and in India. 'Poor things,' wrote Jim, describing the situation, and he and Freda went to call on them.

The ex-Viceroy sailed back to England in April 1916, Jim and family on the same ship, and that is the end of the correspondence. By November Jim was back in Simla, the work 'fast and furious', but undertaken alone and from rented rooms, as he would not allow his family to risk submarines to join him. Besides, there was school in England for the children.

Jim's work was now with the Central Government of India and temporarily as a member of the Executive Council of the new Viceroy, Lord Chelmsford. There were other jobs too, evidently no less burdensome than any he had undertaken in a long service, and his retirement in 1922 was a blessed relief.

Happy the man with interesting work in retirement. For Jim it was to be Secretary and Home Bursar to his own beloved Winchester College from 1927 to 1935. He lived quietly with his family at Petersfield till his death in 1945.

CHAPTER 4

Transvaal Livings:
Mary, Richard (Dick),
Philip, Phyllis

In a big Victorian family with access to education but not to any considerable wealth, it was likely that the older boys would have the best opportunities for successful careers. In this way Noel the army officer and Jim the Indian Civil Servant enjoyed lives different in style from those of their youngest brothers, mainly because their father had been able to start them off in academy or college where they could qualify. If they served the empire in places where the British were disliked and opposed, at least they did so as members of great supportive organizations. And if they were not by nature highly sociable men, at least they were not forced to suffer loneliness. Week by week their letters tell of colleagues and friends, and their personal stories unfold as parts of a much peopled late imperial drama.

The Transvaal chapter of family history is different. The four who found themselves for a longer or shorter time in South Africa were relatively poorer – but not less interesting – than their elders. They too lived in part of the empire where many people on the spot hated the British, but they lived much more exposed to personal contact with those who might hate them, not as a withdrawn élite, cushioned by pay, prospects and prestige from everyday anxieties. Their letters

139

home, regular and factual like those of all the family, reveal Transvaal society in close texture, and the very precariousness of their lives sometimes made their words rough, without the suavity brought by official training.

Mary, an older, unmarried sister, became a school inspector in the service of the Pretoria government about 1906, trekked all over the Transvaal in the course of duty and gave in her letters home a spontaneous account of its human variety. Dick, after a couple of rather obscure attempts in Cape Colony, became a long-term tenant farmer just north of Pretoria. He is less liberal, more 'Boerized', than Mary. Philip tried for a year to work with Dick but wisely went back to Egypt where he will be met later. Phyllis, the youngest of all, spent a short convalescent holiday with the others and manages to convey in her letters a mixture of sharp observation and fey dottiness.

When the regular letters began to be preserved in 1908, the Second South African War had been over for six years, leaving the Boer republics of the Transvaal and the Orange River Colony defeated by Britain. British government had been reasserted against the will of the Dutch settlers, and although it was a mixed government of British and Dutch which created the Union of South Africa in 1910, it was a society divided by terrible bitterness. The war itself had been bad enough, but guerrilla warfare continued afterwards and was only put down by Kitchener's scorched-earth policy which involved taking Dutch families into the 'protective custody' of the 'concentration camps', an expression used here for the first time. There is no doubt that the intention of the British was not the same as that of the unspeakable exterminators in Nazi Europe 40 years later. But bitterness is not always in exact proportion to hurt received. Then was created a perpetual division between communities which in other circumstances might possibly have grown together as a frontier peasant-lordship dominating the Bantu, not unlike the Dutch-German settlers in the primitive Prussia of an earlier day.

As it was, the Transvaal on the morrow of the war was a land of mixed farming and mining, especially for gold. Adventurers made the headlines, as speculators, empire-builders, heroes or rogues. But

18. (Alice) Mary Du Boulay (1894–1950), Inspector of Schools,
Education Department, Pretoria, 1906.

the substratum was of hard rural work. Johannesburg was growing, but Pretoria, according to Mary, was 'sleepy'. Out on the veldt little townships were sometimes connected by railway lines, but mostly by cart tracks, often rutted or boulder-strewn. Inns and stores were very simple, not infrequently run by poor Jews. Dutch and British farm settlement was intermingled. Mines were mainly British managed. Everything was sustained by the vast floating population of Bantu Africans, politically subjected by European weapons and not yet developed enough to be other than a more or less willing supply of more or less unskilled labour. For these the universal term was 'kaffir', derived from the Arabic for 'unbeliever', but used in an unthinking descriptive sense without the intention of personal insult beyond the inborn contempt of European settlers for the primitive capacities of brown Africans whom it seemed natural to address as 'boys'.

These pages centre on the struggles of Mary and Dick to make their livings in the Transvaal, and when the known story begins they had been at it for some years and had formed a good friendship despite the 13 years between them. 'He and I have been through bad times together and we understand each other,' wrote Mary to her mother in April 1911.

For Mary the bad times were a mixture of daily hardships and inner unhappiness, as for much of mankind. The Transvaal may have been a rich colony but its public finance was very restricted. 'My fate has apparently been decreed,' she wrote in September 1908 to her father:

I am not retrenched [i.e. made redundant] but have received an official notice that the salary attached to the post is to be diminished by £100 a year. It will not affect me much for three years, and then I shall have reached the maximum instead of still increasing. And of course it will make a difference to the pension, but the pension anyhow will not affect me unless I can hang on for another 11 years [she was then 44] ... It means they do not mean to abolish this post ... It means one will be comfortable but not rich. I have no expensive tastes and cannot keep a horse (which would be a real temptation) because my work

takes me away so much. So all is serene. The only difference will be in
the amount of money I can leave behind when I die.

These spending restrictions were to be savagely tightened when
the Transvaal government decided that too much was being spent on
education, and in early 1915 all increments of pay and even the grant-
ing of leave were stopped.

There were other comments on her small means in the same
vein, but on this matter Mary was factual and without much bitterness. Christmas 1908 found her shopping in dusty Pretoria for cards:
'this year you must take my love and nothing more', she wrote to all
at home, and she meant it. Her heart was always with her home in
Winchester, and the same letter announced she would probably get
some leave. 'Therefore, O my family, rejoice with me. Only I guess
birthday presents will have to be scarce because I was not calculating
on coming till 1910, and finances are low.'

Want of spending money was far less depressing than lack of her
own settled home in the Transvaal. There was a recurring need to
move her lodging for one good reason or another; even when seemingly fixed up she could write, 'the house has capabilities, and I hope
it may get to feel like a home to other people'. She wrote this when
she was actually going to move for a time into the cathedral precincts
of Pretoria, hardly a 'close' but the nearest approach the Transvaal
possessed, and with characteristic self-mockery she added, 'it makes
one feel one has moved distinctly into the ranks of Old Maids of a
certain standing'.

Despite her fidelity to the Church of England and the friends it
brought, the problem of loneliness was always there, a condition of
which the commonness never removes the poignancy, as when she
spoke of solitary evenings in hotels when she went early to bed.

Happily the expected home leave came about, and a note by her
brother Ralph who saw her in May 1909 at a family tea in London
reads: 'Mary looks well and hard – older-looking – face much lined
and thin – eyes appear brighter and finer – thick dark eyebrows as in
photo.'

When we were small boys my brother and I used to refer to

Aunt Mary as 'The Walnut'. Ralph's description tallies with both the photograph in our family album and the unkind nickname. The South African sun had fissured and browned her lean cheeks. Now one can see it was a handsome face, with firm lips and straight gaze, though not one which responded easily with amusement or warmth. She seemed untouched by any caress.

But this is not a description of despair. Her letters demonstrate ability to love, to be friends and to press on with her work. She loved her brother Dick. She laid herself out to help the unfortunate. She realized and minded that she did not do enough for the native Africans. She was also curiously a child of the early feminist generation who gritted her teeth in the cause: 'I am getting older but I do not want to give up for a year or two ... I do not think they will send me away, because I am more or less of an experiment, but if I fail they will not appoint another woman, so I simply must not fail, either in work, health or tact' (July 1910).

Mary was a school inspector and only occasionally a teacher of needlework or hostel supervisor, and the work which fills the letters was trekking far and wide over the veldt to supervise country schools, British, Dutch and African, as well as those in Pretoria and Johannesburg. Her positive accounts more than balance the regrets and the sadness. They are letters of description and discernment of a kind which could only have been written by a woman who was both clear-sighted and reflective: 'I often write letters in my mind as I go jogging over the veldt,' she confided to Ralph in September 1910. Her own words will be her witness in the scenes which follow.

In Mary's mind an early requirement was to learn Dutch, but in practice this was more difficult than it sounds, not from her incapacity but from the reluctance of Dutch people to address her in their own tongue. 'I am packing up to migrate to a Dutch family,' she said in Pretoria in 1908; 'it is the only way to get to speak Dutch, but it is a plunge *et je n'aime pas plonger*.' Three weeks later she wrote from 'just a room in a Dutch household' at 340 Esselin Street. But 'at present everyone speaks English and I am rather annoyed'. Perhaps that was the idea.

But soon she was off on one of her regular journeys: Fricksburg, Potchefstroom, Christiana and Standerton, all to the south of Johannesburg and some of them over the border into what was still Orange River Colony.

'I have been spending a quiet week at this very pretty place [Fricksburg, Orange River Colony, October 1908]. We look right on to the mountains of Basutoland and they never seem to be the same two minutes running.' Her port of call here was the Anglican rectory and her host the young rector whom she already knew, serving a living set down in the heartland of *Afrikanerdom*.

> The rectory is quite a nice little house with a good bit of ground which is chiefly given up to horses and fowls. The church is quite small but gives the impression of having been always cared for ... Sidney is filling out and getting broad shoulders. He is very much in earnest and reads the Service beautifully, but he has innocent round eyes, and it is difficult not to think of him as a boy, so unselfish and courteous.

It was cold and Mary rejoiced in the coal fire in the sitting room after a winter of an oil stove in one room.

'The Dutch *Predikant* here is a Mr. Kestell.' (The *Predikants* were the Ministers of the Dutch Reformed Church, and leaders of Afrikaner nationalism.) 'I want to meet him and claim cousin-ship,' Mary went on indefatigably, in her good knowledge of family history that Kestells were married into Cornishes,[1] her mother's name. 'I believe he has correspondence with Uncle Rob, without getting any further; his family came from Devonshire originally, – now he is very bitter.' The incident underlines the fact, often unrealized, that Afrikaners were not all necessarily Dutch in origin, but were a tribe that could be joined by marriage and the chances of settlement.

Not that intermarriage was welcomed even between these tribes from north-west Europe. 'A good many of the wives are Dutch,

---

1. A Reverend Cuthbert Kestell-Cornish (1908–98) was ordained a Catholic priest in 1964 by Bishop Gordon Wheeler of Middlesbrough. He served in that diocese until 1973, then retired to die in the Convent of the Little Sisters of the Poor in London.

which is a pity,' she said from the very Afrikaner Heidelberg district, south of Johannesburg, 'but it is a case of "propinquity", as Jim used to say. We have not got enough English girls out here to "propink", and the ones who are here are all congregated in the towns.'

More specific was Mary's disapproval of the teacher she visited at Reitfontein who was 'an Oxford man but has married a Dutch wife who cannot speak English, and has two grubby little Dutch children who also cannot speak English. She is one of the better-class Boers but she is a Boer and nothing else ... a dear little woman but not the ghost of a notion what an English house is like.' This was written in September 1914 when the war had sharpened antagonisms yet further.

Mixed Anglo-Dutch families were, however, the exception rather than the rule, and Mary's treks took her to communities in strong contrast with each other.

In November 1908 she was at Potchefstroom, an old *Voortrekker* township and, for a time, capital of the Transvaal Republic, yet there she stayed with the very English Corbetts,

> such quaint people, – Yorkshire. He has worked himself up into being a first-class inspector, and one would not suspect him of not being a gentleman. She is an untidy, unintellectual, happy-go-lucky person of the 'farmer's daughter' sort of type. It was he who suggested clean serviettes and that sort of thing, but they were both of them as friendly as possible, and the children are great, strapping, fair-haired yeomen who will make their mark in this country. They speak excellent English themselves, but the man who was after Miss Corbett with some prospects of success is a sergeant-major who is not quite certain of his h's.

The modern reader who blushes at these old-time snobberies has more to bear but will realize he is reading a historical book.

Two weeks later Mary was near Heidelberg, centre of Dutch settlement, but again staying with a non-Dutch family:

> such a jolly house, a farm owned by some Irish people called Barron. The elder brother has been over for years. He was scouting for Rhodes during the war as he knew the Kimberley district ... He is

J.P. for his district now. The second brother came out originally as district headmaster with the original batch of energetic young men of the better type. He has lots to say for himself and has got himself elected on the Standerton school board. The third member of the party is a young and lively sister who keeps house, cooks beautifully and plays the piano reasonably well. It was the most refreshing house I have been in for a long time. There was no sitting down and grousing which is the usual way among Britishers just now.

Different again was the trek in February the next year (1909), in driving rain:

The last day we were driving from 8 a.m. to 5 p.m. with two outspans from Vechelvallei to Christiana in the wind, and the rain like a whip ... The driver a very superior Dutchman of Huguenot descent. [Mr Maree] looks a pure Frenchman and has got the French *gaiété de coeur* ... We have seen two awful schools on this trek. Miss Abdy, a niece of John Bonham-Carter, came with me to see what it was like, and she had a good close look ... We found innumerable bugs in the room.

In December 1909, South African midsummer, she was off to Barbeton, centre of the gold rush of 1865. It was a ride in intense heat through a region by this time little populated. Met by a friend, Reggie Hill, 'we drove for hours and did not meet a human being till we got within 50 yards of Reggie's house. We sighted one other European dwelling about half-way [i.e. from Pretoria, to the west], but people as a rule do not inquire into the early history of people who take that house,' she commented darkly; 'it is conveniently remote.' Her friend Reggie Hill was in partnership with a man of whom Mary approved, son of a former Governor of Mauritius and a Creole mother, but like Reggie 'a gentleman'.

'On Sunday Reggie and I rode down to a place called Joe's Luck: we slept at a place called a hotel: there was the proprietor and a raw kaffir in the house, but the former was a nice old Dutchman.' Then they drove on up into the mountains to a place called the Sheba mine, 'a weary road for a cart to go: the last bit from the top of the hill to the school and mine there is no cart-road at all, and coming down we had the wheels tied together to form a drag ... The schoolmistress at the Sheba mine told me she had once been a young lady at Jay's shop.'

Reading the letters sometimes raises the thought that Mary's opinion of those she met was coloured as much by her mood of the moment as by her more settled prejudices, as when in March 1910 she had left a beautiful English type of household and, driving past another house of a very rich woman, thought of her own necessity to turn out once more from her Pretoria lodgings. She halted for the night at a hotel she described as dirty and where she had to share a bed with a young Jewess: 'fortunately she was very clean but the veldt fleas are rampant, and', she added, 'I feel in black despair as to how to dispose of my goods and chattels.'

Yet even through bad times there is a hard, objective core to the letters. In autumn 1910 she made a long trek into the eastern Transvaal. 'I had a big Cape cart and four splendid horses instead of the usual mule, with a gentle kaffir giant with an amiable and child-like smile as driver ... When we went down he merely gave a chuckle and said, "that was a very bad hole, missis".'

> I started from Middelburg on Sunday afternoon and drove nearly due north for 20 miles to a place called Uitkyk where I put up at a store. The lady of the establishment was away, but the old man and his kaffir looked after me ... Next day I continued north over a most lovely mountain road to a place called De Lager's Drift, just short of Roos Senellal. It is a sort of labour colony arranged by the Dutch church: there is a long valley in the hills with a river running at the foot with plenty of water. The river-banks have been divided up into what are called 'parcels', and each family has a house, a parcel of ground well irrigated, and a right to use as much of the open veldt behind him as he likes, either for mealies or to graze his cattle. Each family is also supplied with agricultural implements and a team to draw the plough.

> Two or three valleys have been utilized in this way, and there are arrangements for about 80 families. They are for poor whites, those who have drifted into towns mostly, and it has been found that most of the poor Dutch unemployed are of the same kind as those of other countries, viz: unemployable.

This place is in a most glorious part of the country, good soil well watered with good clean grass veldt for miles and miles. The only real drawback is that it is so far from any market. This makes the small profits–quick returns sort of farming almost impossible, but any man who really put his back into the work could make a very good thing out of corn and mealies.

I stayed for two nights with the Superintendent and his wife, and when we sat on the stoop in the dark he started talking of old days and yarning about life 30 years ago. His work nowadays is very much the sort of thing I imagine an I.C.S. District Officer has to do. He has to see that each family has its fair share of water and makes use of it; to arrange the concerns of the shop and the mill, to look after the kaffirs, to turn out 'impossibles' who have been given a fair trial, and to receive new families in their place; to act as adviser in general and to keep peace and run 3 Sunday schools; also to report to the Church Committee ...

Mr. van Wÿli had known Lorenzo Marquez when there was only one woman in it, a half-caste from St Helena. The first time he and a friend went down there they were arrested on suspicion, and could not explain themselves because they knew only English and Dutch, and the Lorenzo officials could only speak Portuguese and French. Finally, an Englishman attached to some agency turned up and got them out ...

[He and] a good few others were out prospecting ... a rather ungodly lot ... one of the transport riders did a roaring trade in kaffir girls. He bought them down on the coast where there is a very low tribe 'almost like beasts', and sold them to the dig at £5 apiece. One of his friends was a hunter who travelled through Rhodesia and knew Lobengula's father ... and had often spoken of the Zimbabwe ruins.

The third day [we went] across the mountains to Touteldoos. This is an older settlement, land allotted as reward for Burghers who had fought in the old Kaffir Wars ... The present dwellers are mostly a low-class, vicious and thriftless lot [though with] beautiful scenery, plenty of water and healthy veldt.

The present schoolmaster is an Englishman who went up there in

1905. He said that at first he dare not walk out alone for fear of being killed by a stone from behind ... but established his authority in school by flogging and fists. It is now a good school, jolly children, but parents hopeless.

Mary then drove from 4 p.m. till dark to Dulstroom, from where she could go back by train. The railway inspector was a lonely English bachelor, the station-master a Hollander without much English.

Further to the south, from Heidelberg to Standerton, was all high veldt with great sweeping downs and little bald farms scattered about, hardly any trees or stones. 'It is a rich district and gradually getting into the hands of Englishmen [February 1911]. There is one stretch of about 50 miles where there is not a single Dutchman left.' She wished Dick had got into this belt of splendid corn lands and cattle pastures which was being got hold of by English and Scottish settlers.

Mary's own experience that time seems less than to her taste. After missing the woman who was to have met her at Standerton and shown her where to put up, she found the only hotel she knew had been washed away, so went to the Railway Hotel. But there was no one to take her baggage and 'the woman grinned and said the police had taken all the boys they had through the trouble over the liquor question'. Later on she met her contact and found a proper host, who chaffed her, 'for the Railway Hotel is a place of ill-repute and the proprietor is at this moment in jail for selling liquor to natives'.

Mary seemed altogether less alarmed by physical than by social dangers. Discomforts of wagons she endured. She risked assault without qualms and carried a revolver (which her friends said she could never use except on snakes). But evidently she had a horror of Jews, saved only from its own shamefulness by the interest it arouses in explanation. Examples will make this clearer.

On a trek in 1911 she found farm accommodation fully booked so 'I am reduced to a small family hotel kept by a Russian Jew, no other female on the spot, and a sort of family dining-table kept with weird, unshaven fellow-guests who speak bloodthirsty words as to the right way to treat kaffirs.'

Another time she had to stay at a 'Jew-store' near Ongegien where there were only two young men, who explained carefully they were unmarried. With grim humour Mary pointed to her grey hairs and went in. The story gains pathos because the young men were so willing to please. They realized Mary thought the place dirty and rummaged about to find clean sheets. They said they had been sent from Pretoria by their family to run the store, and only charged three shillings for supper, bed and breakfast.

Another time again, in 1911, she put up at a 'Jew house' at Lindequer's Drift on the Vaal River where the two partners came respectively from Riga and Berlin and the latter one, W. Nicolay, gave her a copy of *War and Peace* in German. But Mary remarked on the 'grubbiness' of everything.

The fact seems to be that the Jews of Mary's demonology – and of those English middle-class people like her – were menacing because they were of poor origin, not accustomed to middle-class English ways of hygiene and personal neatness. In this consisted their 'foreignness'. In this context one hears little or nothing of rich Jews. The British insular brand of anti-Semitism at the time seems to have the same roots as the obsession with 'gentility'. Jewish shopkeepers and those who were not 'gentlefolk' shared a demerit in being both poor and dirty – much the same thing – but in a way which was inborn and unalterable by themselves and therefore paradoxically more culpable than any personal scruffiness in folk of good family. There was no theory in this, only a sense of insecurity. People like Mary obscurely understood that families could rise and fall in social acceptability, but were uneasy when watching the process. 'We are going to stay tonight at another farm where they have had just the same chances as the Turners but have never risen above just the roughest and basest necessities of life. They have a crowd of children and I dare say that makes a good deal of difference. A woman cannot be everything, and if she is going through all [the effort] that babies mean, it is impossible.' Mary was addressing this letter to her own mother who had 13 children.

In lighter vein the same point was made in a letter from Mary to her unmarried sister in Winchester:

I am staying with a [school] inspector and healthy, happy family of a huge, fair Yorkshire breed with a touch of Irish. No pretensions to gentility but straight, clean-living yeomen. The only time I feel a bit squeamish with them is at meals, but they are so jolly and good-tempered and I have got to the stage now that I can solemnly hand them a clean spoon if they want to put one straight from the mouth to the sugar-basin.

Disapproval and personal anguish are closely allied. Mary drew the contrast between the comforts of the Gore-Brown household (he was Dean of Pretoria) 'where the house was well-ordered with two white maids, hot water on tap and a huge bath' and the country hotels where she had to stay and where 'the bathroom is a stable-yard and I simply cannot face it'.

It was not all like that. Trekking round the Transvaal to inspect schools and lodging where chance dictated brought great variety, both of comfort and of personality. A hard journey without refreshment in May 1911 brought Mary to Meyerton, near Vereeniging, south of Johannesburg, where 'the little shanty consists of just two rooms, and is inhabited by two old ladies of uncertain age who have bought a bit of open veldt and built this little tin house. They are most delightfully simple and plucky, and have made it really cosy. They are descendants of the Old British settlers of 1828 and have been telling me wonderful stories of the adventures of their grand-parents. The old man with a delicate wife and 13 children was plumped down on a bit of open veldt with no sign of shelter ... left sitting on their boxes and the wagon drove away. What would you have done?' This rhetorical question was to her father, himself of course the sire of 13. 'Well, the wife died after 6 months and the eldest little girl of 13 years had to do house-mother for the whole family ... The grand-mother's side was also British settler, and they say there is money in Chancery in England which they cannot claim because they have no means of finding out the maiden name of the girl that settler married. All they know is that they met on board ship and were married by the captain ... The house was burned down three times by kaffirs and crops destroyed over and over again.'

Sometimes a trek could be made by train. In 1913 Mary travelled on the line east from Pretoria over 100 miles to Wonderfontein, arrived at 5 a.m. in the rain on an empty station where 'an English stranger came to my rescue and carried my bag across to the little hotel ... He was the vet, come down for a cattle sale next morning. The cattle arrived in the rain, lots of them, but there were no buyers at all! Only 2 oxen were sold the whole morning, and they were bought by a man who had come to sell himself but took them because they were going so cheap.' She went on by cart to a farm where a Scotswoman had brothers in the country since the first gold rush (1883) and 'it was delightful to hear her talk'.

There was more good conversation with the old Dutchman further on at De Lager's Drift who had made good and was 'such an old dear and so sweet and courteous, far more so than most Transvaal Boers, – but then he came from somewhere near Grahamstown'.

The same distance westward of Pretoria was Lichtenburg,

a 5-hour trek over the very deadliest and flattest country you can conceive, right away to the Bechuanaland border only 11 miles from Mafeking ... Halfway there is one little iron hand-pump sticking up in the middle of a desert. I spent the evening with a little old English lady who had married and lost her husband out here and had taken to school teaching as a living. She comes of a clever, cultured family and she showed me the photograph of the beautiful house her husband had inherited in England. He was one of the last of the old yeoman farmers in Yorkshire. Now she is living in one room in a very doubtful Dutch house, with Dutch people round her, and she has never learned to talk Dutch, consequently she remains an utter outsider.

The story has unanswered questions about the lady from the clever family who could not learn the language she heard daily and whose late husband inherited a fine English house she could not enjoy, but it was only drifting talk and tales half told.

As Mary travelled, mainly by mule-cart, she seemed always sure of a welcome of some sort, whether with spotless sheets or in a mud-floored cabin furnished with boxes. She spoke with authority of the need for inner resources in the flat dead landscape with nowhere else to go.

The Great War brought its changes here too. One for the better was the greater availability of motor-cars. Her co-inspector in 1915 had one, and ran her to various schools so that she finished her tour in 12 or 13 days instead of 21, though the speed prevented her observing the detail of the country.

The next year, recovering from a near-breakdown, she resolved to get a Ford car 'for which the Government will advance half the money and pay a mileage allowance'. This was 1916, the year Jim in India acquired a car for his work.

A change for the worse was the heightened enmity between the Dutch and British. Though De Wet's rebellion[2] in autumn 1914 brought Mary an official warning not to do any trekking for two or three months after January 1915, she intended just the same to visit a school 33 miles away beyond Crocodile River where the bridge was said to be broken. In fact she went in company with a Mr Stephen, Inspector of the District, and found a way over the river by a detour which crossed three or four smaller streams. 'Our driver was a good boy,' she wrote laconically.

Rebels and loyals she found much mixed, sometimes drinking coffee together and dividing up the area to supply the two sides.

The rebels may have preferred the Germans to the Allies, but oddly enough a long drive in December 1915 to the Twenty-Four Rivers behind a tired and sulky kaffir brought Mary and her co-inspector to a welcoming house of four German ladies. Mary engaged them in conversation about the family's German cousins, one may think not without hypocrisy, but the occasion was delicate, and they received warm hospitality. 'How glad we were to find, a house of that sort to

---

2. De Wet was a Boer farmer and politician who opposed the Union of South Africa's alignment with Britain in the First World War and, in September 1914, joined with other Boer generals in armed revolt after Botha, the prime minister, decided to invade German South West Africa. The rising failed and De Wet was captured and found guilty of high treason but allowed to return to his farm. See *The Cambridge History of Africa*, vol. 7 (1905–1940), ed J.D. Farge, A.D. Roberts and Roland Oliver, esp. pp 558–60.

rest in instead of a Backveldt Boer establishment!' [3]

To meet your foe in his own home is one thing; to cope with him mobilized under leaders quite another. Junior officers like Noel were less bloodthirsty than distant speech-writers, and Mary's letters too show how harsher antagonisms broke out in conferences and schools than in the farmhouses.

Mary herself was by training a peacemaker despite firm views and a sharp tongue. She welcomed an order to do some stop-gap teaching (which would have postponed a holiday) in Heidelberg, 'in the very middle of the opposition Dutch, so there would be some triumph if one could win through on friendly terms with everyone'. The College there was to be a Dutch one under the eye of the *Predikants*, the clerical leaders of Dutch nationalism, but it was the Dutch Principal himself who asked Mary to go, which was a good testimony to her quality.

The new College at Heidelberg for Dutch students was opened in March 1909. Confusion reigned during the first days:

> Into this confusion comes a very precise and strictly brought-up Scotch lady, my co-adjutor; she has spent the last five years at Stellenbosch in the oldest and most precise Dutch Seminary in S.A. She 'does not wish to make a fuss, but objects to rugs of different shades of blue in her bedroom!' The opening ceremony was performed with interminable speeches in Dutch and English. The only ornament in the assembly hall was a huge motto and the Old Transvaal colour with a huge mourning ribbon stretched across the front.

After giving tea to the Director of Education and the Education Committee,

> we hung round ... seeing men students where they should not be and girl students in the wrong places, but with no authority to stop

---

3. Mary's great-uncle, Thomas Du Boulay of Sandgate (d. 1872), had had a daughter Harriett who married *en secondes noces* Karl August Alfred, Baron von Wolzogen, of Kalbsrieth, Prussia (d. 1883), and they had children who made German marriages.

anything because the Principal hoped to come round presently and discuss regulations.

The most trying time of the day is meals. Breakfast and supper end with what is called 'Devotions' – a chapter of the Bible and a prayer. Mr. Douglas asked me to take the first evening and I could not find my prayer-book anywhere. One suddenly found oneself faced with the necessity for extempore. I got through somehow, and I feel the necessity will recur, as set prayers are not approved of in this community.

Mary liked the girls very much but not the need to make up two extempore prayers a day. 'I wish one could unite in worship without feeling so uncomfortable.'

Heidelberg College provides a good illustration of antipathies sharpened by external practices – as it were, the alienation felt through different liturgies rather than through different underlying beliefs. Mary was all her life conscious of the family's Protestant forebears, and the more proud of them because of her own Protestant outlook, and she genuinely wished to make a bridge with the Dutch Reformed believers in spite of their dislike of set forms. Conversing a year or two later with Lord Methuen she recalled, 'we were talking of the Boers and I said my Huguenot ancestry was a great help sometimes, and he said, "Yes, that would be a great bond. I have not got that, but we are clothiers, you know, Flemish clothiers originally, and I bring that in whenever I can."'

Real hostility was of course political, and boiled up over the changes made in the Pretoria Education Office when Mr Clarke the Secretary became Inspector of High Schools, and the secretaryship was given to Mr Scott. Hertzog, Afrikaner leader in the government, attacked both appointments in a public speech on the grounds that neither was an Afrikaner or knew Dutch, though Mary wrote that Scott in fact spoke Dutch fluently and did nearly all the Dutch-to-English translations in the Education Office. 'That would not prevent Hertzog asserting that he knew no Dutch,' was her comment.

Hertzog was leader of strong opinions not their creator. Strife at the centre was reflected in bitter local conflicts. In February 1914

Mary was spending a few days' rest at Heidelberg, 'this inner fortress of Afrikanerdom', as she called it.

> There is a certain famous *Predikant* here named Loun, who is monarch of the district, bitterly hostile to anything English. They have started a Normal College here in opposition to the one in Pretoria because at Pretoria there is an English Principal. They have an enormous *Volk* school, and every child who enters the door reads overhead 'To the Memory of ... (a long list of names of men killed in battle) and of ... (a much longer list of women and children done to death in the camps).'

She summed up Meneer Loun's preaching: the Boers as noble saviours even of the British who were trying to drive them from the country. He preached too on the deliberate failing of Afrikaner children in the Cape matriculation exams. 'Does he really think the examiners take the trouble to look up which numbers on the papers belong to Afrikaners and deliberately fail them? He must know better yet calls on God to witness the truth of his words!'

At Christiana too, on the western border between Transvaal and the Orange Free State (as it became in 1910), the dissension of years boiled up in early 1915. The Dutch objected to the English Principal, Mr King, and got the school divided with a great wooden partition across the hall, and a ten-foot iron paling across the playground. 'The school has to support two Principals and a double staff "for the sake of racialism". A third investigation has again exonerated Mr. King of every charge, but ordered the school to be again amalgamated and the Principal's post advertised.' Later Mr King 'was given another post and left Christiana after many years effort by the Dutch, [who] called a prayer-meeting to thank God for having rid them of that damned Englishman'.

Naturally the war in Europe and the failure of De Wet's rebellion in South Africa (1914–15) brought the bitterest words to Afrikaner lips, like those of the lawyer in Ermelo who said in spring 1915 that the sufferings of Belgium were nothing compared to the outrages of the British in laying waste the country and maltreating Dutch women and children. 'The English response,' wrote Mary to her mother in

England, 'is to smile and hope feelings will improve.'

The apportionment of blame cannot be a matter for a historical memoir which tries to record the evidence of the letters, but at this long remove it may be pointed out how important emotionally the 'rape of Belgium' in 1914 was to the Allied cause against Germany, so that to meet it in South Africa with a *tu quoque* from the Dutch is some measure of hatreds.

The country was also divided within the Dutch community. At one extreme was the concert organized in the Town Hall of Krugers-dorp in 1915 and advertised by one general leaflet and another secret leaflet. The second was circulated to Afrikaner sympathizers as an invitation to watch a re-enactment at the concert of the execution by shooting of Fourne, who had been court-martialled at the begin-ning of the rebellion. At the other extreme was the depressed Dutch schoolmaster who confessed to Mary that the country was not a place to live in because it was all politics, race against race, neigh-bour against neighbour. 'My friend cannot sell oranges without being asked "are you for Botha or for Hertzog?" and the sale depends on the answer.'

The other problem to which the answer was and remains even more obscure was of course that of the 'natives'. During these years Mary, like thousands of others, spoke with the voice of a liberal who carried a gun.

A young missionary of her acquaintance in 1909 made her 'feel rather miserable about the natives. He says that if he mentions "black work" among white people he is promptly cold-shouldered, and I know myself that I do absolutely nothing for the natives. There is also the "coloured work" which has to be taken quite separately. The Wesleyans have some big work going on, and our Government school here [Pretoria] is run by a Wesleyan who does it *con amore*, but most whites say "leave the natives alone".'

Everywhere the family letters show the two-way pull. Jim in India argued for justice to the Sikhs; Dick in the Transvaal, as we shall see, was more or less a Boer; George the missionary had died among his flock. And Mary? Her longest attempt to express feelings is in a home-letter of 1911:

> There has been a great fuss lately over what is known as the 'Black Peril'. A poor little old English governess was knocked down by a kaffir and badly treated. There have been rather hysterical meetings in Johannesburg. I am glad to say that the women's mass meeting talked sense and kept away from hysterics. One very good point has come out, and that is pretty straight talking about the white man's behaviour to black women and the white woman's behaviour to black men. Poor Lord Gladestone [High Commissioner] is in hotter water than ever for reprieving a black man in Rhodesia, and the heroine of the day is a lady in Rhodesia who shot a kaffir dead on her verandah.

> My own experience is that as long as you are quiet in your own behaviour the kaffirs are perfectly civil. I have to tell a man sometimes to take off his hat, but he always does it and looks sheepish. I always carry a revolver just on the chance that one might light upon a 'beer-drinking' somewhere. I am not a bit afraid of a sober kaffir.

The world knows the problem is not yet resolved and the uncertain standards of those early days signal inner confusion. Mary wrote with obvious distress about the 'native-girl' question – she meant prostitution in towns – and about bands of white hooligans who rounded up black men to beat them. But how did you behave towards those you employed or were educating?

A characteristic vehicle of management was the *indaba* or discussion, and Mary describes two, in illuminating contrast:

> I am writing on Ralph Turner's stoep [13 May 1915] listening to Mrs. Turner holding an *indaba* in fluent kaffir. She sits enthroned on a red cushion behind the teapot, and seven stalwart Zulus stand uncovered before her, one after another bringing forth his request or desire for advice ... The hut tax is coming on next week, and they all want to borrow money to pay it ... The last subject to come up is the story of a baby girl who has swallowed a shilling which according to them has stuck in her gullet and produced pneumonia, Mrs. Turner is recommending salad oil, and we are to go down and look at it [sic] this afternoon.

Three months later she wrote of an *indaba* concerned not with a white farm but a black school:

> I have been doing some native schools this week. At the last we had to go to the chief's house for an *indaba* over a girl. The Chief was the most repulsive-looking object, dirty and drunk. Three chairs were brought out into the courtyard, one for the lady missionary, one for myself and one for the Chief. The rest of the women squatted on the ground and the men stood respectfully with uncovered heads.

Mary cannot be summed up from these letters home, filled week by week with descriptive snippets, insights and sometimes sad reflections behind the brave exterior. There are doubtless things to dislike: attitudes of a past age, perhaps, and little weapons forged in her own disappointments. Yet it would be unjust not to recognize a spirituality: the fortitude of trekking, the quiet generosity which bought little bits of handiwork from children she wished to encourage, and the way she could speak of good men she admired, not flinching from the word 'holy'. She was a woman of inner resources.

Between Mary and her younger brother Dick, six other brothers and sisters took their place in the Winchester family. When these were growing up, South Africa appeared a land of opportunity to many different kinds of people, and from Britain alone were attracted both rich and poor. Entrepreneurs were brought by the prospects of profitable mining or large-scale landownership. The stories of Mary and Dick, and indeed their own persons, are evidence of many immigrants without fortune.

It is equally clear that those with little property of their own might come from quite different British backgrounds. Some came from the ranks of the gentry and from families which for historical reasons tended to stick together and to possess links with county and even aristocratic families. At the same time there was often an economic chasm between men who came from the same social origins. The generation before the Great War was in any case a highly class-conscious one, and these tensions were extreme in South Africa as penniless English men and women of good social education strove to support their social dignity – all they had in their treasury of

19. Richard (Dick) Du Boulay (1877–1949), farmer in the Transvaal;
2nd Lt. RASC, Transvaal, 1914–19.

self-esteem – by cultivating their own kind and mentally relegating the others by the use of 'gentlefolk' as a technical term. It was the difference as it were between those who travelled on the same liner but either in first class or steerage.

The simile is especially apt in the case of Dick. In September 1908 he travelled out third class on the SS *Dover*, while the Bishop of Zululand, with whom he was on speaking terms, travelled first. The point is made by the incident of the bottle of port:

> I had several talks with him but his conscience annoyed me when I asked him to get a bottle of port wine for my friend Mrs. Newby. We cannot buy a bottle of anything down here [third or steerage class] without a written order from the doctor ... annoying when one does not know how much to drink and has to pay for port at 6 pence the glass instead of 4 shillings the bottle. And a lady is not prepared to go and interview a doctor to get a medical order for port. All the bishop had to do was to buy a bottle and send it to me by his steward, instead of which he interviewed the Chief and the doctor, etc. etc ... I now get 'My Lord' into the conversation as often as possible.

Shipping-line rules were evidently general that third-class passengers were likely to run amok after more than a glass of wine, for in 1910 Philip noted that some who brought wine aboard from a shore trip at Tenerife had it confiscated and thrown overboard by the officer on duty. Curiously it was often the third-class passengers who were going to walk armed against kaffir beer-drinkers.

More immediately, this is an introduction to Dick's character. Dick's original emigration to South Africa is now shrouded in obscurity because the collected correspondence beginning in 1908 makes only oblique reference to it. He went out to Cape Colony in 1895 at the age of 18. As a boy he was good at games but not especially bright at school work, and some sort of opening was found for him by his family who numbered among its friends the 2nd Earl of Selborne, old boy of Du Boulay's House at Winchester, who had just become Under Secretary of State for the Colonies.

Dick's first and only real love in the world of work was farming, but a single early letter of 1900 to his younger brother Philip was written on active service in the Cape against the Boers. Dated 'under a blooming truck' it starts 'Here's a letter from your brother what's a bloomin' Trooper in the army of the south' and goes on in a simple but entirely literate style to explain that he was one of a flying column of 42 men with only three light carts for their gear. He rode his own pony, a little Basuto mare which could be left standing or shot from without a movement, unlike the old crocks the government was supplying. Each man wore a slouch hat turned up on the left side, khaki tunic, riding breeches and putties, and carried 100 rounds in a bandolier (9lbs) and another 100 in saddle bags.

But while the letter fits into the family pattern of regular writing, it adds in Dick a character different in interesting ways from his brothers and sisters. It says several times in various ways that though he was only a trooper he was considered a cut above the rest, always put in charge of details and expected to get his sergeant's stripes soon. Though he had had typhoid he was as fit as could be, and loved the outdoor life. The letter is doubly datable by its reference to 'old Jim' getting engaged, which was in 1900.

All in all, it is the same Dick so much in his dignity eight years later, the active farmer, consciously 'colonial', slightly aggressive, uncertain of himself and at the last the lonely widower, retired and with nothing to do.

Let us return to 1908. Steaming towards South Africa in the SS *Dover*, he was making a journey he had made twice before. He had learned the elements of farming but had failed financially when starting on his own in 1905. Now he was returning with his love of the life undiminished, aged 31 and with just £500 of capital. His older sister Mary was already in the Transvaal, and it was there that Dick's search for work was to be. Mary would keep a motherly eye on him, advising him, rejoicing when things went well and remaining quite unhurt by his moody character with its bouts of euphoria and outbursts of temper and gloom.

If farming was to be the life, the first task was to earn some cash. The way to do that was to get a job in a mine, as he had done before.

There were numerous gold mines in the Johannesburg area which depended on Africans for unskilled and semi-skilled labour and employed Europeans at a fairly lowly level to supervise and perform the more responsible tasks either for a wage or by means of a contract system in which their pay was calculated according to the quantity of ore produced.

As soon as he arrived Dick contacted the mine he knew, but on 3 November 1908 wrote, 'they cannot start me immediately as they are fearfully short of kaffir labour ... but I shall get the first possible chance as I am wanted for the cricket team of which the mine captain is captain'.

This takes us straight into the Alice in Wonderland world where dangerous work was given to desperate young Englishmen who would play for the works team, where they worked long hours underground in bad conditions and bicycled back in dinner jacket after a night out to go on early shift, where they drove and taught their 'boys' hard, yet risked their lives to save them in disaster.

Dick got a job quite quickly. 'I started work on Thursday here,' he told his father on 2 November, writing from Village Main Reef, Johannesburg:

It is my old job running hammer-boys. I have got the stope [gallery underground] just below my old one with only 19 boys and those good ones and the best boss-boy on the mine; the result being that my job is as near a sinecure as possible. I have to climb down about 50 feet on a chain, and there is hardly a place in the stope in which one can even sit upright, but one very soon gets used to that sort of thing ... In getting my job the mine captain added, 'Now you understand you have got to turn out for cricket.'

He did not exaggerate. Mary, ever-accurate, said, 'Dick got his place on the mine chiefly for his cricket but it means that he was wanted back for his own sake, which is a most satisfactory condition of things.' But Dick's remark about a sinecure was a joke. He was told to put the 'boss-boys' on to drilling while he himself helped to put in the timber props and to cut pillars. Morning shift started at 7, for which his 'boy' awakened him. The manager gave him the measurements to be cut for the month and he had to keep account of costs underground as the stope was worked. On day rates he made £22 (presumably a month); if he could contract to do piece-work this might become £30 or £40, though management was always trying to lower the rates.

'I shall be on shift on Christmas Eve and Boxing Day,' he wrote ruefully, meaning his sister Mary would have to come over to him on Christmas Day. Christmas Day and Good Friday were the only mine holidays: 'the Battery and cyanide people don't even get these days,' he explained.

'My work has been going quietly on and I am becoming an expert at going on all fours, as the greater part of my stope is only 27 inches high now. It is fearfully difficult for the boys to get their holes in, cramped up like that.' He resented chiefly the bad weather which prevented cricket as a relaxation after nine hours underground.

There was tennis too, but it was hard to arrange when his friends mostly lived some way off the tram-line and his own shifts were all day and with no long weekends. This meant late nights if he wanted company, 'and with cricket all day on Sunday I like to go to church in the evenings here'.

Christmas Day 1908 gave Dick the chance to meet his sister at early service on the mine, but he had to rush off at once afterwards to breakfast with Mr Dove, the agent who was helping him fix up a suitable farm tenancy. This was the whole plan: to make cash on the mine till the next winter (i.e. about May) and then to get on to farming. 'I wish this life suited me,' he said, 'as it would be delightful to be able to earn cash at it, for a year or two, but I have already got a cold again.'

Even this makes it sound too easy. When the supply was good the mine constantly took on new Africans as hammer-boys and turned the machines off; the Africans had to be taught; they crowded out the stope and slowed up production.

The Transvaal was as subject to sudden floods as it was to droughts, and Dick wrote in January 1909 of the outcrop mines caving in. 'We are fairly safe, as our top level is 600 feet below the surface, but one burst dam flooded a mine and drowned 150 natives and 7 white men. Two of the white men were last seen rushing into danger to save their natives. The last white man to escape came out with all but four of his boys, having rushed down his stope and got them out, minimizing thereby his own chance of safety.' No wonder Dick was longing to get the plough in.

It took Dick a year to find a farm he was willing to take on. The journeys, enquiries, disappointments and irritations occupied autumn to autumn 1908–09 – a period when the youngest brother Philip was also experiencing black disappointment in Egypt. But Dick was rightly cautious. He had a capital of only £500 and there were many decisions to risk. Which part of the Transvaal? Or should it even be Rhodesia where farms of 3,000 to 6,000 acres were going for one or two shillings the acre? Should it be cattle, lucerne, mealies, ostriches or some combination? What about the outgoing tenant – why was he leaving? Was he sound? Should he take in a partner? 'A farm-partner is the nearest approach to a wife in wanting careful choosing,' he wrote. Communications with a market, rainfall, water-level, soil type, available buildings and stock and labour supply as well as financial terms were all churning through Dick's head as he hacked away below ground, played tennis with friends on the Settlers' Board and found time to talk to his friendly lawyer. When possible he got leave to go and look for himself at likely farms. His letters at this period are filled with technical details and his thinking on paper.

At last, in the late South African winter of July to August 1909 the search lighted on the little settlement of Naboomspruit, some 100 miles north of Pretoria. Later Dick was to call his farm here Ridding Mead, after Lady Laura Ridding his patroness (possibly godmother) and Mead his mother's middle name. This was easier to say than the Dutch place-name. But first a little explanation is needed about the Ridding connection.

It was told in Chapter 1 how one of Grandfather Du Boulay's closest friends at Oxford had been George Ridding, whose father-in-law, George Moberly, had brought Du Boulay to Winchester. Ridding's first wife had died young, and much later, in 1876, when

Second Master of Winchester College, Ridding married the Hon. Laura Palmer, daughter of Lord Selborne. She thus became known as Lady Laura (Ridding). The first Lord Selborne was Chairman of the Governing Body of Winchester College, and his son entered Du Boulay's House as a Commoner in 1873.[4] In this way there was a family and Wykehamist bond between the Selbornes and the Du Boulays. It is another example of the unequal brotherhood spoken of above which existed so often in that world between men of a like social background, some rich and some poor. In this way we can see the 2nd Lord Selborne as in due course Administrator of the Transvaal and the Orange River Colony in 1905 after their conquest from the Boers, and then High Commissioner for South Africa after the Act of Union (1910), as well as Fellow of Winchester College (1904), while Dick, 17 years his junior but fellow-Wykehamist, became a protégé both of Lord Selborne and his sister Lady Laura, who may possibly have been his godmother. Grandfather had of course been housemaster to both men.

If for a few years the one was the supreme political figure in South Africa while the other was an obscure tenant-farmer without resources, then the relationship can be understood, and with it something of the small but layered society which guided the late British Empire.

Lord Selborne and his sister, Lady Laura, obviously took a kindly interest in Dick's struggles to establish himself. They wrote to him with advice and encouragement, never overbearing nor constraining him to follow any particular course, but (Lady Laura especially) urging him to get into the farming he so obviously loved. They received him and entertained him: 'Dead-beat after seven sets of tennis with Selborne,' wrote Dick to his father in February 1909. 'I had all the time the feeling that I did not want to beat him badly.' But the sentiment was not servility, merely a natural courtesy of an athletic young man towards an opponent of middle age.

The Selbornes were generous too. 'I am feeling somewhat

---

4. For all this, see Laura Ridding, *George Ridding, Schoolmaster and Bishop* (London, 1908), esp. pp 139–44.

overwhelmed by news from Lady Laura this week [November 1908] in the shape of a draft for £460 and a further letter from Lord S. enclosing cheque for £40 which he had received for me. £300 of this is gift and £200 a loan at 4%. Have you ever heard of such kindness? It is quite beyond my ken and I don't know what I have done to deserve such luck.' This was at the moment Dick had got his job in the mine.

Later, when Dick had started on his farm, he wrote to Selborne to give an account of how things were going, 'and he has answered very cordially and also told me to have my house made completely mosquito-proof and send the bill to him. It's a most noble offer' (1910).

On the Du Boulay side deference stopped well short of servility, and incidents described in letters would be wrongly interpreted as such by readers unfriendly to old-world manners. Mary, for example, spent a morning in February 1909 when the Selbornes were in Pretoria chatting with Lady Laura in the churchyard where she was sketching a grave. 'I sat by her side holding an umbrella over her head. She was very nice and there were no pauses in our conversation.' It was a hot day in summer which Lady Laura, older than Mary, found hard to bear. But they were deep in conversation about the country, and especially the native question, which concerned Laura.

The Selbornes preferred Johannesburg at that season, which is where Dick saw them:

> I went to Lady Selborne's At Home on Saturday afternoon and had the honour of being the only man in a straw hat there. There were about 8 not in top-hats, but it was distinctly a top-hat affair. However, they don't know how to look after their hats, and the fit of their frock coats with a few exceptions was atrocious, so I felt quite happy, especially as Lady Laura gave me far more attention than she did anyone else. She is most tremendously keen for me to get fixed up before she leaves the country.

This was Dick at his most characteristic, mingling bravura with uncertainty, asserting bluff colonialism and patrician *savoir-faire* all at once, feet firmly in different worlds.

The farm which Dick eventually bought was being sold by a young widow, Betty Grigson (*née* Douglass), whose brother was a Crown Prosecutor in Pretoria and whose husband had recently died, not before investing a lot of his own money in improvements. 'The deed is done, and I am fixed up here for the next six years and a bit, if all goes well.'

Dick had clearly hit it off well with Mrs Grigson from whom he bought the lease and who had been farming there successfully with her husband until his unexpected death. There is no inkling in the letters of this time that Dick might ever become her second husband, though it is clear that a liking existed from the start.

There was certainly a liking for the farm. Dick's early letters are euphoric, but he had reason to be happy as he had got more or less what he had come back to South Africa to find.

He had little capital: he mentions £500. He agreed to pay £800 for the lease of something over six years, and of this money £200 was cash down and the rest in £50 instalments at six-monthly intervals. To the owning company he seemingly paid an annual rent of £150. The stock, valued at £1,000, was to be paid for by a loan at 6 per cent interest a year, repayable in four instalments beginning in December 1912.

The farm's acreage is unfortunately not mentioned in the letters and one cannot follow the farm's finances in detail, any more (it must be confessed) than could Dick himself. Mary took an interest and gave him her advice. Philip during his year's stay did some work on the books. It was, as Dick said, a living. They were poor but not desperately so, and to him it was quite proper to be poor in South Africa.

The farm was fenced, divided into three parts but not all at first cultivated. The farmhouse soon got fenced against cattle, and a vegetable garden cultivated within the compound. Bore holes were sunk and before long piped water to the house laid on, pressured by a little engine he bought.

It was a mixed farm of dairy cattle, cereal crops (mainly mealies, or maize) and ostrich bred for their feathers which commanded a good price from the feather-brokers until the trade collapsed at the outbreak of the Great War.

At first Dick was milking a dozen cows, but he gradually increased the herd to about 150 head which flourished reasonably well despite the prevalent East Coast fever. Butter and cream were taken twice a week to the railway station four miles distant – also whole milk in winter – and sent to the Pretoria dairy, which paid carriage as well as a fair price for the produce. It was this which produced regular cash for wages and living expenses. The crops and the feathers fetched larger payments at longer intervals. For the ploughing, mules were trained and would turn at the headlands without reins or leader. Dick or a white helper generally held the plough.

Beyond there was good shooting which went far to supply meat, and also provided extra income when Dick organized shooting-parties for holidaymakers from town. There was buck and guinea fowl and the local variety of pheasant in abundance. 'A new law says the occupier of a farm may shoot game all the year round, which is a great help as I shall not have to buy any meat, but I don't approve of it as I am afraid the Dutchmen will abuse the privilege and shoot unnecessarily.' Dick often cooperated with Dutch farmers and even liked the occasional Dutchman but was deeply imbued with the belief that only Englishmen of a certain kind were ideal human beings.

Beyond again were the mountains. 'From my plough I have an almost uninterrupted view of about 40 miles of mountains, and the evening hues are exquisite.'

Looking back on the South African farm from early twenty-first century England, the most exotic features are the ostriches and the use of native African labour. Ostriches, both grown and chicks, were bought from a reputable breeder, fed as carefully as possible to make them breed and produce fine feathers, watched to identify the nests and to prevent thefts, and plucked at the right time, feathers unspoiled by rain or dirt. They are strong and violent creatures and only pictures of the nodding plumes of debutantes or field-marshals can explain the trouble lavished on them.

A month after signing the lease Dick expressed his joy at finding

a month or so after the plucking, when the quills come out quite easily. They round up an ostrich and then 2 or 3 boys catch it by the wings and tail while Dick gets the head and wraps it up in a red flannel hood. The ostrich kicks all the time. It can't kick backwards, yet its jumps are so powerful the boys go flying in all directions.'

One time an ostrich tore its gullet and therefore could not feed and Phyllis, fresh from her nurse's training at Guy's Hospital, volunteered to stitch it up, which she did successfully while others held the bird and stood round, and one of the kaffirs, Moses, watched 'with tears running down his cheeks, saying over and over, "Oh poor, poor dead man"'.

The feathers were attractive to Africans and although each bird had about 160 to be pulled, Dick did not trust the kaffirs to do this. Feather stealing was stamped on. 'One unpleasant thing,' in a letter of 1912:

> I found a dead bird in the veldt which should have been in full plumage, and it had just had every feather taken. So I searched the huts and found the feathers in my cattle herd's coat, and a lot more stuck in the roof. I had him arrested at once, and he confessed to having taken them and also to having pulled out odd feathers from other birds while they were feeding, which accounts for a lot of blanks I am finding on the birds. It is a very serious business if natives are going to do that.

In the event the case was tried at Nylstroom and the thief got three months' hard labour, his youth and previous good conduct being taken into consideration.

The basic labour which kept South African farms going under white men's supervision came of course from the native Africans who lived then as later in two worlds: that of their own kraals and that of the white men's economy. The idea was that the 'kaffirs' did three months' work for no pay in consideration of their living on the farm with their families and stock and having lands to plough.

From the beginning Dick had a semi-Boer mentality:

> My boys are shaking down into real useful servants [he told

Winchester in September 1909]. But the amount of indaba i.e., sit-down discussions, one has to go through with these natives up here is appalling. They seem to think they are on the place solely for their benefit. I am applying for leave to have some more squatters on the farm, which I have no doubt I shall get, as I want considerably more labour than I have at my command now. This is a real hard life, but worth it even if one can only make a living at it.

The Africans were evidently not servile in attitude, and Dick spoke off and on of 'trouble with the boys', calling them 'idiots', and it is a matter of judgement how far he spoke out of ordinary European assumptions, and how far out of his own impatient nature. The next February he wrote:

I am having a sort of strike among my boys, who only want to work three months a year for me. I am insisting on 6 months: 3 months unpaid as rent for their ploughing and grazing, and 3 months at the current wage of 30 shillings a month.

They are sending a deputation to the Native Commissioner, who is a friend of mine, and can only advise them. They will probably settle down to my terms in preference to being turned off.

The basic difference between this mentality and that of English liberals of the day could be seen in striking miniature when Dick was visited by his younger sister Phyllis, and this will be described in a moment. But at this point it is of interest to set down Dick's own words on the problem to show how far the later formal doctrine of *apartheid* had taken shape in Dick's not very original mind. In March 1913 he wrote to his old father:

Government seems really determined to tackle the native question at last. The proposed temporary bill of Sauer (a professed negrophilist), whilst a commission is sitting, seems to me a very wise one, unexpectedly so coming from him. He states that in all his dealings with natives he has preached to them that it is to their interest to keep quite separate from Europeans socially. Now he proposes to prevent all buying of land by natives from Europeans and by Europeans from natives, also leasing of land in the same way.

Natives ploughing on shares will come under the head of leasing. Their only means of living on a European's land will be in exchange for their labour. If they want to live without work they will have to go to territory set aside for natives in which Europeans can have no holdings.

Some immediate steps are necessary. Lately, natives have been buying land in the middle of white settlements at three times the value of the land, knowing that in a very short time all the land round will fall into their hands at a cheap rate. Everywhere this has happened sheep-farming has been killed immediately by the enormous loss from stock thefts. Native when collected always have big beer-drinks, and then they will have meat at any price, and one native has been known to eat a whole sheep in one day after a beer-drink.

The question has to be settled now whether it is to be a white man's country or a kaffir country. If allowed to slide for another four years legislation will be almost impossible. In England people talk about [South Africa] being their country. The present kaffirs only conquered the country a few years before white occupation, and <u>destroyed</u> the old inhabitants. We have occupied the country and given them peace in which to multiply. There is still heaps of room for them all, but it is an impossible thing for the whites to have natives living on equal terms alongside of them, and under English rule equality is the law, so that the only solution seems to be a separate white and black, allowing them to mix only for trade and labour, so that the native who is ambitious may come out of his own territory to work and earn money and return to his own land rich in cattle when he likes.

Rarely did Dick write at such length on a general topic. Usually his views were expressed in action, occasionally in an exasperated quarrel. Right from the start he used natives as stockmen and labourers (the farm was unsuitable for sheep) but would not pay them as much as £2 a month: 'very few boys can earn that on the mines nowadays … their food is very cheap … Here we only feed mealie meal which I grind myself.' He hoped to get more than the six boys he started with but to put them the other side of the railway 'so their stock etc.

won't get in my way at all. It will be many years before the stock has increased sufficiently for me to want to use that part of the farm.'

To Boers these views were a matter of the obvious. The historian of the present day has to think away the years which have brought the terrible and well-known tensions, and to see that even before the Great War differences of opinion could bring quarrels within loving families. Even Jim in an India of white supremacy thought Dick's views untenable. The clash on the spot came with Phyllis, the youngest of all, idealistic, untrained but eloquent.

Phyllis and Philip paid a visit to the farm throughout 1910, and this is a distinct episode in the family's Transvaal story which is best related now as a whole, for it brings together in time and place the four contrasting siblings: Mary, Dick, Philip and Phyllis.

Between the years 1908 and 1910 Philip was having the greatest difficulty in finding a job in Egypt, and since Dick wanted help on the farm, and especially with the sort of book-keeping, vegetable planting and lighter manual work at which Phil was good and he was not, it was somehow suggested that the younger brother should come south and try his hand at becoming a South African farmer.

Phil's temporary job was to end in October 1910, and rather characteristically he puzzled Dick by not writing a full letter saying what he would like to do, but cabling in Latin that he would be coming by October: 'Migratio citra October'.

Philip did not mean to tease Dick; that was not his way. He was trying to be brief and definite. The scheme that they should join forces in the Transvaal and incidentally give their sister Phyllis a holiday to convalesce from a serious illness, shows the family at its best.

Ralph was an intermediary, trusted by all, who advised in place of the elderly parents, lent money to Phil for the journey and received an unusually personal letter about it all from Dick. On 18 March 1910 Dick wrote:

My dear Ralph, ... I am very glad to hear that Phil is definitely coming ... My idea in getting him out is not to do manual work or riding, but to do all the pottering jobs round the homestead and leave me free to do the manual work. My presence in the working gang is worth several boys, – not that I do all that work myself, but that everybody is doing a good day's work; and if I have to look after seed beds and the dairy, books and house, I cannot possibly do a fair day's work as well. My idea of Phil is that he will exactly fill the niche, and I shall not interfere with him at all.

The only possible way for two men on level terms to run a farm is each to have his own department and discuss everything in a friendly spirit, but realize that they have got to put up with the other's methods and mistakes if he insists on making them, and that it all comes in the day's work.

Financially, Phil's legal position for the present will be [as] my overseer with a share of the profits and right to run stock of his own. Privately we share everything on equal terms. He is coming in, I take it, without any capital; most of mine is borrowed or owed; I am bound hand and foot to the Company and Mrs. Grigson, and can only sell stock with the Company's permission and for the purpose of either paying off money advanced or buying other stock. Phil will have no legal responsibilities until I am free of the bonds, but will actually be on level terms with me and morally responsible for half my debts which have to come out of the farm. If he came into a legal partnership with me at once he would have to sign a general bond to the Company and Mrs. Grigson, which in his penniless condition would be a useless expense, and I see no use in both of us going bankrupt if things do not turn out right.

I have sent him a full statement of how I stand, and the prospects of the farm, so he knows exactly what he is coming to. This is a country where one does not mind in the least being poor. A retired Major, a real good chap, is living miles away from anyone about 40 miles from here, in tents, and educating his son at home with his pension. We agree it costs about £2 a week to live.

Father asks me whether I realize that I am accepting the responsibility of all Phil's expenses for clothes, journeys, etc. and all that makes life worth living. I can only say that I don't know what makes life worth living for Phil, but that we shall practically for a bit have a common purse, and have to recognize that every penny we

spend on ourselves might have gone towards buying another cow.
For personal needs the want of cash never worries me; it is just a
question of Phil's fitting in with the happy-go-lucky S.A. existence.

Dick went on to write of getting a housekeeper to look after the
hoped-for paying guests during the shooting season, and ended by
saying, 'I have written more fully to you than I am doing to anyone
else, as being I believe most in Phil's confidence and knowing more
of his ways of life and thought ... Personally, I prefer my affairs not to
be too generally discussed.'

Shortly before Phil was due to start, the idea that Phyllis should
travel out from England with her brother Phil (who had gone home
for leave) was thought up by the family. Dick seemed delighted but
slightly puzzled, probably not realizing how ill she had been. He
suggested she could get maternity work at £4 or £5 a week by reason
of her hospital training, and also sounded a bit dubious how she would
get on with Jeffery, one of Dick's white workers and a rough diamond
who 'chaffed girls and is no respecter of persons'. The sequel was
rather different.

In October Phyllis and Phil travelled from England to Cape Town
on the *Dover Castle*, Phyllis first class, Phil third, a voyage made disa-
greeable to Phyllis by 'unmannerly children' and to Phil by all the
other passengers, whom he found 'uninteresting to the last degree'.
But to arrive was wonderful, Phil speaking Arabic to bemused cab
drivers and luxuriating in the comforts of dry land and the Cape
Town hotel.

By 9 October the train had brought them to Naboomspruit and
Ridding Mead, to Phil 'a most magnificent residence ... Barring the
hard red soil we might be in the Sudan. The landscape is full of flowering acacia trees, with low scrub or grass all burnt up by the drought
... the atmosphere almost unthinkably dry. Tomorrow I shall begin
to prepare a small patch of ground for vegetables just for the house.
They are badly wanted and can be irrigated from the big tank which
the windmill keeps filled.'

'Eustace and Jeffery,' he continued, speaking of the two white
boys who were helping temporarily on the farm, 'are in one room,

Mary in the spare room, Phyllis opposite in one of the big bedrooms which will also be the office.'

To Mary, the loneliest member of the family, it was a happy occasion. 'Can you not imagine what a jolly party they will be in that farm?,' she had written in anticipation. 'Just the three who were in the nursery together! I shall be able to manage ten days with them at Christmas, but it will be something to be able to think of them even if I cannot be with them.' She went to help greet them when they arrived in October, concerned for young Phyllis who was at once scouring the veldt for flowers to put in rooms.

Whatever Phyllis's faults – impulsive fancies and inability to stop talking which always maddened her brothers – she knew how to put together a factual letter with an eye for detail. After a week she wrote home to her sister Bee an account of the daily round. Breakfast was of coffee, mealie porridge, egg and bacon or some other dish, bread and jam. 'The bell rings at 12 for knock-off. Dinner is bully-beef, buck, guineafowl, partridge or any other game shot. Phil talks of getting cold-store meat sent up, but Dick scouts the idea.' One morning they had an ostrich-egg which fed six people and the housekeeper's little girl with some left over. 'At 1.30 the bell goes for the kaffirs to start work again, but the others mostly loaf on their beds till about 3; at 3.30 there is the bell for the cows to be brought in. Then tea. One of the youngsters (Jeffery or Eustace Halifax) superintends the milking. The sun sets just after 6. Supper comes at 6.30 and is of tea, a made-up dish, and bread and jam, eaten round the table with collars and coats put on.'

Personal relationships became difficult quickly. At the centre was Dick's quarrel with Phyllis, which was fundamentally about the white attitude to the African: an individual version of a global grief.

Phyllis had arrived, nervy and touchy, to find a brother who often exploded with impatience, but also to encounter for the first time a population of black people who seemed to her to be 'always laughing, unlike Arabs' but incapable of doing all the work pushed on to them by their white masters. She was not completely idealistic, for she spoke with the two voices, of irritation at the black boys' feck-

20. Phyllis Du Boulay (1883–1956), nurse and Franciscan nun. Founded St Giles Homes for Lepers, East Hanningfield, Essex.

lessness and dishonesty and of a motherly compassion at their childish simplicity.

The row is best pieced together from the family letters, too well-bred to shout. Dick's comes first, written to his mother on 20 November:

> Phyllis left here rather a white person, as Mary had the house [in Pretoria] all to herself. I think Phyllis had a touch of the sun, but she had been doing altogether too much. An English person coming out does not at first realize that the wily kaffir will appear to work hard, but will at the same time leave everything undone that he can get anyone else to do for him. The boy has been serving up quite decent meals and doing all the rooms as well since Phyllis has been away. Phil seems to be a bit better too, and has got rid of his cold at last. We are probably going to change rooms a bit, Phil sleeping in the spare room except when it is wanted. We don't suit each other as room-mates, as I don't sleep well unless I have a gale blowing in my face, and Phil being used to mosquito-nets cannot stand a draught at all.

If we now turn to Phil's letter written on the same day to his brother his first ostrich nest, 'and now there are 5 eggs in it, which means that two hens are laying in it, as two eggs were laid in one day. This means being able to start my incubator as well as leaving eggs in the nest.'

The parents, ever interested in practical details, asked about costs. 'They were bought in Cape Colony as young birds at £25 apiece,' Dick replied. 'Half of them are now old enough to breed, and a cock and two hens are doing so. If I wanted to buy this set of three in Cape Colony now I should have to pay £150 to £250. A good cock fit for breeding would be about £75. One very good bird still too young to breed he would not sell for less than £200. The feathers from these birds got first prize in Johannesburg show this year.' News of the birds' progress and mishaps peppers the letters. One or two incidents will be enough for the picture.

In the breeding season ostriches are moderately dangerous, as the cocks have a violent forward kick. Sometimes they wandered into the veldt and had to be found and brought back. 'One found me,' wrote Dick in April 1910, 'and removed one trouser leg and made a hole in my other leg, luckily not laming me, and I led him off ignominiously by the neck to solitary confinement in the breeding camp, where a hen will join him as soon as I can get a double fence through to prevent him fighting the cock in the next camp.'

Experiments were tried with feed. As well as rape he tried velvet beans, but kept a control batch off in order to see what sort of feathers they would grow on the bare veldt. He concluded that nothing equalled 'good green feed'.

There was little doubt, though, about the superiority of Cape Colony feathers. Dick spoke of the fine quality of the local stock at the agricultural show, 'but though I could grow as good feathers as those that won the prizes, some which arrived late from the Cape put the others in the shade and are far superior to any of mine ... The Cape people are all driving motor-cars now [1911] on the proceeds of ostrich farming. One man has reared 400 chicks which he won't sell under £15 apiece.'

It took a visiting observer to give mundane details in her letters. 'Dick is pulling the ostrich quills,' Phyllis wrote home; 'they are done

Ralph, we find a similar story but put in a different way:

> Phyllis has been a bit off-colour and gone up to Mary for a bit. She
> is certain to stay until the 26th [November] ... It was a good thing
> she went, I think, because she was getting beyond bearing things,
> especially Dick who hasn't been very easy to live with owing to
> temper. But I've had a good row with him and the atmosphere is
> cleared all round, thank goodness!

Phyllis herself had been writing home of Dick's temper and Phil's
level-headedness since within two weeks of her arrival, as well as
of the difficulties of catering for numbers of people including unexpected guests, and the work expected of the boy. Finally, from Mary's
house in Pretoria, she wrote to her sister Bee on 18 November: 'I
walked in here last night at about 7.30 to find myself very welcome
but quite unexpected as my letter had gone astray.' She wrote of her
violent headaches, and of going back to the farm when the new housekeeper had got there. 'I only trust the boys [meaning her brothers and
the others in the house] won't starve before the new house-keeper
arrives; the present boy's cooking is of the weirdest, but I left them
with bread to go on with and a large lump of salt-beef, not to speak of
bacon and eggs and heaps of butter and milk.' There was then a story
of the kaffirs on the farm stealing what they thought was salt but was
in fact Epsom Salts, and she ended with a complaint about the usual
badness of the railway.

Finally there was Mary from her rented house in Pretoria writing
the next day to her father about a week of surprises:

> On Wednesday Phyllis turned up. They are without a house-keeper
> for the moment, and I think Phyllis got a little overdone. It was
> rather comical to hear the two sides of the question. Dick [who had
> obviously just written to Mary as well as to his mother] thought it
> would be a good thing for her to come away so that the newcomers
> could find out what the kaffirs could do when left to themselves
> and put on their mettle, and Phyllis told me she thought her coming
> away would be a lesson to Dick who seems to have no idea of the
> many things the kaffirs could <u>not</u> do. Anyhow, a new, capable house-
> keeper is going up this week, and meanwhile I am scoring.

The quick-tempered incident was obviously soon composed and Phyllis went back, but only to witness another personal *contretemps*, this time about the housekeeper herself.

Housekeepers were hard to get for the pay and conditions Dick's household offered. In spring 1910 Dick had managed to engage a Mrs Shepherd, a widow with a little girl of three, and was delighted to think he had got a 'treasure'. But he added in his letter 'They are going to meal in their own room and will be just superior servants.' To him it seemed a natural arrangement as well as a good one, as Mrs Shepherd had already been in service and was going to work for £3 a week, roughly twice a kaffir's wage. As Saki wrote, 'a good cook as cooks go, and as cooks go she went'.

The interim without a housekeeper was not a success. Phyllis complained she had to produce a square meal out of an empty larder and that Dick was 'a most impatient young man who thinks food falls ready cooked from heaven'.

Eventually, in November, Mrs Proctor arrived, also with a child, the four-year-old Kathleen. She had been engaged by Mary who vouched for her capability and her ability to get up at 5 a.m. Unfortunately, it was the gentle Phil this time who sailed into the storm, directed, one must suppose, by Dick as master of the household. 'I had an awful quarter-hour when I found she had laid a place for herself at table, and an immense amount of diplomacy to convey to her that she wasn't expected to meal with us. She has never been in service before and I am afraid she felt it, but it had to he done.'

It is easy for a modern observer to reply that it hadn't to be done, and that the family should have accepted her expectations of social equality. But it was a family not only imbued with the class *mores* of the age, but not at ease with itself at the time. Feelings between Dick and Phyllis had come to a head, Phil had been trying to make peace, and now, doing what he thought expected of him, he was to be hounded by Mrs Proctor.

Dick was not told of the terrible embarrassment. He wasn't an intuitive man anyway. If Mrs Proctor took it out on Phil who had snubbed her, Dick was clearly amused at getting his own back too on the Phil who had stood up for Phyllis:

> We have installed a new house-keeper who has frightened the life
> out of Phil ... She calls him 'young man' and takes her own way,
> Phil submitting meekly. She is a middle-aged Newcastle woman,
> thick in the beam and as strong as a horse. She is quite all right
> with me at present and I like her, but she is distinctly forceful in her
> dealings with the others. Phyllis I expect will manage her all right.
> Otherwise she proves to be a treasure, as she is an excellent cook
> and likes doing all the work herself, and only wants the boy to be
> within hail for odd jobs ... She talks Zulu and the boy runs when she
> opens her mouth. She cleaned and scrubbed the house from top to
> bottom after her arrival last Wednesday evening and would not let
> the boy touch a thing until she had satisfied herself that everything
> was clean. But I howl with laughter when I return from the veld and
> Eustace tells me stories of the way she sets aside Phil's suggestions,
> and the meek way in which he takes it.

As to Phyllis 'managing' Mrs Proctor, the letters do not record,
but she learned from Phil what had happened, saw that Mrs Proctor's
feelings had been severely hurt and wrote home that she, Phyllis, was
being kept firmly in her place.

Christmas 1910 smoothed these unhappy relationships with the
enactment of the old festive ceremonies from home. Shoes were put
outside doors to be filled with presents, and little Kathleen Proctor
whose mother had told her Santa Claus would not be coming this year
was filled with joy to find it not true.

Mary tuned her viola early in the morning and 'Hark, the herald
angels sing' sounded out with voices and string as it had done so often
at Winchester in former days. Even Dick was genial at being part of
what he called 'a thoroughly jolly English pitch-up' and at 'the many
joys to be got out of a big house'. Perhaps the interlude healed hearts,
but there were longer decisions to be made. The futures of Phyllis and
Phil lay in England and Egypt respectively.

In a way these two youngest members of the family reacted in
opposite ways to the Transvaal life. To Phyllis there were sights to
see and fresh society to embrace, even though she had sensed the life

was not for her. With Phil there was only a deepening depression that stemmed from being out of place. His mind and heart longed for the quicker exchange of Anglo-Egyptian society and were numbed by 'colonial' life. So their letters home throw criss-cross beams of light on society in Naboomspruit and the Transvaal.

At the end of January 1911 Dick, Phyllis and young Eustace Halifax made a weekend social trek round the neighbourhood. It was a little summer holiday and perhaps also a peace offering between Dick and Phyllis. Certainly it was within the customary practice approved by Dick to call on his neighbours in colonial fashion, without invitation or pre-arrangement.

Phil preferred to spend this weekend at home, minding the farm and nursing his dull spirits: he made his own trek later and, alone. But Phyllis wrote about it all gaily to Winchester:

> I suppose we did a good bit more than 50 miles all told, – tandem mules, Eustace and Dick riding the mare in turns ... in among the kopjes, climbing through drifts and the boulder-strewn road, down to green plain, grass over our heads in places and big trees instead of stunted ones.

> They first called on a typical Scotch couple, sort of front-parlour business, but most hospitable and delighted to see us ... The poor little woman was only just out of hospital, put in the train by a nurse and had 11 hours' journey by herself with a change in the middle, arrived at Naboomspruit with no-one to meet her and a good 15 miles home in a rough Cape cart.

On they journeyed to another valley where a Captain and Mrs Groves were farming:

> We were amused to find 3 visitors there already, all of whom had just been staying with us! The Groves have only got a mud-hut with two small and two little brick rooms for Mrs., but they gave us a hearty welcome and promptly killed a sheep. I slept with Mrs. and the baby, one boy went into a tent, and the rest took the floor and couch ... We meant to stay only one night but they pressed us, so we stayed two ... Poor little Mrs. Groves is a regular pretty little

butterfly, and there she is, alone most of the day and doing a large part of the housework. They are trying to raise funds for her to return to England for the birth of her baby.

When they pushed on they lost the track against wire fences 'and found ourselves bottled up in a fruit-farm with no road ... a house bolted, barred and empty, with one mournful little terrier'. They outspanned and ate apples, figs, pears and peaches. 'We found out afterwards the place belonged to a man who is more or less off his head and is trying to sell but believes there is gold on it, so is asking absurd prices and meanwhile letting the place go to rack and ruin.' They found a gate but no road and 'finally got put right by some kaffirs. We turned up at about 5 at a bachelor's house, Dawson by name, a really nice fellow; his father was at Exeter [College] with father, and his boy had not lost his polish as most have out here. He has got a nice little four-roomed house ... and is painting it ready for his bride. I only hope he has struck a girl with enough grit in her to face the lonely life.' (Dick considered Dawson 'out and away the best farmer among us'.)

Again the party stayed the night at their host's insistence and were well entertained with food and conversation. The next morning brought them to the Allen family:

> Mrs. a cheerful American with two very American girls of about 15, and a quiet husband. We only stopped for a cup of tea, but it is delightful how one is welcomed everywhere.

> We got to another fruit-farm in time for lunch, – typical English yeomen, nice simple people, rather distressed at not being 'ridded up' for us. The son was busy building two rooms on to the house ... They settled here six years ago in dense bush, cleared the trees entirely themselves, and planted pips, stones and slips of all sorts of fruit trees ... This year they are coining money: plums, apples, oranges, lemons, figs, bananas ... They only had bread and cheese to offer us but turned us out in the fruit trees afterwards, not to speak of giving a great basket of figs to take away. They say it was a pure fluke trying there.

Most of our route has been rough track and some times open veld. Once we were going down a precipice when I fell out at the right moment, which righted the cart. It was exciting with Eustace driving tandem for the first time in his life and a very young mule in as leader for the first time.

This was nearly at the end of Phyllis's brief but turbulent stay, a month before she paid a last visit to Mary in Pretoria and then sailed away for ever to become a Franciscan nun (in the Church of England), nursing lepers at East Hanningfield in Essex. It was a house she helped to found.

Her comments on the Transvaal form an interesting contrast with those of her brother Philip: hers enthusiastic, even gushing, his reserved, precise and sad. Both of them found the Transvaal on closer inspection intolerable and Dick impossible.

More exactly, there is a whimsicality about Phyllis's letters which is irritating because it sometimes tried to hide what she felt. 'I shall be leaving a great many friends behind as well as the boys [i.e. her brothers],' she wrote to her mother; and two days later to her brother Ralph, 'I have many dear friends amongst both kaffirs and animals to part with.'

Yet the silliness is balanced by more factual observations made in her last batch of letters home. She saw the hardness of a tenant-farmer's life – 'to go on improving the place and then to have to pay through the nose for every improvement if they eventually want to buy'. She saw the isolation. Sunday service if wanted was organized in the dairy, with the milking bell for summons and the whole stock of seven chairs for pews, about enough for 'neighbours' who would have to come a minimum of 13 miles. She saw too the interior isolation bred by the class sensibilities of the day, so that easy talk was too rarely possible: 'I am afraid I am not in love with Colonials, and Phil feels it too, very much … It is either a case of front parlour and edges of chairs, or else the most appalling familiarity and jocoseness.' And at the very centre, within the homestead, the 'Philistines' found actual philistinism. 'There is a lack of outside interests on the farm, no conversation, the re-reading of novels.'

Philip was a different creature from his younger sister. The thin, slight body was indubitably masculine and the good head held steady thoughts. But his reaction to the Transvaal was if anything more negative than that of Phyllis and his disillusion swifter. The diet of shot birds irritated his rebellious insides, but worse than that or the tedium of butter-making was the isolation from a world whose spinning-round activities were dear to him. 'I get the hump most frightfully at times, but gardening or a thunderstorm generally clears it.' This was from a man never given to complaining. But a week later to his mother whom he loved he confessed, 'I am quite buried here and can give no outside news. There are heaps of little things that I would naturally write about, but I've hardly time to appreciate them … They are all bottled up and will burst forth some day to make a decent letter', and he went on to describe his efforts to reach mentally out of his cage, resigned to having an *Overseas Daily Mail* he couldn't afford. 'Our present daily paper is a piece of extravagance on my part, as it costs threepence a time, but we had to see how the world moved.' By 'we' he most certainly meant 'I'.

The next spring Phil did a little trek on his own, but suffered from cold and indigestion as well as losing his way. But 'it was a great change mentally and I enjoyed my trial'. His purpose had been entirely praiseworthy: to see some neighbours. Even though he 'detested the Colonial', he felt there must be people about with whom he had things in common. 'I hunger for information and object-lessons that I can't get here.'

Not that Phil was an 'intellectual' in any sense, good or bad. He was intensely practical like his brothers and sisters. Barred by physique from heavy labour, he was adept at skilful planting, curious about the world and admiring of those who possessed technical knowledge. Once when Dick was absent from the farm the general manager of the owning company (Dormer) turned up with his wife, and 'I wasn't much impressed with his knowledge of the trees or crops.' On the other hand, there was Mr Moray. 'He is a Dutchman of Scotch descent and stayed here last night with his son. He is our Resident Magistrate, and is about the most interesting man I have ever met. He has been everywhere, read everything, and will talk. He happens to be a hypnotist and a great deal of a doctor as well as a distinguished lawyer, and is also good at natural history.'

Obviously this life could not go on, even though Phil had not (as he told Ralph) 'a brass farthing to get out of the country'. There were wild thoughts of British Columbia, but salvation came, as it ought to have done long before, from Egypt.

On 17 September 1911 Phil received an obscurely worded cable: 'WRITING OFFERING BILLET ACCEPTANCE UNITED ADVISE – LOWE.' In clear, this was an offer of appointment as assistant manager of the United Egyptian Salt Company from its managing director, Phil's old friend A.J. (Tiny) Lowe. He and Lowe had been together as teenagers in the office of a dubious City businessman; Lowe had been helped to his job in Egypt by Phil and had quickly shown his flair for money-making; now Lowe was mounting a rescue operation. Within days Phil had written to accept. On 25 October he joined the *Avondale Castle* at Delagoa Bay where before sailing north he was able to meet his brother Noel on his way back to Mauritius for a day's reunion. Contacts re-established, Phil sailed with a lightened heart. We meet him again in Egypt.

Whatever his faults, Dick was not ungenerous, least of all towards his younger brother whom he respected for his capabilities about the farm. 'A great relief having Phil to leave behind' he confessed after a rare holiday: 'I feel that I need not think.' And again, after a crowd of guests had gone, 'Phil put a tip-top lunch on the table.'

When the job in Egypt was offered, Dick said at once he was right to take it and 'go back to Egypt which he knows and loves as I do this country. From the business point of view I don't think the farm will suffer,' but 'he has been a delightful person to have in the house, and excellent for me to have someone living with me who goes his own gait regardless of my opinion in the matter, as one cannot help becoming autocratic in a country where one has to plan everything to its smallest details and one's white helpers are practically pupils whom one dare not leave to their own devices.'

When events mark a turning-point in someone's life, surprising

21. Cape Town from the *Edinburgh Castle*, 1911.
Sketch by Noel Du Boulay.

him or her with happiness, as with a good marriage, it is always open to speculation how far the lucky ones had planned it. 'There is a time to love,' said the Preacher (Eccles. 3), suggesting how the moment brings the person. Certainly Dick's long and contented marriage to Betty Grigson, from whom he had not long since bought his farm lease, came at the aptest time, yet with the amazement of discovery and a glow of astonishment which the letters convey. The idea was timely, but has left no trace of calculation on Dick's part.

As late as November 1910, just after the row with Phyllis on the farm, Dick had written to his mother, 'I am glad Mrs. Grigson has had another stay with you. Poor woman, I wonder how she will settle down to Capetown life again. She is such a typical farmer's wife.'

If Dick were already thinking of marriage to her, he was keeping it within himself. Most likely he was honest when he later described her as too good for him. Yet two visits to old Mrs Du Boulay on a single home leave suggest an interest on Betty's part, prompted or not by signals from Dick.

Mary also had taken a deal of trouble with her brother, whom she loved dearly, and when she heard of Phil's return to Egypt, which she approved of for Phil's sake, she added how desirable it was that Dick should get married 'to a clever woman he absolutely trusted. Then I should feel a sort of "Nunc dimittis". As it is I am distinctly low in my mind about him, for he is not strong enough to live alone.' (This incidentally throws a good light on Mary who knew herself to be a clever woman and could selflessly envisage her own wasted virtues in a partner for her brother.)

Very likely Phil's imminent departure stirred Dick to boldness. Anyhow, he was amazed at his good fortune. Faithful to the family custom of celebrating one another's birthdays, he wrote on 8 October to Ralph:

> Mary, Phil and I drank your health and many happy returns of the day last night, and when you get this you've just got to drink our health, i.e. Betty's and mine. Mrs. Grigson has been brave enough to say she'll marry me. She's yards too good for me, and besides ... the pluckiest little woman [she was very short] and an ideal farmer's wife, loves the life and could manage it very nearly as well as I can with all her woman's disabilities. At present we are only telling relations, and the telegram office here is by no means a safe place for secrets. I hope she will up here within a fortnight, when I shall try to fix the day for very soon. She has promised not to keep me waiting long. I'll shut up now before I begin to babble ...

In the later twentieth century it was not quite easy to realize there could be a South African happiness. Dick's was this. As well as the toughness, even the brutality, of Transvaal farming there was an evident joy in it caught by his phrase about Betty: 'she loves the life'. Further, his judgement that she could manage it 'very nearly as well as I can' was not a personal arrogance but a plain recognition that the job took a physical strength and instinct for command more usual in men than in women. Readers of the letters will see no male pride but rather the heroine-worship of a working farmer who struggled with his simple accounts for a woman of the world on familiar terms with those who had been making South African history.

Though her parents then lived in the Cape, Betty had been brought up in Grahamstown (Natal), where she had been 'Lizzie Douglass', daughter of a man also said to be 'the father of ostrich farming'. There were new brothers-in-law too for Dick, whom he valued to the point of indiscretion: 'I hope you managed to meet Frank Douglass,' he wrote to Ralph in 1913; 'he is my particular pal who taught me to work at Cranemere [an earlier farm]. He is a very prosperous and successful farmer, cursed with the fool of a wife, a spoilt child utterly wanting in balance.'

The spurt of savagery in a way lights up his idealization of Betty, whose letters to Winchester began now to take their place in the family correspondence, injecting their sense of happiness at Dick's good health, his better meals, and to the improvements to the house furnishings.

Mary as usual is a witness worth hearing and was soon sending good reports of Betty: 'one of the helpful kind ... I went with her to see the theatricals and chuckled at the way she looked after me as if I was a young and tender babe and had not had to look after myself for 25 years. She realized the reason of my laughter, but we both gravely agreed that the quality would come in very useful on the farm.'

The old Douglasses lived at Claremont, Cape of Good Hope, where the wedding of Dick and Betty was performed by the Archbishop of Cape Town. This was at Christmas time 1911, and Mary went down for the occasion and revelled 'in the beauty of this old Dutch estate with great oaks and stone pines and the house full of flowers, Transvaal life is interesting, but oh, – so ugly'.

She and Dick were shown around the Alphen vineyard by Mrs Henry Cloete, wife of the great winegrower of Cape Town. 'Tell father to try some Alphen Burgundy – they are now selling the 1906 vintage – the later years have not been touched but are reposing in enormous oak barrels.' Mary was the only one of the family to show the smallest interest in wine (though Noel seems to have enjoyed Lord Wolseley's Cyprus wine on the desert campaign).

It was a golden interlude, for Mary herself was happy at her young brother's good fortune, and as so often her happiness spilled into affection for all she saw; for Mrs Douglass, 'a sweet old English lady

with no colonialism about her in spite of all the years out here', and
also for the preacher on Sunday morning at Claremont, for it was a
sermon 'on joy from a man whose own wife was gravely ill'. Mary
was not, however, losing her bite, for she commented at once on the
evening sermon at Wynberg – 'a very evangelical one with exact
details of the Day of Judgment. I do not quite know where the information was procured, but the preacher was in deadly earnest.'

The marriage itself was the culmination of festivities. 'You could
have lighted a candle at Dick's face as they came down the church
together.' This too was followed by a shrewd remark. 'The chief sign
of colonialism in this family is their open admiration of each other. So
different from our own home upbringing.' This was addressed to her
mother, then aged 69.

The marriage of Dick to the widow Betty Grigson marks in many
ways a high point in his life on the Transvaal farm. He was given
to strong enthusiasms and deep discouragements. These continue
indeed after 1911, with swings up and down. But the correspondence
in general becomes a kind of switchback as forebodings and misfor-
tunes run on into actual gloom and the eventual failure of the estate.

Some of the letters provide interesting and measured comment.
In August 1912 he wrote home:

> I think the days of boom are passed and we are now building
> ourselves up steadily and surely in a way which does not appear much
> in the papers. In a few years' time we shall probably have a very
> large mealie export, and within my lifetime I prophesy that our beef
> export will be one of the big ones of the world. There are millions
> of acres still unoccupied up this way, all capable of producing
> superb cattle, and ground is being taken up daily. Mary notices the
> marvellous increase in acreage ploughed over as she travels about
> the country, and everywhere one meets men who started after the
> [Boer] war with 6 or 7 head of cattle and have today 60 or 70. South
> Africa is going ahead alright slowly but surely instead of in fits and
> starts with awful periods of depression in between.

But the bland generality was too easily upset by personal setbacks.
Within a couple of months Betty's reaction to the Transvaal summer

heat triggered a change in the tone of her husband's letters; he began to speak of going south rather than of buying more land in the Transvaal. It was a bad year, even 'for the kaffirs with their hardy little beasts'.

The year 1913 brought renewed optimism: the land filling up, and the ultimate paying off of his debt something he could envisage. He wrote longingly of being able to afford a car suitable for farm use, and described the 1913 Ford five-seater with its powerful engine and high clearance, available new in Johannesburg for £210.

But the old enemies, climate and politics, remained, and in 1914 they began to get the upper hand. They have to be written about as separate circumstances but of course were effective together in destroying farmers. Too much rainfall or too little might with a little bit of luck be survived, but war in the wider world affected markets and by stirring disaffection and rebellion at home upset the balance of a country where stability was precarious enough anyhow. Defensive movements of white men sent black men into terrified posture too, and white society became even more fissured.

In January 1914 there was a South African railway strike which caused widespread alarm. There was the problem of bringing provisions to scattered settlements and also the problem that some country people got frightened of possible 'native trouble'.

Different preoccupations are reflected in the letters of Dick and Mary, brother and sister, brought up in the same household, yet chalk and cheese, the one a Boerized farmer, the other an educator who had tasted Oxford lectures.

'A big meeting was called at a farm 15 miles out to discuss organizing the district, that is, of those men who did not already belong to shooting clubs,' Dick reported on 20 January 1914. 'A few of us as Naboomspruit people got together and sent a Dutchman out as our representative to say we were willing to act in concert with them, and would have a meeting to elect a commandant and choose a place for a laager if necessary … I was put in the chair and elected Commandant unanimously in face of two Dutch names proposed.'

Dick then took a party to Nylstroom to try and get recognition, guns and ammunition, but they were told there was no fear what-ever of the natives and they could not be recognized as they did not belong to shooting clubs. 'But I intend to keep this organization up, as although I am not in the least nervous or expectant of native trouble, we must be outnumbered by them in the district at least by 1000 to 1.'

In a couple of weeks the rail strike was broken, but Mary's reac-tion was that this had been 'the most high-handed use of power in this generation outside Russia'. She also noted that in the Piet Retief district the Boers were so afraid of the natives that they went into laager, while the kaffirs were equally frightened, not knowing the meaning of all the arming of the Reserve Defence Force, so they too went into war formation and slept with assegai in hand for two or three days simply for defence purposes.

In February Mary was writing:

> Smuts has made a great speech in Parliament and I have no doubt he will carry the Indemnity Bill, but I was glad to see that Patrick Duncan spoke up against the principle of imprisonment and deportation without trial, however great the offence. I am entirely with the Government in wishing to get rid of those particular men, – they were simply agitators, not the real workers; but we in England fought many years for our Habeas Corpus Act, and one does not like to see the principal charter of democracy given up without a word. As far as I can make out, I am in a minority in these views. I can only think the others have not read history.

These alarms coincided with financial setback on the farm. The price of ostrich feathers slumped and cows were dying of an undi-agnosed disease, which led to a fall in the monthly amount Dick received from the sale of cream. Drought threatened. 'I shall make no attempt to pay my bills' was the desperate comment.

There is a break in the correspondence till September 1914, and by then of course the Great War had broken out. Dick's next letter was full of war fever. He was easily excited at the best of times, but now his world was polarized between the sturdy and cheery English (sic) troops preparing to go and fight and the hostile, uncomprehend-ing Dutch. Some of the Dutch were fortunately 'splendidly loyal', but 'a good deal of treason is being talked round here'.

As a man typical of his generation and place in society, Dick's attitude is quite understandable, and our own possible views of it are in
any case not relevant. But at the time Dick was clearly correct. Rebellion was indeed being prepared by some Dutch leaders and was to
break out in the incident known as De Wet's rebellion[5] that autumn.
Martial law was proclaimed and by October 1914 Dick was a lieutenant, in charge of a rifle club, and also 'a sort of senior special policeman' with orders to try small cases himself and power to administer
corporal punishment, though he added that the thrashing was not to
be overdone.

Fear of the Dutch was paralleled by fear of the natives. The kaffirs
who lived on white men's farms were disliked by native chiefs because
they did not pay them anything. Hence, ran Dick's argument, farm
boys were unlikely to welcome a rising.

Dick himself was genuinely at his wits' end to continue the farm's
activity which was his livelihood, and if he exulted in seeing men go
off in uniform while he stayed around making speeches, his view-
point was consistent. He wanted bonds between Dutch and British
cemented for the sake of security, and for all his English patriotism and even arrogance he never really hated the Dutch, whom he
regarded as co-workers in opening up the Transvaal.

This made De Wet's rebellion all the more serious to him. On 4
November 1914 he wrote home, 'The call has come, and I am off to
defend my District against the rebels. It has been sudden – rebellion
has come to a head in the last couple of days ... I have been O.C.
here for the day and am tonight in charge of eight men to help defend
Nylstroom. Must stop as I have to parade my men in 10 minutes and
truck horses.'

From now on the letters present a state of excitement to be
succeeded by anticlimax, frustrations and disappointments, and in
this the letters are an accurate enough account of what Dick's life was
like.

The rebellion made them all jumpy: full of righteous hatred for

---

5. See p 154, note.

the disloyal Boers, deeply anxious about their own farms, keen to show prowess in this chance of military expression and bitter about their own higher command and their lack of recognition.

Betty was left to run the farm during the emergency, and Dick wrote to her, describing how he took his party off on that 4 November and dismounted at the district capital of Nylstroom in Poht's Hotel yard. They drew rifles and got their horses valued in case of loss. His own 'Punch', he noted, was written down as £27.10 shillings.

From being a local lieutenant he found himself a trooper attached to Willy de Klerch. He was, as so often, much on his social dignity: 'the men treat me as though I were a lieutenant'. It is a replica of his position 14 years earlier when he longed for rank in the little troop he joined in the Cape. Why was he not now an officer? One can only speculate that the demands of the farm had prevented him training with a shooting club. He was, it seems, the familiar type of barrack-room grumbler too, full of complaints at the lack of clear orders and at the 'messing about' which is the military experience of other ranks since war began. Of course, he could have been right.

They were sent out to scout, rather haphazardly, but with success, for the rebels were located and they advanced against them in open order, shooting at the gallop and standing up at intervals in the stir-rups, reins flying, loosing off with their rifles at Boers some 300 yards ahead. They captured the occasional Boer on the run. Some of their own horses bolted in terror at the racket. One party of English charged a kopje of stones and seized it from its Boer defenders, where Durance was shot through the heart at 12 yards. Lieutenant Besten on his right was shot through the hand – 'these were our only casualties'. Of the Boers, ten had been killed, several wounded and some 20 pris-oners brought in. The next four days saw further skirmishing. Dick missed a fight in which the English lost 12 killed and 12 wounded as against the rebels' loss of 137 killed and wounded. Then it was a case of chasing stragglers while the government offered the rank and file a chance to surrender. Dick and his comrades were hungry, worried about their homes and fed up with 'rotten mismanagement, every-body arguing'.

Civil war brings some problems more terrible even than those of international hostilities, and if Dick could write of lack of discipline and of provisioning he was surely referring to the kind of consequence that must follow a breakdown in society. The legacy of hatred too is not in doubt. Mary had been in England but bravely sailed back to the Cape in January 1915 to hear reports of a country 'rotten with rebellion'. She spoke of the harm it did: old scores paid off, brutalities committed, mines closed down and the desperate efforts by government to heal divisions. Belgians were sent round to lecture in Flemish to the Dutch on the horrors of a German occupation far away in Europe.

By December 1914 Dick could go home to his Transvaal farm, raging against the rebels, and with new contempt for the Dutch: 'my opinion of the courage of the Boer has sunk to zero after this affair. Many of them are stupidly brave but the great majority take very good care of their skins ... They simply ran away when we charged.'

He also thought the rebels' punishment had been ludicrously light. Though he does not mention it in his letters, De Wet in fact had been found guilty on eight counts of treason, but sentenced only to a fine of £2,000 and six years' imprisonment, which was cut short by his parole the next year on his promise not to agitate. He died on his farm after a peaceful retirement.

But the rebellion was both a sign of Afrikaner consciousness and a strengthening of its resolve. The Nationalist Party De Wet had helped to found now passed on to other leadership and made great strides, as the world knows.

Englishmen like Dick who might so easily have been incorporated into the Nationalist movement were made sharply aware of the conflict of loyalties all about them but were themselves never anything but British who snarled at traitors: 'some Boers tackled me to sign a petition asking for more leniency for the rebels,' he wrote in April 1915, 'but I refused point-blank and said they were being treated too leniently already; that as long as men in this country saw they could rebel and break laws without punishment, they would continue to do so on flimsy pretexts, and that the whole country wanted discipline, which entails punishment for wrong done. They did not like it.'

Meanwhile the war went on. Despite the rebellion, Dick hoped desperately not to be sent in the expedition against German West Africa, for the sake of his homestead. As a married volunteer he had been paid five shillings a day, but his presence was needed for the farm and for the lonely Betty. 'The farm cannot be kept going without me,' he wrote, looking round at the unchecked weeds and fields unsown.

His pessimism turned to his age:

I cannot stand heavy work as I used to [he was 38]. The difficult part of Transvaal farming is that one is always changing boys and no sooner have you trained a boy than he is called away to do his 3-month free labour on the farm on which he lives in lieu of rent. So it often pays to do the manual labour yourself rather than train new boys. In Cape Colony a boy took up his abode on your farm as a labourer with his whole family and probably stayed many years with you.

To catch up on work not done during the rebellion, Dick even had kaffir beer made to tempt a gang of some 20 boys and women to get on with the weeding, but rain came and thwarted the work. Where the work was done, the mealies were wonderful.

So Dick and Betty continued to farm with frugality and economy, concentrating on crops and cattle and getting in some cash from shooting parties. Cattle disease was being tackled by building dip-tanks.

On the surface Dick seemed a moderately successful tenant-farmer with time for tennis on some days and bridge in the evenings. But the passage of years, bad teeth and a natural tendency to depression brought out his latent ill-humour with the world. Betty wrote of him as overwrought and nervy. He himself could write, 'Betty's family were all well-to-do men looking down on our methods', but 'we are paying our way ... we live far above the average for people in our class in this country on farms.'

He got very irritated with some people called Cresswell who let it be known they expected two days' notice of a visit. 'We like people to drop in and have never been used to letting people know in this country.' The colony of people up 'the hills' he thought too prim and proper. It was not just inverted snobbery, however, for, as he pointed out, you cannot live by 'society ways' in stock-farming country, and the free and easy behaviour was both necessary for the requirements of the cattle and also, to him, its own compensation. In this way they went on through the war, getting about in a Cape cart with two big horses, no Ford motor-car, and selling dairy produce to Pretoria.

Suddenly it came to an end. The letters get few, but in August 1917 Dick wrote that he had been in Johannesburg to have all his teeth extracted, and with a Du Boulay fortitude that it was all satisfactorily done: 'I have been staying with my dentist, and am beginning to munch solids again.' In the same letter he reported his intention to get out of the farm as he was no longer solvent. This was after be had noted a profit in 1916.

The real trouble seems to have been that ostrich farming had never properly recovered, and its slump had wiped off £2,000 of Dick's working capital. However well the cattle farming went, the farm was under-capitalized. He needed more animals but could not afford them, and the company's rent and interest continued to rise.

In addition to this basic problem, Dick was feeling his age. So he and Betty decided to take a small house near Pretoria along with Betty's young sister who had a little girl but no husband. Betty would look after the house, Dorothy would look for work and Dick would try to get into the Labour Corps as an NCO at £5 or £6 a week and run a smallholding too.

The pathos of these plans does not lighten. A letter to Philip in 1936 shows Betty ill and the couple running some kind of smallholding. He had bought eight cows for £80 and was pleased at getting £101 compensation for the wayleave of an overhead electric cable: 'I hope to start a flutter on the share market when it comes.'

That is really all. Hard-up for cash, Dick and Betty nonetheless managed to visit England in 1936 where he seemed to one young observer a quieter and glummer lookalike to his brother Philip.

Betty died and Dick followed her soon after, in early 1949, looked after by his lifelong friend, Mrs Adelaide Newby, of Isipingo, Natal. 'He was a lonely old man really,' she said, 'far older than his years. I think if he had had some occupation he would have been happier, but he never wanted to bestir himself. His house was only a few doors away and he used to turn up at all sorts of odd hours, out of sheer boredom.'

22. Philip Du Boulay (1880–1960), the author's father. In Egypt 1899–1928; First World War Lt. with Egyptian Labour Corps; 1916 Capt. at Gallipoli; 1917 Major with Desert Column of the Eyptian Labour Corps.

CHAPTER 5

Man of Egypt: Philip

The youngest son in a family of 13 has awesome problems but also a few advantages. There is not often much money to keep him in coats and shoes, let alone fit him up with professional training. Brothers and sisters already on the scene may provide warning object-lessons or (perhaps harder to cope with) models of success and of superior behaviour. On the other side, there is the friendship and help of the family network where the bond of love as well as of kinship ties them together.

There was always a special friendship between Philip and Ralph despite the 11 years between them. Ralph, creator of the family letter collection, had gone out to Egypt in 1891 to work in the Egyptian Government Salt Department, concerned with the great saline lakes along the coastline. In 1899 the Egyptian Salt and Soda Company was formed as a private venture, and Ralph moved into this. By means now obscure a post was also found for Philip, then 19, as private secretary to the company's general manager, Ayerst Henham Hooker, on the very first day of the company's existence. It was centred on the Wadi Natrun (the soda wadi) near Alexandria and the settlement there was known as Bir Hooker.[1]

This was Philip's beginning in Egypt, and it was a stroke of luck for him. At the turn of the century Egypt was not a welcoming country for Englishmen without fortune, and even those with connections and money had to steer a cautious course in a land which was growing

---

1. E.M. Forster, *Alexandria: A History and Guide* (Alexandria, 1st ed, 1922), p 201.

tired of foreign dominations.

Egypt was not part of the British Empire. Its ancient civilization, the wealth of the Nile, and its crucial position between east and west, south and north, had always attracted the domination of conquerors and the penetration of commerce. From 1516 to 1914 the nominal overlord was Turkey. England fought Napoleon there and French political influence was second only to that of Britain. Underneath all this a struggle for national independence developed from the middle of the nineteenth century.

In the reign of Edward VII at the beginning of the twentieth century the British virtually ran Egypt under King Edward's Consul-General Lord Cromer. Turkey's nominal viceroy, called the Khedive, was dependent on the advice of British civil servants. And when in 1914 Turkey entered the war against Britain, Egypt was declared a British Protectorate by the occupying power. But the government of the country, in effect Anglo-Egyptian, was both sparing with public money and careful to promote native Egyptians as far as possible to public posts.

This is the background which makes Philip's early life intelligible: his struggle for employment and also his close involvement with the people of the country once he was employed. Men like him who served the country were in some sense serving an empire which considered itself to have a mission. More intimately, Egypt was a land full of potential friendships for those willing and able to go out and meet its inhabitants in town and village on personal terms and learn to speak with them.

Grandfather Du Boulay understood much of this in his fatherly, donnish way when he wrote to congratulate his son Philip. It was a letter of relief that the last boy was off his hands, but of loving advice also:

> I wish you all sorts of happiness. You have got interesting work and plenty of it, a liberal paymaster, and it is delightful for you to be living in the house and under the care of Mrs. Hooker. I suppose that you are picking up colloquial Arabic, and I shall be woefully disappointed in you if you do not work hard at the language. It is

your only chance of making anything but a temporary career in Egypt.

The advice was heeded, and Philip was the only one of the 13 brothers and sisters to become really fluent in a foreign language, though he never learned to write it.

From the beginning, when he was employed as personnel officer of the company's soda works at the Wadi Natrun just west of Alexandria and on 'extraordinary duties' as they were mysteriously called, he became in his heart a man of Egypt who learned to like and respect those among whom he worked, though he sometimes longed to get away from them.

This description of Philip is of his personality, a quick and sympathetic intelligence in a slight thin frame, a man to whom Egyptian workers and soldiers turned in confidence. It is not, however, a description of 'success' as the world understands it. It was years before he had anything like a secure job, and he never rose to a very well-paid one though he served in the country for nearly 30 years. In the end he was forced to leave Egypt through poor health and the need to make a home in England for his young family.

During that last part of his life in England, from 1927 to 1960, he dwelt a great deal upon what he had left, as was clear whenever he reminisced, his face alight with the memories.

Mr and Mrs Hooker took good care of Phil, trusted and recommended him and looked after him over the time when he had all his teeth extracted in April 1900. 'My dear Hooker,' wrote Dr Seymour Dolley from Cairo, 'I do not know how to get at Du Boulay; please tell him I will give him chloroform on Monday at 11.30 at Wallers. Bread and milk for breakfast only, at <u>7.30 on Monday</u>, and not too much of it. Kindest regards to you all.' Phil's older brother Dick, it will be recalled, had the same operation but much later in life, and stayed with his dentist in Johannesburg till he was over it. Expatriate medicos easily became family friends.

With hindsight the early connection with the Hookers and the new company might with advantage to Philip have been continued. Nowadays a job in business life may well seem less secure than a post

in government service, yet given Phil's efficiency and obvious likea-
bleness he could have progressed up the ladder of responsibility to an
'executive' post, acquiring Arabic and expertise on the way, as he did
in other circumstances.

So far as one can see, his disastrous changeover to government
employment was an accident, and the name of the accident was Ernest
Ayscoghe Floyer,[2] scholar, explorer, scientist and inspector-general
of the Egyptian State Railways and Telegraphs. Doubtless it was all
well meant. Floyer, a remote cousin of the Du Boulays, had heard
good reports of young Philip and invited him in 1900 to become his
assistant secretary. It was no trivial offer. Floyer was by all accounts
a remarkable man, and among his other achievements he had run the
Egyptian State Telegraphs so well that he had converted an annual
loss into a surplus, out of which he had persuaded the government to
devote funds to an experimental desert plantation. In this way he had
set up Planter's House to grow cactus for fibre, Casuarina trees for
telegraph poles, and other plants. This was at El Katta or Manashi, in
the desert outside Cairo, where Phil rapidly found himself employed
in congenial if lonely work by a man who was high official, affectionate relative and scholar all in one, and who, moreover, wrote to him
in friendly and familiar terms:

> My dear Phil [he wrote on 25 August 1900 from Planter's House], I
> have been hoping to hear from you. You may come any day you like.
> My mail and provisions leave Cairo for Barrage every morning at
> 8.30 a.m. I can lend you temporarily a bed, chest of drawers, chair
> and table. But no washing apparatus. I have spare mosquito curtain.
> I hope to leave for England on 11th September. But I do not see why
> you should not stay on with my inspector. Yours truly. E.A. Floyer.
> You will have to pay something for your messing. But we do it as
> cheap as we can.

What Philip could not know was that Floyer had heart disease,
of which he would die in 1903. This misfortune did not for the time
being take away Phil's job, but it removed a man who was a consid-

---

2. For Floyer see pp 24–5 above.

erable figure in the difficult economic and social world of Cromer's Egypt who might have been able to save Planter's House, and who in any event could have remained a powerful patron for the young man whose services he quickly came to value.

In the short term Phil did very well as Floyer's subordinate in the Egyptian State Telegraphs. What he had already learned in Salt and Soda was put to good use and improved at El Katta, both paperwork and the physical activity of working in the heat and often in solitude. Floyer must have shown Phil's father some specimens of the young man's business letters, for he wrote from Winchester to congratulate his son on the good impression he was making and begging him to pay more attention to his food and not to lose weight.

This was in 1902, and the next year Floyer was dead. For the time being the work at Planter's House went on, and Philip was made director of the Plantations Department of the Egyptian State Railways and Telegraphs, though without success in getting included on the government's pension list.

Little survives from this period of Phil's life save for a handful of yearning love letters to Mercy Friend (who broke their brief engagement for ten years) and a rough crayon sketch by him dated January 1904, showing a flat-roofed pinkish house, a water-reservoir on one part of the roof, and the whole surrounded by a rigid green network cage structure within which plant and shrubs were growing; also short green trees outside the cage and a few figures either carrying water buckets or, clothed in *galabeeah* and *tarboosh*, gravely conferring.

The letters tell of a life which was isolated but in itself satisfying. A little railway connected the semi-desert villages. Mahmoud, whose own wife could not stand the solitude and departed for Cairo, kept Philip company and served him well. The place bred loyalties as well as the experimental plants, and as late as 1909 Mahmoud gave part of his 15-day holiday to travel up to Beni Suef above Cairo where Phil was then working just to meet his old boss for a couple of hours and bring him magazines.

In 1912 Phil had occasion to pass again by Planter's House, and wrote to his sister in England how he mourned to see seven miles of his beautiful trees cut down 'and the place where they stood as bare as your hand, sand-dunes forming all about and canal banks falling in'.

In the catastrophe the culprit was 'government economy'. The period 1908–09 was one of intense restriction in government spending which under Cromer and then Sir Eldon Gorst admittedly brought greater solvency and order. It also saw a marked increase in nationalist and specifically anti-British feeling. For these reasons it was especially difficult for Britons who were employed by the nominally Egyptian government rather than by some private concern, yet had no formal training which might prefer them over Egyptians, whose country it was.

This was the position when in 1907 the Department of Plantations was transferred to the Ministry of Finance and from 31 December abolished outright. Philip was granted full pay for six months, but the job was over. In March 1909 he was curtly refused the use of a truck to take his furniture from El Katta to Cairo and was told the site was for immediate sale. Its dereliction has already been noted.

These events were the beginning of a black period in Philip's life, some of which is chronicled in surviving letters but never with the note of complaint. In 1907 his engagement to Mercy Friend had also been abruptly broken off by her, though in fact they married years later, in November 1917. The year 1908 was spent job-hunting in Alexandria.

With no money but what he had from 'severance pay' (as it is now called), Phil was given a little room in a flat set up by his old friend Lowe and a man called DesClayes. This was just outside Alexandria to the east, near the Sporting Club, and from here he journeyed in daily 'billet-hunting', as the phrase went. In the afternoons he and Lowe generally met for tea at the Union Club and went to watch the skating until it was time to go home for dinner.

Some interviews were quite encouraging. Phil felt he was well in with the men in irrigation, but the weeks went by without an offer; 'hope for work gets dimmer,' he wrote in November 1908, 'as the Ministry of Finance are cutting down budgets right and left. Is there anyone at home such as Lady Laura Ridding who could give me an introduction to Lord Edward Cecil [financial adviser to the Egyptian Government] out here? He could give me letters to people who won't speak to people who have not a title … Yesterday I had an interview with Colonel Macaulay, the General Manager of the Railways. He held out no hopes whatever, for the eternal reason that I was an Englishman.'

This was a cry of desperation, not only at the unemployability of Englishmen without formal qualifications but also in his own uncharacteristic attempt to fall back on the old-boy network. It seems indeed that letters were sent. On 16 November 1908, Mary Lady Waldegrave, sister of the Wykehamist Lord Selborne, was writing to Lord Edward Cecil about the Winchester family of Reverend James Du Boulay with the phrase 'all the sons and daughters are made of first-rate stuff'. The upshot of this embarrassing communication is unknown, but when Phil was promised a small office job on the new drainage scheme at Port Said about the same time, it seems the offer had been made through an introduction from his own brother Jim, then on his way through to Bombay to become Political Secretary, to the government official at Port Said.

This hope too was cruelly dashed as the post was first postponed and then refused on the ground that it must go to a trained Egyptian accountant. But even in his disappointment Phil considered it had been shameful that a government man should recommend a man to a contractor, and that had he been taken, it would have been jobbery ('a form of *bakshish*').

Life without resources was not all gloom. Phil had a love of good company and a vivacity of observation which bring back the sparkling sights of pre-war Alexandria more effectively than do works of political history or the fancies of fiction.

There was the official entry of the Khedive into Cairo for the Season, in a shocking bad temper at not being met by the British consul-general and ignoring all the reception committee but the British general. Then there was the craze for roller-skating in Alexandria, looked down on by supercilious Cairo. There was tennis at this club and that, and parties at the houses of friends who had employment in Salt and Soda or the Customs Service, such as the Ludolfs and Gordon Morices (who were still sending handsome Christmas presents to the present writer in the 1930s!).

Alexandria as a strategic port in a troubled world could expect all kinds of naval visits. Just before Christmas 1908 'two officers from H.M.S. *Aboukir*, the Duke of Connaught's boat, walked into the Club the other day in peals of laughter with a clockwork teddy-bear which they proceeded to wind up in the middle of the floor. In a minute the whole club was round it helpless with laughter, – it all happened so spontaneously.' Two weeks later four Russian battleships were expected for a fortnight's stay, and Lowe was to be in the thick of the entertaining owing to his flair for keeping people amused.

Back in the flat they all had a craze for air-gun shooting at a target: 'so far I am unexpectedly good, and can knock out a drawing pin at 36 feet a good average number of times. We put up a shilling a side and it has paid for all my Christmas cards and postage. Shocking gambling!' At the same time the three men were looking out for anyone stranded at a loose end in Alex to ask to Christmas dinner. It was a clubbable society amongst the expatriates.

Temporary relief came in February 1909 with a little job as commercial agent with James Waterlow, at £15 a month and 2½ per cent commission on anything he could sell 'from paper to portable buildings'. The money, he said, was practically not a living wage though theoretically it could just be done, nor did he think Waterlow would keep him on during the slack summer months, nor was Phil very keen on 'travelling in lines'.

The incident is interesting for two reasons. One is that Waterlow, son of Sir Sydney Waterlow, Bart., who had died in 1906, was head of the well-known firm of government printers with interests in the Near East, and hence one of the entrepreneurs of all sorts who were attracted to the honey pot of Alexandria. In March 1909 Waterlow had taken on a big printing job for the government which kept Phil busy 15 hours a day, with a hacking cough on him and not much pay for the hour but the promise of a bonus and good praise for the way he had handled it. Ironically, the work was for the Drainage Department which was failing to honour its promise to Phil of a job. Another striking instance of foreign business in Egypt was that of the Bavarian Hess export concern in Alexandria, where the notorious Rudolf was born in 1894 and worked in his youth.[3]

The second point of interest in Phil's connection with Waterlow is that it forced on him yet once more the errand of mercy in looking after a sick man struck down in an unhealthy climate. In 1903 he had been at Floyer's death bed. In 1906 he had taken his future father-in-law from a stay at Planter's House to die in a Cairo hospital. Now on the morrow of his appointment by Waterlow he had to take his boss to hospital with pneumonia and pleurisy; 'but being a strong, clean, energetic man, he is getting along all right'. 'And the great thing,' he added, 'is I am earning something.'

In spring 1909 better days dawned when Phil was offered a post in the Egyptian Irrigation Service. Admittedly it was not a permanent, let alone pensionable post, for he was not a trained engineer and could not be given established status. But it was much better paid than Waterlow, and took Phil into a job he understood, in the heart of Egypt, and amongst the men of the country with whom, however exasperating he could find them, he could speak on easy terms.

'Rejoice with me,' he told his sister Bee on 10 April 1909, 'I am getting out of Cairo and into the country again ... away from catalogues, typewriters, drawing-paper, calculating machines, and pay that can't last out the month, and into a temporary job:- "4th Circle, Irrigation Service, Beni Suef, Upper Egypt".'

He spoke of the need for diplomacy with the natives, but 'I get along pretty well with them', which was saying a lot in the tense political atmosphere of the day when armed British soldiers were sometimes used to control rioting nationalists.

The diplomatic touch was not required of him, however, in matters of politics but in matters of water, as he showed in the lucid descriptions of his work sent home to parents who relished every factual detail of their children's lives.

---

3. Obituary of Rudolf Hess, *The Times*, 18 August 1987.

Writing from Bibeh in May 1909 he explained to his mother:

My work is roughly this:- A canal is designed to water so many acres, but the *felaheen* [Egyptian peasants] have put in pipes leading from the canal to the channels in the fields mostly far too big for the area to be irrigated, and generally without permission. The result is that the people at the head of a canal have more water than they can do with, and let the surplus off into the government drains, which eventually discharge into the Nile lower down. Those owners of land at the tail of the canal hardly get any water at all. I have to re-pipe the canal so as to ensure each owner according to his acreage (and not according to *bakshish*) gets his proper and ample share. It is not at all an easy job. The first thing I have to do is to go out with two chain-boys, start at the head of a canal, and measure the distance between each existing pipe – and note what kind of a pipe it is – then home to plot my results out on survey maps and make lists for filing.

Next, I must call on Native heads of villages and owners of land to meet me in their different 'parishes' on certain dates. Then the fun begins. Arguing where the new pipes are to go, how many acres they are to water, and working out the proper size of pipe … When you have argued the matter out with them and with great difficulty convinced them they are not being done in the eye, then the pipes must be brought up and a contractor found to put them in. He has to be watched with an eagle eye or he will take *bakshish* to put in larger pipes than necessary.

That finished, all the lists must go up to the *Mudir* [provincial governor] who makes the *omdehs* [headmen] of the villages responsible for the new pipes.

I shall be jolly pleased when I have completely finished one canal, for at present I feel as if I was floundering a bit. It is a very hot day with a hot south wind and I don't feel a bit like work, especially as I have to tackle a particularly cantankerous *omdeh*.

A fortnight later he continued the story from the village of El Fashn:

My work isn't a bit easy and requires all the self-confidence in me to

carry it out. I arrived here last night in the starlight and rowed down
in the luggage-boat sent to meet me against a soft north breeze ... It
has been 102° to 110° F. for a week, and damp, – quite exceptional,
but now getting back to a normal dry 95° F. in the shade.

Despite the heat he took time off to play several good sets of tennis
at Beni Suef, where there was an Irrigation Department rest-house
and headquarters. The food was poor though the tennis good, with
the result that Phil got even thinner and put in a letter his suggestion
that he label himself with marking-ink lest he got sent to the wash
with his wringing-wet clothes. When he was not up in Alexandria at
the docks or at some railway station taking delivery of thousands of
iron pipes from Europe, he was most of the time at work in the fields.

Tomorrow morning [22 May 1909] I have a big meeting of *omdehs*
and owners of land at a village about four miles away to discuss water
arrangements for their fields. There will be awful ructions when
they discover I am putting in a 6-inch pipe where an 18-inch one was
before. Once the positions of the pipes are decided, I should like to
wave a magic wand and find all the old pipes out and the new ones
in before anyone had time to complain. Instead of that I must tackle
contractors and listen to endless complaints from the villagers.

Even so, he preferred to be right out on the district rather than
at headquarters, free in the hot breeze and cool at nights, meeting
the *omdehs* whom he mostly liked and able to expand his thoughts in
the open before having to return and cover pages of foolscap with
columns of figures.

Egypt was for amateurs like himself 'hopelessly un-permanent',
and more than once he exclaimed that nearly all Englishmen wished
they were out of it. There were frustrations too, part of the imper-
manence: 'it astonished me to find how hopelessly under-manned the
Irrigation is. Nearly all the native engineers are both incompetent and
overworked, and the Englishmen working all day and every day have
to let many things slide in order to keep up with the most important
matters.' For all that, Phil felt he was dealing with real people and
vital problems.

He bought a mule. 'One was brought to me just now which might do, and during my short interview with it, it did not seem to have any enmity against me. It will mean keeping a *saice* but after all pay is calculated for that purpose.' 'Send me books,' he pleaded to his brother Ralph; 'being no longer near a book-shop I cannot choose.'

Though uncertain of the future, the letters are not those of a bored man. 'It is not dull a bit, and as I get things organized I hope to get more time to myself both for working and reading. In a month or so I hope to take on a man who can read and write to relieve me of some of the routine work of copying lists of figures. On my present job I am bound to be irregular in mails, as sometimes the Post Office is 20 miles away and there is no available messenger.'

It was only to be expected that an inspector like Phil would be a target for bribery or threats. In June 1909 he reported home that the land-agent of Egypt's prime minister had called on him, complaining of the size of pipes allotted to his land:

He was tall and dressed in *stambouline* [official frock coat] and *tarboosh* and had a demure and dignified bearing (hands folded in front sort of thing) at first sight. But on closer inspection the wickedness and cunning on his face eclipsed anything I have seen in a native. He tried to talk me round into giving him more pipes, using every kind of argument, and I had to use first of all proofs, aided with large-scale maps, to show what pipes were due to him, and then extravagant politeness.

He got up after a bit rather suddenly with a nasty leer and went through the form of leave-taking, and as we reached the door he turned and threatened, 'I shall be on the fields tomorrow to stop your contractors' work by force.' More from irritation than presence of mind I opened the door and repeated what I understood he had said in front of several of my people outside, and he was so angry that he said, 'Yes, that is what I mean.' Then I bluffed and said I should know how to deal with the emergency. Whether he went to the field this morning or not I don't know. If he did he must have been sick because I had all his pipes out and new ones put in. All I do know is from a report that came in tonight that he had been hanging round the telegraph office all day, waiting for instructions from Cairo.

In the charged atmosphere of Egypt, hostility could erupt in other ways, though the Englishman's security was generally ensured through the informal roughness of a police which obeyed the government. One day Phil was returning with a friend from a tour of inspection and had sent their baggage and servants on ahead. Nearly home, they stopped for their sandwiches and a bottle of beer when one of the *saices* dashed up to them hot and excited to say they had been stoned and whipped and the baggage cart pushed into a courtyard.

This wasn't good enough, so I sent for the chief of the local police-depot and asked him to send and recover servants and baggage. However, it all turned up before the police got there; but I still insisted on an enquiry, as my long man (6 feet 3 inches) had a bruise and wheal across the back of his hand and his clothes were torn.

I think I can reconstruct the story of what really had happened. They were passing in front of some native farm-labourers' dwellings owned by an *omdeh* who is a great friend of mine. There the children greeted them with a shower of mud and bricks, and one of the children got cuffed for it. Thereupon the women joined in and made a noise which called the men out, and so the row began. When the police arrived on the spot all the men had disappeared, so they left my man, one policeman and the sheikh of the *ezbeh* [village] to wait for them. They were all successfully caught and taken to the *merkaz* [police station] where my friend the *omdeh* was waiting for them. He took the sheikh by the moustache and shook him; then he took each of the offenders and beat him, and finally chucked them head under in a very nasty pit leading from the police stables. He sent a message through to me that night to Beni Suef saying he would have them all put in prison if I liked, but added a rider that he thought he could deal better with them himself. It's been left at that.

Friendship was given as well as accepted. One hot September day in 1909 Phil was taking a little local holiday working over his garden and training flowering creeper over a pergola to make shade for potted seedlings, at peace with his plants and the world, when his boy came running up out of breath to say that the *ghaffir* [watchman] of his house was on the point of death. 'I sent for the doctor and bolted round myself to see if there was anything to be done. He was very bad indeed, in great pain, and seemed to have made up his mind to die, and twice during the hour before the doctor came I thought it was all up. But hot fomentation and massage did the trick, and he is now doing well in hospital. I wish I had more knowledge of First Aid.'

The Samaritan's story did not end here, for a month later the *ghaffir* died. 'His people insisted on taking him out of hospital, though I fought against them for two or three weeks. He had an intermittent heart. He himself told me in hospital that he would far rather return to his house and die.'

It was a full and happy life so far as it went for a man like Phil who could understand Egyptian feelings yet also relished the conversation and company of his fellow Europeans.

In September 1909 he wanted to get a series of village meetings over quickly as 'the fast of Ramadan begins in a very few days now, and I am anxious to do as little as possible in the way of meetings during the month, as then the people get muddle-headed and very often hot and cross, and we should never be able to decide anything'.

He pleased his native gardener too by the working interest he showed in his own patch of ground, while at the same time rejoicing in a forthcoming holiday trip to Cairo in a friend's steamer, which would be 'delightful as the Nile is at its highest and best now, and I have never seen the scenery' on that stretch.

Now at 29, mind on the job and fit in body, there was a mental vigour about Phil naturally attractive to intelligent seniors:

> The Inspector-General for Upper Egypt turned up this afternoon and was particularly nice to me. The last time we talked together was about a month ago after dinner in the dark on the balcony here (at Beni Suef); there were five or six others and he started on trees and agriculture and in my opinion talked through his hat, and I couldn't resist joining in, with the result that we became politely heated. Today he hinted it might be a good thing for me to go to Asyut for a day or two and vet the barrage garden there.

At other times Phil would consult with men doing the same job in other provinces, like 'the young and lovable Irishman entirely wrapped up in horses and hopelessly unmethodical', and would make other social contacts like dining with the resident judge to talk about gardening. For this sort of thing there were no Sunday breaks, but time off during the week could be arranged.

It was a thousand pities that the Irrigation Service could offer no certain career to a foreigner, still less an unqualified and junior one. Urgent work done so quickly and well like the canal re-piping merely shortened the time for which temporary employees were needed. Even the inspector-general sent in his resignation when passed over for promotion, and Phil again commented, 'there are precious few Englishmen in Egypt who would rather not be out of it'.

For this reason the idea of leaving Egypt had to be seriously considered, and the proposal to join Dick in the Transvaal was made. This year's interlude was fully described in the previous chapter. Although it was a depressing time for Philip, there is a kind of continuity in his life-story, since South Africa was only a short episode and was bridged either side by supporting years of happiness. In the year before leaving Egypt, for instance, there was picnicking with friends at his old Planter's House where he could bury his inner regret under the regal spread provided by his cook; and there was a tennis tournament at Beni Suef in the scorching heat but dinner afterwards on the lawn in the cool, with 25 diners, and 'I don't think one person stopped laughing the whole time'.

Eighteen months later Philip was on his way back again, the fare from Pretoria to Alexandria generously lent by brother Ralph, his own heart light at the prospect of a new and more hopeful life in Egypt.

The mechanics of the change were fairly simple. The United Egyptian Salt Company was doing well and making money. Tiny Lowe, Phil's old friend, was the boss and knew that he would have in Phil an experienced man with fluent Arabic to look after the coastal salines and other installations on which the business depended. The company was therefore able to offer Phil the post of assistant manager, starting at £E25 a month plus 15 shillings a day travelling allowance when out in the provinces. 'It is a great relief to me to know that I

can occasionally have jam with my bread and butter', and Phil's exclamation to his father was from the heart, though he correctly did not
consider the position very lucrative. Through experience and through
opportunity Phil's promised land was Egypt and his return was to a
land of friends, not a strange people.

There is a corresponding lightness of mood in the letters which
record the northward journey up Africa's east coast. At Delagoa Bay
he was able to spend a day with his older brother Noel, homeward
bound from Mauritius, and to see the sights of Lourenço Marques:

> it is a pleasant, very clean town, and the Portuguese government
> is making efforts to entice people from the Rand to spend their
> holidays and money there. They are opening up a magnificent beach
> just outside the town and intend putting up a regular Monte Carlo
> casino. From the Cardosa Hotel where I stayed there is a magnificent
> view over the bay and country beyond. I should think the bay could
> hold comfortably all the navies of the world.

Beira reminded him of Ismailia except for the streets 'which are
deep in white sand' and 'trolley lines run all over the place and the
trolleys, much like those at the Barrage, are all owned by private
people.' This was a specimen of African coastline during the European scramble for Africa: 'only 50 white residents in Beira and
certainly more than 50 bars', but worth a sea-traveller's visit for the
sheer exercise of being swung into a tug by a big basket while the
steamer lay seven miles out beyond the shifting sand-bar of Zambesi
alluvium.

On board it was cramped in second class but the company pleasant – 'a nice Miss Spink' – and in the first class an American Admiral
Bleeker and his wife who loved to have Phil over to talk.

Mozambique, a 'funny little place on an island' offering cheap
shells and coral trinkets in the sun's glare, was hardly worth seeing,
but Zanzibar excited him. To start with he entered again the network
of family and friendships, never far away. He went ashore with a first-
class passenger he had struck up with, named Shore, a distant cousin
and from the Teignmouth family, well enough off to voyage round the

world to recover from a concussion. On Zanzibar island itself a Dr Aders he had known in Egypt tapped him on the shoulder, asked them to dine and put them up for his club; 'he was living in an extraordinary old Arab house with magnificent carved doorways'.

These genial meetings took place in an air heavy with the scent of cloves from the miles of plantations where the trees stood 40 to 50 feet high. 'The cloves are picked as unopened flower-buds, then women rub them off the stalk with a single motion of the hand and put them on mats to dry in the sun.' Phil the planter revelled in the flora, decorating his letter with sketches and drinking in the vista as he was driven along roads shaded by casuarina, mango, coconut palm and others he had tried to grow at El Katta. His very driving companion reminded him of Ernest Floyer 'under whose auspices my life among plants had begun'.

Here at Zanzibar too he met a Miss Gibbons who had been very ill at Magila when Phil's missionary brother George had been brought in to die (1895), but now it was the living rather than the dead who had his attention: Knollys 'whose clothes I used to brush (at Winchester) was port engineer at Port Sudan, 'looking fat and well liking', and Mure of Culver House, Winchester, working with a land company in Egypt, who came aboard at Aden'.

It was October 1911, and Italy was at war with Turkey, so the skipper had an anxious time picking his way up the Red Sea which he did not know and where the belligerents had put out most of the lights. But there were still three years before Egypt was engulfed in the wider war, and this period saw Phil happily at work again round and about the country.

The work was mainly to inspect the company's agencies and. installations, but there were old friends and old haunts to look up too. 'How heavy one's legs get on a donkey without stirrups, and how hard and angular the native saddle.' But he got about, to 'see my tree and garden' at Beni Suef, to stay with the Friends (Astley and Kate, uncle and aunt of Mercy whom he was to marry) in their delightful house on the Nile north of Cairo. Astley was another engineer, a man of value in Egypt. Phil passed also by Planter's House where he felt his heart shrivel to see the desolation where once he had made the desert bloom. 'It's a discordant, screeching shame,' he wrote.

Though El Katta was going back to sand, Heliopolis up in the desert behind Zeitoun where his brother Ralph had built himself a house was now quite a big town with 'a huge hotel, many times bigger than Shepheards or the Continental'.

Workaday life was often one of movement, not so much on the back of an animal as by little railways and the shallow-draught Egyptian sailing-boat called a *dahabia* or the smaller, un-decked *felucca*; in these could be navigated the great salt lakes along the Egyptian coast and the canals which in places linked them.

In March 1912 Philip made a trip with his chief Lowe to Damietta which he had never seen before, 'to find out what progress our only competitors are making in creating new salines on private lands. Damietta is about 10 miles from the coast, on the Nile, and has quite a big trade of its own with Syria. At certain times small ships can get through the bar at the mouth of the Nile and sail up to Damietta, and it is curious to see these little "Spanish" galleons moored against an Egyptian setting.' He observed too that Damietta people are hard nuts to crack.

> We stayed in the coastguard rest-house outside the town and looking over Lake Menzaleh. It was originally a summer palace built by some rich Pasha and is on a most lavish scale. The landing on top of the stairs is about as large as the Shawford parish hall [near Winchester].
>
> The fish-market is under the windows. The lake fisheries is a very big industry. Many of the fishermen carry a mascot on board in the shape of a pelican tethered by one leg ...
>
> On Sunday morning we got on board a lake steamer, an ugly, flat-bottomed stern-wheeler with a raised deck and cabin, and slowly churned our muddy way for 4½ hours across the lake to Matarieh, where I had the pleasure of seeing the toy-train I was to have caught steam out of the station as we tied up.

A couple of months later Phil was again on Lake Matarieh and made Matarieh his base of operations. It was a large fishing village on the western side, and from here he had to inspect all the natural salt-pans to see they were properly guarded.

> At this present moment [he wrote to Noel on 8 May 1912], I am sailing slightly south of the direct line [north-eastward] to Port Said to inspect all the little islands. After that I don't know in what direction I go, as I am in the hands of our local native inspector and the wind and depth of the water. It is very shallow indeed all over the lake and the *dahabia* is continually scraping the bottom. It is my temporary home and more or less comfortable, the weather perfect. I don't expect to be back in Matarieh for 4 days, and then expect to be there for 3 days during rides into the interior to see more big salines. We are tacking round an island and I must go on deck in order to keep my bearings, as half the islands are not marked on the small map I have, and I am trying to get them in approximately.

Three days later he continued his letter, 'After writing the above I got separated from my *dahabia* by wind and water for ten hours. It was so shallow that I had to get into a smaller boat to visit certain islands, and a big wind sprang up and I could not get back.'

Five days later again he started a letter to his mother, still on the *dahabia* on which he had been living for 12 days but now at the village of San, four hours up a canal from Port Said and near a hilltop crowded with obelisks and broken statues of Rameses:

> Probably earlier a branch of the Nile ran this way, where is now fine dark dust. The Bedouin inspector is going to ride over tomorrow to discuss plans for watchmen. Tomorrow I must bargain in Port Said for a horse for the native inspector; then by train to Salhia, thence to Alexandria and then again, I'm afraid, to the Fayum to see how their new man is getting on.

Lowe was sailing on leave shortly, so Phil was having to complete all the inspections in time to take charge in Alexandria.

Working at company headquarters in Alexandria meant sociable ways of spending time off. Sailing was cheap: a boat for eight people could be hired for seven shillings the half-day, and there is a happy account of a nude (all-male) bathing-party at Agami, the point to the west of Alexandria. Lowe, about to go on leave, was full of himself, 'crowing as usual' and the friends had some modest wins at the races to add to their good cheer.

They talked politics in a gossipy sort of way, wondering what Lord Kitchener was going to do next as consul-general in Egypt. 'He has made a tour of Upper and Lower Egypt, is now (12 May) at Malta, and will be back again on 3 June. The native is aghast at the speed things are being done and simply worships him. The Egyptian likes being governed with a strong hand.' This was a refrain in Philip's writing and indeed reflected a fixed family concern with firm authority, often expressed as disgust with indecisiveness, dishonesty and all kinds of chaos.

Alexandria itself was not a cheap place for taking time off as there was no countryside just outside in which to wander at leisure. But with a couple of days' leave Phil could take the train halfway out to Aboukir and then walk along the coast eastward to Aboukir itself for lunch. Sometimes after a storm there were 'anteekas' to be picked up on stalls for sale along there.

It was the early days of the cinema, and sometimes the Baron (Hirsch, who with Lowe was the third flat-mate) would take a box and invite a party of friends. 'There are heaps of Cinematographs in Alexandria now, and all crowded. The native simply adores them and it is wonderful how much he has learned to understand. Heroic deeds are tremendously cheered, and if the hero gets into trouble the villains are hooted.'

Egyptian society itself was very stratified, from the 'pashas', rich businessmen, officers and politicians down through the more or less literate clerks to the *felaheen* or village cultivators. When Phil wrote in his letters of 'the native' it is usually the townsfolk he meant, employed in one way or another in the service of the urban and business economy. His paternalism sounds condescending. It was sometimes exasperated or even angry, but never mocking. In a poor society one expected dishonesty and dealt with it as best one might. But from the letters there emerges no sense of the natives as primitive human beings as in South Africa but as members of an ancient and alien culture and religion. They were also people with whom Philip could speak.

The case of the embezzling bookkeeper is one illustration. Phil cursed in his letters the employee who had vanished after receiving his September salary, taking the apparently important sum of 12 shillings, and he expressed pity for 'his poor old mother, going blind, with whom he lived'. In due course the case came before a court and the absconder was sentenced in his absence to a year's hard labour, a £20 fine and costs. There was no trace of him, and as they hadn't any interpreter in court Phil had to do it, and 'it felt horrid to get up and tell the whole story in Arabic. However, I got through.'

Underneath the upper crust of government and commerce, highly cosmopolitan though English dominated, it was of course a Muslim society in which nationalist fires had been lit to smoulder and then flame with the *Wafd* party and much later on with Nasser himself. Probably not much of this was understood by the average British businessman up to the Great War.

'The holy carpet came through yesterday from Cairo,' wrote Phil to his mother on 10 October 1912. 'It proceeded down the quays where it was put on board a steamer en route to Mecca. We rather expected a row and many shops put up their shutters, but everything passed off quietly. I saw it from the window of a hotel. There was only one attempt to start the shout of "a Christian!", and the crowd was much too good-tempered to take it up.'

Turning to thoughts of Ralph now in London and the house he had formerly built himself outside Cairo, he wrote, 'People say that Ralph's old house at Zeitoun is the centre of a big Mohammedan secret society for turning out the Europeans from the whole of North Africa.' This was at about the same time that Freda in India was lugubriously expecting the massacre of all white people. Perhaps those imperial servants with the greatest dedication were the most conscious of their unpopularity.

For a little while longer there was a peaceful life of provincial inspections alternating with Alexandria jollifications before the war came. A pleasant trip took place in October 1912 to the great Lake

Boroullos (Burolus), separated from the Mediterranean by a narrow strip on whose western end stood the town of Rosetta:

> I have been out nearly the whole of this last week making an inspection at Rosetta and Lake Boroullos [Phil told his father]; ... slept Sunday night at a rest-house at Rosetta and next morning sailed 2½ hours up the Nile to the place where Nile and Boroullos most nearly meet, and from there I rode a donkey for about an hour until the *dahabia's felucca* was reached lying in a small marshy inlet. My servant and provisions for a week follow behind and he, three sailors, food and self managed to crawl into the small, flat-bottomed boat which was then poled out to the *dahabia* lying about ¾ hour away in deep water.
>
> It was then about 5.30 p.m. and my boy got to work on dinner at once, and jolly hungry I was, as I had had only a biscuit and some chocolate for lunch. With the greatest difficulty I stayed awake till 9. We set sail about 4 hours after, and that waked me for a few minutes.
>
> It was delightful waking early next morning on the water. We were moored close to an island I wanted to have a look at in case there were salt deposits, but there was nothing worth bothering about. Bettim at the far eastern end of the lake was reached about 3, and I went ashore and inspected the agency, books, etc.
>
> Next morning was spent riding about 15 miles to see the condition of various salt-pans. The country was delightful and most unusual in Egypt: low, rolling country of clean sand, small water-courses, and covered with palms. It was a good time to go as the dates were fast ripening – crimson ones and yellow ones – and little groups of people gathering them brightened up the scene. Every few minutes we were hailed to come and eat of the harvest. The only unpleasant part of the trip was the last night on board when we were sailing and poling up a canal to a station on the south of the lake. It was as pretty as could be, winding through the marshes under the moon, nearly full, – but the mosquitoes! They had beaks and stood on their heads and feasted and sang all night long. I took the precaution of taking some quinine and no ill-effects have arisen.

The trip took the staleness out of me, and I was even glad to get back to food which didn't come out of a tin.

A month later Phil was en route from Alexandria to Port Said and Lake Manzaleh where the company's new *dahabia* was to take him round all the salines and see how well they had been guarded during the summer. The task was to keep the number of *ghaffirs* to a minimum while ensuring the security of the salt-fields. This time being alone, without Lowe, he made his way by coastal steamer from Alexandria to Port Said, a journey of 15 hours and a dull one. 'The First-class was empty save for me, the English captain and the Greek doctor, and we dined alone.'

Once again Phil found himself needed to take a man to hospital – a comment on the precariousness of health in such an epoch and climate. He had arranged to meet the company's superintendent at the agency at 10 a.m. but 'found him rocking with fever'. Without much surprise he found he knew the doctor at the hospital – the same Dr Hayward who had once seen him through typhoid – though this time the diagnosis was less certain and Hayward himself was too ill to do the test at once. In the late afternoon, however, Phil called at the hospital where after a long wait an Egyptian doctor escorted him to see Hayward who was in the middle of a post-mortem. 'You don't mind bodies do you?' The post-mortem was a native murder case and Hayward insisted on showing Phil the 'bits' of proof. 'I had wondered what Manzaleh smelt of!' Later that Sunday evening Phil went to church 'for the first time in Port Said, – a mosque-like little place but somehow much more home-like than the usual churches of hot countries'.

The inspection was an uneventful one except to see the fine new *dahabia* being built for the company to rent. It was ready at Easter 1913 when Phil had a happy time cruising about Lake Manzaleh, fitting her up and teaching the crew how to keep things clean as well as how to sail. 'The *rais* [skipper-steersman] is a particularly good fellow. He is a Gyppie of course but rather of the Bow class of men. [The implication was that third-class passengers travelled in the stern.] I was able to help him with the medicine chest Hubert gave me – a rare reference to the oldest, medical, brother – and he will now go to any trouble for me.'

'We have had exciting times too. One morning we started at dawn and I never got breakfast till 11 o'clock. We were hanging on by our eyebrows the whole time, hoping and hoping we should not blow over. Being in a new boat we did not know when the last straw might upset us. She was nearly flat-bottomed, and her mast is 25 feet high, and that carries a lateen sail with a yard 76 feet long, so you can imagine the sail-surface is fairly large.'

In September 1913 he was out again with Lowe, staying with the commandant of the Suez Canal police for the Bairam holiday. 'We sailed over from Damietta with a splendid breeze behind us, doing the 35 miles in 7 hours which is quite good going for a boat of that sort.'

To the 'natives' with whom he worked Phil's attitude was a mixture of friendship and exasperation. Negligence always irritated him. He worried reasonably enough about the bad storage of the gunpowder used by the company and was for ever lecturing native agents on government regulations. 'The other day I found an agent who said that ever since he had been in our service (years and years) he had always opened a powder barrel by bursting in the end with a hatchet borrowed from the carpenter over the way!' Sometimes a barrel vanished, likely enough to turn up stored in a horribly dangerous position as cement.

Dishonesty brought a different kind of anger. There were great anxieties about salt thefts, which meant hours every day of investigations and ended in the dismissal of long-trusted employees. 'We are advertising for a Britisher as inspector and can find nobody in the least suitable.' This was after the war had started. 'We are fed up with natives. Both the men we have dismissed have had every chance, have been well paid and backed up in difficult positions, and then when they thought they were trusted servants of the Company they go and behave like silly fools.'

One new applicant in December 1914 was noted by Phil with the words, 'he reads and speaks English, French, Italian, Arabic and

Turkish, and speaks Greek, and he is not uncommon here', but it is not recorded whether he was suitable.

At the same time Phil looked after the well being of his men with a friendship amounting to affection, and this was known and admired by his superiors during the war; it is evident also in the letters of warm thanks he continued to receive after retirement in England, accompanied sometimes by photographs of company employees solemnly posed in tarbooshes amidst their numerous families.

In the year before the Great War broke out the letters portray a kind of hectic gaiety in Alexandria society, less perhaps a reflection of any social change, let alone of any inkling of the future, than an expression of Philip's own enjoyment of social events at that time in his life. It is strange to look back on this, remembering him in later years as a man of retiring and even withdrawn demeanour. But his taste was always for occasions which were 'merry' rather than 'smart'. When he referred in letters to important people he encountered it was for their associations not their *cachet*, and their antics were told for laughter not conceit. In other words, he was not a name-dropper.

In November 1913 Alexandria was visited by the Fleet. Everybody got up early to watch from the harbour mouth as the warships steamed in, and evening after evening was given over in private households to dinner parties:

> On Monday night I found myself next to Commodore R.F. Phillimore who knew Noel at the Summer Palace, Pekin. On Sunday night Major Rhodes, brother of Cecil and Herbert, dined with us ... I don't think I have ever seen such an old-looking man for 55. The great night was the last the Fleet were here ... when the British community gave a ball on a magnificent scale and I was astonished to see Kitchener starting it with the Lancers and appearing to enjoy it. Prince Albert [King George VI] was dancing it too, looking very shy, and he got hopelessly bewildered. There must have been 1800 to 2000 people there. Carola told me she took the Prince in to supper and said she had her work cut out to entertain him as he stuttered and stammered so much.

Back in the bachelor flat 'the Baron [Hirsch] and I have been returning some of the hospitality shown to us, and on Monday and Tuesday we sat down ten each night, and Bridge afterwards. We generally choose a time when Lowe is away as he does not care for ladies' society.' This private remark to his sister was purely factual, without the innuendo so often assumed today. Lowe was a great eater and *bon vivant*, full of organizing ability and no misanthrope, but though he was later happily married and with children, he had not been brought up to the gentler, courtly graces.

Philip with all his diffidence was the organizer, at various ladies' request, of a supper for the English company of actors who had been playing to rather small houses; and he did this with enjoyment.

The other side of him was a quiet but keen desire for educated society. 'I have been breaking new ground with friends and acquaintances. Last week-end I spent with Levereux,[4] a lawyer, who has a beautiful flat full of books and pictures. He himself is a reader and a man of taste, and one of the most unselfish men I know. It was a very pleasant change.' It is easy to see why Philip had languished in the Transvaal; the comment about unselfishness too is a little signal of an integrity he never lost while at work in an acquisitive society.

The war brought no heroics with it into the letters from Alexandria but an edge of determination to hold against any Turkish–German attack and – if one may guess at a mood – a lowering of esteem towards political Egypt.

The first wartime letters allude to events without much discussion or explanation of them. There was an amazing exodus of Egyptian princes:

> they seem to have gone for reasons of health, ... Egypt is buzzing with excitement about the new proclamation that is to come out on Sunday morning ... It is generally supposed we shall declare a Protectorate and that Hussein Pasha Kamel will be instituted as sultan of Egypt and the Sudan. I don't think the average Egyptian cares a pin what happens as long as it doesn't touch his pocket. The

---

4. Possibly the theosophist Levereux. See P.N. Furbank, *E.M. Forster: A Life* (1978), pp ii, 44.

European is likely to be taxed properly at last, and a good thing too. We have not paid enough hitherto, thanks to the Capitulations [agreements between Egypt and foreign governments about their communities in the country].

These events are matters of history. So too is the expulsion of Germans and Austrians. 'On the way to the office this morning [26 November 1914] we passed 40 or 50 being marched off to some ship under armed escort. They had evidently picked the biggest and smartest Territorials for the job. It will do the native good to see them.'

For the time being the routine of company work went on. It is interesting here to compare the attitudes of the brothers towards 'joining up' in the early days of the Great War. Noel, the regular officer, already serving, referred to nothing but the alternating dullness and excitement of military life. Jim in India was loudly agitated in his pleas to go and fight, which the Viceroy forbade him to do. Dick in South Africa alternated between a wish to serve and fear for his lonely farm. Philip was wistful but level-headed. He responded to a call for volunteer observers from aeroplanes and hydroplanes in the Suez and Sinai districts, but 'Lowe won't let me go at any rate for the present. We have just been obliged to dismiss our Inspector and another superintendent, and he says I must stop or we shall lose control of all our staff in the provinces.' This was explained to his father in January 1915.

The war did not deprive Alexandria of its attractions: it was rather the reverse, in providing comfort for men with grim duties in the surrounding desert. Early in 1915 the Turks were said to be in retreat on the Sinai side of Egypt to the east, and Alexandria was gay with flags to welcome Sir Henry McMahon, the new High Commissioner who had taken over from Kitchener.

Phil found a new flat which would be home till he got married, and it was one he both liked and could afford, near the office and overlooking the roof-tops to the sea. Gas and electricity were laid on, and there were polished wooden floors.

This time he shared with his friend Felix Powell, later Director of the Alexandria Public Works. They shared humour too, rejoicing in the white plaster statue of Napoleon left behind by the previous tenants, and giving house room to Powell's parrot who lived in the dining room or on the balcony and 'could do everything from a dog-fight to "three cheers for Lord Cromer, hip, hip, hurray"'. It was a bird called Coco, which the present writer remembers from boyhood as it blinked gluttonously when offered banana. It eventually died in the wholly unexpected attempt to lay an egg.

Powell had lost his wife and child 15 months earlier and was much broken up, but told Phil he already felt better for coming to live once again in an English flat. 'Of necessity we live carefully, and hitherto our sole amusement has been to go to a cinematograph on a Saturday night. After dinner he plays patience and I read, and we are generally snoring soon after 10 o'clock.'

In Alexandria there were some duties in drilling and shooting practice, but work as always lay chiefly outside. In spring 1915 Phil took a new native inspector to the desert, west of the Suez Canal, to show him all the salt-fields there and the arrangements for guarding them. It was an eight-day ride by camel, averaging 25 miles a day, 'and I am still very glad to lie flat on my bed,' he wrote afterwards, 'for I have had a satiety of sitting. It would be nothing on good camels, but good camels were not to be found as the Army has comman-deered them all.'

Quick to blast off at 'Gyppies', Phil was also quick to give credit where due. The new native inspector was an old servant of the company, now promoted and made to ride a camel for the first time: 'he has shown grit and brought new ideas to bear on the work. We have shared the same tent, food and livestock. I can recommend the desert as a good place to get to know a man thoroughly.'

One night they stayed with an old Bedouin sheikh, a keen sports-man whom Philip asked about his hawks. 'Ah,' he said, 'I have some new ones promising well but I have given instructions to stop the training, for who has the heart for pleasure in time of war? And also the locusts are upon us and I must look after my people.'

It was true about the locusts. The next day they rode an hour long across a cloud of them. The road was greasy with them and the two men had to wear cloths across the face to stop the buffetting.

That day too [Phil went on], being the lightest of the party, I had a perilous experience, being carried over a swift-running canal on a man's shoulders in order to visit a saline. He was up to his neck, slithering about on the muddy bottom, but we did the return journey safely, only to get soaked in a thunderstorm half an hour afterwards.

We finally rode across the desert to Ismailia where, after a magnificent night's rest, I was lucky enough to get the loan of a coastguard launch and went down 15 miles of the Suez Canal and saw all the trenches and wire entanglements and a field of battle. Except for many hummocks the field is marked by only one cross where a German officer lies. We passed two French men-of-war, acting I suppose as floating forts. Another attack is expected soon, but everything is ready for manufacturing 'Turkish Delight'. Most of the troops I have seen are Indian, but everything is so cleverly hidden that the layman can gather no information of numbers and the kind of troops employed.

This was the area west of Romani where the battle of August 1916 was to drive the Turks back from their assault, but by that time Phil was more personally involved.

In summer 1915, though, attention was focused on the Allied landing in the Dardanelles. Egypt received thousands of casualties and Philip helped a doctor friend he had known in Winchester with surgical dressings at his hospital. It worried him to have to go off once more on provincial inspections when there was so much to be done for the wounded.

Almost at once Philip resolved his dilemma by persuading the company to let him go. In July 1915 they gave him indefinite leave with pay, and at once he was commissioned into the newly formed Egyptian Labour Corps. Lowe wrote generously that Phil was very bucked and looked fine in his uniform.

For once the army fitted a round peg into a round hole. Phil was a fluent Arabic speaker who was deeply attached to his Egyptian workers. These were enlisted by timed contracts of service to do practically any work in war-zones that might be performed by sappers or pioneers, though they did not undertake to be ordered under enemy fire unless they specifically volunteered. Since he was with this corps almost from its beginning, Phil's personal story and that of the Egyptian Labour Corps move closely together.

His first assignment was to Gallipoli with 1,000 Saidis, leading them as lieutenant under Captain Holland as officer commanding. In August 1915 they were on Lemnos, treeless, scrubless and parched:

> Our day begins at 5 a.m., and I felt at first it was always 5 a.m. We walk miles every day controlling our gangs of Gyppies, and the going is atrocious. On the stony ground pick-axes bend, yet latrines must be dug. Water is rationed to a gallon a day a man for everything, but it is very hot and our camp is on the sea-shore and our men can bathe and keep themselves clean. Rations are good but not as well-provided as in other war areas, – in general, bacon, beef, sometimes beans or potatoes, bread, jam, rice and raisins, tea and sugar. Flies are a scourge. A loaf of bread left for a second is covered with a black pall. The grass-hoppers too are hard-up for food, and there is now one engaged in eating the bristles of my nail-brush.

After four weeks he moved to Imbros, and wrote asking Lowe for winter uniform, cigarettes, newspapers, plain chocolate and more whisky. 'The last six cases I handed over to the Mess at Lemnos and we live on luck here.' The letter also shows that Phil was aware his father was dying at home in Shawford.

On 28 September 1915 Phil landed on the mainland at Anzac as officer commanding a detachment of his corps who had volunteered to work under fire. After two weeks they were learning not to duck at the whizz of bullets and to smile encouragingly at newcomers. 'The men stand it well in spite of a few casualties.'

A big Turkish gun called 'Beachy Bill' lived in a tunnel some seven miles away and was trundled out to shell the beach with shrapnel a few times every day, 'what time everyone who can gets under cover and swears or jeers. We have topping dug-outs where we can sleep peacefully at night except on rare occasions when there is too much noise outside.' Here at least Phil had a camp bed with blankets.

He wrote in positive, courageous vein to his mother: 'how you would love to see the glorious sunsets here. They are so beautiful that they affect one in a rainbow-like way and assure one that the deluge won't come and that this enormous war is but a tuppeny-halfpenny affair in the scheme of things.'

'Had tea with an R.E major today in his tiny little dug-out, and his servant got from another servant two helpings of home-made, whole-strawberry jam.' His own Gippy servant who had volunteered to come had turned out a trump: 'he does my cooking and washing and saves me the very worrying job of measuring out the rations for the men'.

Phil was there with one other lieutenant organizing the volunteer detachment of the Egyptian Labour Corps in cutting terraces for stores, making dug-outs and huts, draining saps and shifting stores. The terrain was uncomfortable: practically no beach, and that shelled all the time, so cover consisted in trying to get flat against the hill or into a gully. 'We keep our respect for shells and instinct shows one a friendly inequality in the ground in the twinkling of an eye. We live up a gully called Shrapnel Alley, and the enemy front trenches are about 800 yards away.'

He wrote that the men responded to cheeriness, 'but if a shell got into the middle of them it would not be possible to get them back to work for several hours'. Casualties were dealt with by the Beach Field Ambulance, and serious ones sent out to one of the hospital ships which were always standing off shore.

Philip's service at Anzac was terminated by a dysentery almost as sudden as a bullet. His brother officer looked after him during two nights like a bad dream before the bearers came to carry him down to the beach; and there too there was a horrible eight-hour wait before the steam barge could get him to the hospital ship. 'The sick and wounded were packed like sardines in the Field Ambulance Clearing Station ... No conveniences, and somebody would whistle very low just out of tune.'

This was on 24 October 1915, and the ship called at Lemnos and went on to Malta instead of Alexandria. Philip was given the option of going to England but chose to stay on Malta in the belief it would be easier to get back to Alex when he was better. He knew well enough that his fate was not in his own hands, and took with gratitude what Malta had to offer: the Blue Sisters' nursing, and the pyjamas, dressing-gowns and slippers provided by the Red Cross for the officers who had naturally arrived with nothing.

Hopes lay in the brilliance of Kitchener who was (mistakenly) supposed to be returning to the Middle East, and anger was expressed for the Gallipoli debâcle, especially for the supposed muddlers who sat safely in charge and issued lying reports.

Stretched out in hospital as thin as a wraith Philip had to mourn the news of his father's death and to feel the lack of any Anglican service in the hospital. Mails were slow, organization makeshift and opportunistic, and men were ordered to leave with almost no notice.

None of this was surprising in wartime, and as so often in such times bad and good news came when least expected. 'I had almost despaired of getting away for weeks when my doctor came along smiling and shaking himself by the hand to say that I had to be aboard in two hours. He fondly imagined it was a hospital ship but it wasn't, so I lay low, and so got here for Christmas, – an unexpected bit of luck!' The letter is written from Alexandria on 27 December.

The voyage had not of course been a pleasure cruise, what with no lights after dark and the need to be able to grab the life-belt in a moment. But now the dark sea lay between the constrictions of hospital life and a month's compulsory convalescence in the Alexandria flat. Powell and he made up a jolly Christmas party by finding two homeless men to invite, though he was tired to death by early evening.

In mid-February 1916 Philip was passed fit again for full duty, and about the same time started a small docket-book for his letters which left carbon copies still preserved.

Already he had been doing a period of light duty, which meant some ten hours a day at the Egyptian Labour Corps base office in Alexandria, and the experience taught him what so many of his family found at different times, that the happiest work is outside, on the ground, rather than stuck fast in office paper. 'I have been living in a maze of giving and taking orders by wire, telephone and letter, and can sympathize with Noel a little. It is not my job, and I long to get out to work again outside.' True to form, the army wired him to take over a camp at Suez, floated a captaincy before his eyes and then sent him westward instead to Mersa Matruh.

Here amidst desert scenery familiar to a later generation of British soldiers Philip got down to his old double task. To understand this we have to visualize an enemy presence (Turkish and German) in the Western Desert as well as in the Sinai area east of Alexandria. There was no powerful equivalent to the Afrika Korps of the Second World War, but there were some hostile troops, some airfields and numbers of native Bedouin in Egypt and Libya who could and did help the enemy. Ultimately the British thrust was through Sinai and up to Jerusalem, captured by General Allenby, not without the help of the Egyptian Labour Corps in laying the railway and other lines of communication. But for the time being in 1916 the western approaches to Alexandria had to be protected against attack or subversion.

So Philip's job in March 1916 was to set his Egyptian Labour Corps to their many tasks, and also to act as intelligence officer to interrogate the refugees and travellers who were intercepted.

Here we do all sanitary work, defences, building sheds and stores, reservoirs, unloading and loading ships, carpentry, quarrying, blacksmithing, tinsmithing, digging graves, and transport. We run from ordinary labourer to skilled traders, and can hardly cope with all the demands made on us, as well as taking on new men in place of those time-expired.

We start at 7 a.m. sharp, have two hours off for lunch, and then on again till 6, when of course office work, orderly room, etc. has to be got through ... I am in charge of our Corns here now. The Brigade Major told me that if it hadn't been for E.L.C. they would have required another infantry battalion here.

There was competition for this labour, and the only way to supervise it was from horseback, 'but I shall never enjoy riding a horse', he confessed to Lowe.

The other half of life was spent 'sitting on a biscuit box for hours in the evening interrogating refugees and either giving them passes or having them arrested. The work would take much less time if they didn't lie so much – surely a police platitude – they are terrified of telling the truth. Most of them that I allow passes to have probably been forced into fighting against us, but there are some who are laughing in their sleeves at the way the British Government is dealing with them.'

Government policy was in fact reasonably crisp as it was stated in an army instruction from HQ Western Frontier Force, Mersa Matruh, 7 March 1916. Egyptian Bedouin were to be orally interrogated and searched to discover if they had been with the enemy, and records were to be kept. *Muhatzia*, employees of the Egyptian government and convicts were to be sent as prisoners of war to Alexandria. Sheikhs without safe conduct and Bedouin who had fought against the Allies, or had probably fought, were to be detained pending orders. Evidently innocent Bedouin were to be given passes to proceed eastwards to Hamman and arrangements were to be made to feed the destitute. Officers were reminded that almost all the Egyptian Bedouin coming into Matruh were followers of the Senussi and presumably had been assisting them, though in some cases against their will, and some had suffered at the hands of Tripolitan Bedouin. The order concluded by saying the enemy was at Sollum, Siwa, Dakhla, Tarafra and Bakkaria, and that information was wanted about them, and about any enemy submarines.

I saw some prisoners yesterday [Phil wrote home on 9 April 1916], Sheikhs of a certain standing. I had arranged certain things for their families, and when saying good-bye the archest hypocrite of them all said to me, 'If I come back here I will give you anything you want.' They were very frightened, and with reason. If you could only see what I do with regard to the treatment of Bedouin women and children by their own kind, you would want to have real justice meted out to ringleaders. However, to my mind war is necessarily a very objectionable form of insanity.'

The sentiments were decent if hardly either illuminating or relevant, for the Bedouin were not being interrogated by marriage guid-
ance counsellors. If they presented a threat it was military, as Phil
himself showed in a letter about the same time:

> It behoves us to be careful still with these unreliable Bedouin. It
> is naturally not safe to go out alone into the desert, and only one
> juggins tried it. He got shot at 2 yards range and the bullet went
> through his sleeve and never touched him. He had to gallop for his
> life away from camp and had an anxious time getting back in the
> dark. I think I've got the aggressor.

Three weeks earlier the intelligence job had seemed interesting
but by April he saw it prevented him attending enough to his other
work and hoped for relief.

Desert discomforts were small compared with being shelled or
bombed. Washing had to be done in sea-water, as sweet water rations
were sometimes down to ¼ gallon a day per man. Dust-storms (*kham-
seen*) could fill a room with dark khaki sand in ten minutes, stopping
work and cooking, and reducing rations to bully-beef and biscuits.

Early in May Sollum was evidently clear and Philip relieved
Captain Holland there in a happy camp, more sheltered from dust
and unspoiled by officers who idled and bickered. He had spent Easter
Sunday there and wrote to his mother:

> I had a curious experience. One of my head men with 24 natives
> and Syrians asked me to arrange for a special [Easter] Communion
> Service for them. The chaplain was a trump and agreed to hold it.
> They were very mixed Christians, of all sorts of Oriental churches,
> and didn't know English with the exception of the head man, who
> knew a little and was the only actual communicant with me. But
> they said 'Ma'alesh [never mind] – we can at least say the prayers
> that are in our hearts'.

But there was a restiveness in Philip's mind. Sollum was not bad
and he could look at it sometimes with peacetime eyes, picking out
the possible cliff-scrambles and the good bathing spots. In his quarters his old toolbox which he had been taking round since he was ten

did duty as a safe, and the letters he wrote by candlelight recurred to the swift passage of the years.

One of these Sollum letters, written on 19 May 1916, was to Mercy Friend who had broken her engagement to him ten years before but whom he was to marry the next year. He had gone on corresponding with her at intervals in an affectionate, rather guarded way. Now he wrote:

My dear Mercy, – It is positively awful the way the weeks go by and never a letter from me to you. But, me Boy, I am doing all the Adjutant's work and am O.C. too, and have to keep an eye on everything, so that by evening I am too sleepy to think any more. Outside work I manage to scrawl to Mother or Bee about three times a month.

You would like this place – for a bit. It beats Mex hollow,[5] and in one direction there are real rocky cliffs, – fishing and bathing topping, or would be if one had time.

It's an awful nuisance not being allowed to write details because one can't give any proper idea of the work or place.

I am just beginning to feel a wee bit as if I wanted a holiday right away from the 'Gyppie'. He is beginning to pall. Three years at a time is quite long enough to be with them and keep fairly sane.

We have just got some papers about the trouble in Ireland, so I suppose Uncle Lovick[6] has got his hands full and has indented for an extra large pair of regulation boots to stamp it out. I believe the consular people in Egypt are finding out all about the remaining

---

5. Mex, a salt-lake settlement near Alexandria, owned by the Egyptian Salt and Soda Company, where the Friends used to stay.

6. Sir Lovick Friend was one of Mercy's uncles and, as a Royal Engineer, was largely responsible for rebuilding Khartoum after the battle of Omdurman (1898) at which he was present. In January 1913, already Major-General, he went to the High Command, and when the BEF was mobilized in 1914 he succeeded to the command of British forces in Ireland. The *Times* obituary (21 November 1944) says that the Easter Rebellion in Dublin was firmly handled by him. Family tradition is that the executions disgusted him, a gentle soul, and he asked to be relieved of his command early in May 1916.

men in Egypt who are not serving, with the idea of roping them in. They will find a curious collection of British subjects but very few Englishmen who can be spared.

I must stop and get on my old gee and ride round all our jobs. It will take about a couple of hours, and then I must be back for Orderly Room and try the little peccadilloes of the men, and settle squabbles, and then food and bed soon after. So the days fly by.

Best love to you, Boy, and Mummy and Dobs [Mercy's younger sister Norah] and don't think me an utter outsider for missing so many mails. Your loving pal, Phil.

If Phil was still after ten years holding a candle for Mercy, his tone is reticent, even enigmatic, but this is not the place to speculate on private hurts which he himself chose to conceal. But there is a contrast of phrase when he writes to his widowed mother at Winchester saying that her regular letters are 'almost my only joy and recreation for the last month'. They relieved the arduous routine of replacing his time-expired men and teaching the new ones.

But a change was coming. In early July he was recalled by telegram to Alexandria for a special job, he didn't know what.

The next letter in the series is dated 14 August 1916 from Romani and told Lowe mysteriously of 'strenuous and exciting times', after which they had marched to Port Said, having received small casualties in relation to the amount of 'noise and metal knocking about'.

The next leaf in the docket-book is signed 'P.H. Du Boulay, Lieut. O.C.E.L.C., Romani North but at the E.L.C. camp, Kantara' and it is an order to the Egyptian Field Force Canteen at Kantara to supply the bearer, his servant, with one case of Dewar's White Label whisky and one case of gin, for money which the bearer has.

The mystery is resolved in the next two letters, both to his mother, one dated 4 September 1916 and not sent, the other dated 16 September from Port Said and presumably sent, as only the carbon copy remains. What had happened was the battle of Romani, which on 4 August pushed the Turks out of Sinai and from Gaza up northward and ultimately out of Palestine.

Then something else, another kind of noise, began, familiar to me at Anzac. Shrapnel and high explosive began to pour in.

Our camp was on a long sand-dune in full sight of Johnny Turk and their German leaders. We were in an excellent position to see it all.

Just after 8 my belated orders to move arrived and I started my officers and men off marching in twos down to the sea. I had to wait a bit to bring up the rear as there were a few men coming in from the works.

Having had no breakfast I went into our Mess to search for something to eat and there found my black messenger solemnly collecting odds and ends. They were half tins of marmalade, bits of bread, etc. I found a small bottle of stout and some biscuits which restored my courage. I confess I was feeling a little peevish amid all the din.

This was the second time we had had to evacuate in a hurry, the main reason being the water difficulty. The men behaved very well, and when we reached the sea we dished them out with water and rations, and I went off for further instructions and got them after about a couple of hours.

I reported at HQ where they were all very calm and collected and took the trouble to let me know how things were going and what the plan was. The General who was running the show was pointed out to me; he was in his shirt-sleeves walking about and chuckling to himself, 'just let them come one more mile, one more mile'.

Our orders were 'March to Port Said as we haven't got water for you today'. Port Said seemed a long way off at that moment, 41 km. We did most of the march at night, right along the edge of the sea, and all the little crabs came to look at us all the way along.

Half-way we luckily found enough water to give the men a drink. We got to our resting-place at Port Said about 7 a.m., and we officers were splendidly done by some French people, and we had our first decent breakfast for many a week.

It was a very busy day, and when I turned in at 9 p.m. I was fully prepared for eight hours' solid sleep. Not a bit of it. At 1 a.m. a signal came in to send off a stretcher-bearer party of 90 men under an officer back to the front. You can imagine my feelings going out in the pitch dark to get my 'Gyppies' to volunteer, and they had to get a train at 4 a.m. some miles away. Luckily I knew two good head men (*Raisis*), and those men filed out and never raised their voices above a whisper. It was a very proud moment.

I found the young officer whom I had selected to go with them. It was pitch dark. I noticed he was a bit halting in his speech and didn't like trusting his voice. I lit a cigarette, and to my horror discovered the tears were trickling down his cheeks. To my great relief he stammered out that he had just fallen down a cement lime-pit six feet deep, and that it was really nothing. He was a plucky boy, – a Maltese.

Later that morning special arrangements were made for the rest of us to cross the Canal where a special train was waiting to take us to Kantara.

In November Philip was promoted captain and was sent to Suez, but, bored with inactivity, volunteered to go eastward again and was given a stretch of some 50-mile line of communication to organize. Here he got back his old horse and lived most daylight hours on its back, returning at dark to the hut which was both mess and office. 'He is learning this country as he did Romani, and I am teaching him to go home like a dog by tucking the reins under the stirrup leathers and giving him a friendly smack. He has never been sick or sorry and has an extraordinary knack of getting on with other horses.'

Telling the story how a single officer of no great seniority was moved about to various jobs in a world at war might well sound like an impersonal reading of destiny. Yet it was an older world than ours and a less mechanical one than that of the mutilated Europe a week or two away from the deserts of the Near East. In a less teeming theatre of war, more men knew each other as individuals.

Even so, it is with some astonishment that one turns up letters from the Egyptian Labour Corps's commanding officer, Colonel Hicks Paull, handwritten to Phil personally and asking unofficially whether he, then a lieutenant (July 1916), would like the inspectorate of the Basra wing of the corps with the rank of major, suggesting his health was perhaps not strong enough, and saying he might well get his majority without leaving Egypt. A later letter (5 October 1916) from Hicks Paull thanked Philip for his loyal support during the Romani action and added: 'I appreciate very much the way you have of getting on with Senior Officers and with the rank and file of the Corps.'

The upshot was that on 21 December 1916 the Colonel ordered Philip to take charge of the Desert Column Branch of the Egyptian Labour Corps based at El Arish (or Rafa), and he was in due course (1 April 1917) gazetted major.

Here he was responsible for a section of the Palestine line of communication supporting Allenby's thrust up to Jerusalem. The orders were specifically to be out on the job as much as possible and leave the office work and routine returns to junior officers. The need now was to drive the railway and road northward, and the means required to mobilize this effort through a competent officer were the rare combination of a good horse and the Arabic language.

'If only I could get more Arabic-speaking officers things would be easier,' wrote Phil to his mother in January 1917 from El Arish. And with his horse friendship grew. 'He is most amusing these cooler winter days. Firm and level stretches are few and far between, but when he can get a gallop he loves it. He prefers to start by ducking his head and kicking up his heels, and then with a squeal he is off!'

These were happy days if not golden ones. El Arish, his headquarters, was near the sea and there were palm groves in the wadi. 'The relief from sheer dust is immense.' The staff were energetic and peaceable, and there were eggs for breakfast. 'Owing to local knowledge we live far better then the average General'; but then, Phil could speak to them in his modest way and in their own Arabic, which the average general probably couldn't. 'The inhabitants,' he commented, 'are more picturesque than the Nile valley people. They go in more for colours in the dress, and I should think were far better educated in the art of doing nothing. The real Gyppie *fellah* [peasant] has to work hard to keep body and soul together.'

So the days passed well enough. 'My job reminds me of a game of patience more than anything else, played with many packs of cards, and the court cards (officers) don't turn up at the right moment. Just as everything seems to be going nicely somebody invents a new rule which upsets one's schemes.'

It was a line of communication, fought for and worked at over the arduous months of 1917, bringing supplies by extension of railway and road and the precious water to Jerusalem by pipes screwed together under the blazing sun. At one end was Phil's home in Alexandria, comfortable but usually far away and rarely to be visited. At the other end was the moving 'front', hardly to be alluded to in his letters save in riddles to lull the censor. But the letters embrace in their subject-matter these wide desert horizons of his experience and were themselves a line of communication to those he loved across space and time.

At one moment Phil was asking a friend to return his copy of Chardin's *Travels* to Bimbashi (Colonel) Felix Powell in Alexandria 'who will put it among my books'. At another he was writing to Powell himself, yearning for a leave he had not had in months: 'I would love to come and hear your disgusting language again.' Even that good moment was not delayed beyond May when a spell of leave allowed him to walk out of the war for a while and nurse his ill-used stomach: 'my saving dish is thick lentil soup with sippets of fried bread'.

So in the end the war was for Philip a desert column, as it had been in the beginning for Noel, both serving the same army and – though they did not use the word – the same empire. But what a world of difference between the forlorn expedition of 1885 where every formation and every blow might be described freely on paper, and the hard but victorious advance of 1917 shrouded in secrecy.

But being of a letter-writing family, Philip was at no loss to keep in touch. 'They have made me a Major, and my responsibilities are very great – to me. The promotion was quite dramatic, and my crowns were provided in the Promised Land, and from the shoulders of my own Officer Commanding.'

But where? All he would say to his mother was that 'Samson must have been an awful nuisance to the countryside I now know pretty well. I wonder how he caught the foxes? Just think of him sitting on a hill and watching the blaze through the barley lands.' Old Mrs Du Boulay would have picked up the story in Judges 14 and 15 and been able to trace with her finger the village of Thamnatha some 20 miles south-west of Jerusalem.

So in the end we leave Major Du Boulay with his Egyptian Labour Corps easing General Allenby into Jerusalem in December 1917. The Turks had been driven out. Allenby is said to have entered Jerusalem on foot in Christian humility. My father was there too.

23. (opposite) Marriage of James Du Boulay to Freda Butts Howell, 31 July 1901. Back row from left: Philip, Freda (bride), James (groom), Hubert, Isabel, Harriet, Ralph. Front from left: Phyllis, James T. (grandfather), Alice (grandmother), Beatrice.

APPENDIX 1

Family of Reverend J.T. Houssemayne Du Boulay and Alice Mead Cornish

James Thomas (Reverend), B.A., M.A.

b. 26 July 1832, Heddington, Wiltshire. *Educ.* Winchester College, Exeter College, Oxford (Fellow & Tutor 1856–62). Holy Orders, 1860. Housemaster (and founder) Winchester College, 1862–93.

m. 9 Feb. 1860, Alice Mead Cornish (*b.* 13 Feb. 1841, *d.* 8 Nov. 1925), youngest daughter of Rev. George James Cornish, Vicar of Kenwyn and Prebendary of Exeter, and Harriet his wife, daughter of Sir Robert Wilmot, Bart., Chaddesdon.

d. 13 Oct. 1915, Shawford, Hants.

Hubert, M.R.C.S. (Eng.) hon., L.R.C.P. (London)

b. 8 Dec. 1860, Oxford. *Educ.* Winchester College, Royal College of Surgeons, Guy's Hospital. Surgeon-Lieutenant, 1st Dorsetshire, R.A. (1897–1900). Consultant ophthalmologist/G.P., 1889–. J.P.

m. 21 Jan. 1899, Katherine Mary Young (*d.* 7 Apr. 1926), eldest daughter of John Young, architect of Guildford Lodge, Brentwood. *Issue*: Hubert James, Elisabeth Mary, Philip Frances.

d. 1 Mar. 1955, Chandler's Ford, Hants.

Noel Wilmot (Brig. Gen.), C.M.G. (1916)

b. 25 Dec. 1861, prob. Oxford. *Educ.* Winchester College, Royal Military Academy. R.A., 1880–1918: Nile Expedition (1884–85), Military Attaché Japan, Sino-Japanese War (1894–95 – Japanese War Medal), Special Services Peking Legations (1900–01 – China Medal with clasp), served in First World War as Staff Colonel, France (twice mentioned in dispatches) then Portsmouth.

d. unm. 25 Nov. 1949, Winchester.

Isabel Aimée

b. 16 Jan. 1863, Sidmouth, Devon. Co-founder with husband of Horris Hill preparatory school, Newbury.

m. 4 Apr. 1888, Alfred Henry Evans (*b.* 14 June 1858, *d.* 26 Mar. 1934), third son of William Evans, M.D., Inspector-General of Hospitals, Madras. *Issue*: Alfred John, Mary Winifred, Ralph Du Boulay, Catherine Isabel, Beatrice Alice Houssemayne, Margaret Du Boulay, Martin James.

d. 10 July 1956, Shawford.

Alice Mary

b. 14 June 1864, Winchester. *Educ.* Lady Margaret Hall, Oxford. Schools Inspector, Education Department, Pretoria (1906–)

d. unm. 18 Sept. 1950, Shedfield, Hants.

George Pascal Keble (Reverend), B.A., M.A.

b. 1 Apr. 1866, Winchester. *Educ.* Winchester College, Exeter College, Oxford. Holy Orders, 1889. Universities Mission, Central Africa, 1893.

d. unm. 1 Apr. 1895, Magila.

James (Sir), C.I.E. (1906), K.C.I.E. (1911), C.S.I. (1916)

b. 15 Apr. 1868, Winchester. *Educ.* Winchester College, Balliol College, Oxford. I.C.S., 1887–1922: Bombay Presidency (1897–1900), Private Sec. to Governors of Bombay (1901–10), Private Sec. to Viceroy of India, Lord Hardinge (1910–16), Lt. Col. Indian

Defence Force.

m. 31 July 1901, Freda Elais Butts Howell (*b.* 1874, *d.* 2 Sept. 1957), third daughter of Alfred and Beatrice Howell, of Boyle Cottage, Thames Ditton. *Issue*: Gwendolen Meada, Freda Wilmot, James Drury, Michael Hardinge.

d. 26 Nov. 1945, East Meon, Petersfield.

Ralph

b. 7 Oct. 1869, Winchester. *Educ.* Winchester College. The Hampshire Militia, 1887–89. Egyptian Government Service, 1891–99. Egyptian Salt and Soda Co., 1899–1934. Imperial Order of Medjidieh (4th class) (1900), Imperial Order of Osmanieh (4th class) (1906).

m. 21 July 1898, Ethel Margaret Thurston (*b.* 10 June 1875, *d.* 13 Nov. 1961), only surviving child of George J. Thurston, N.D. of Sandown, IoW). *Issue*: Guy George, Alison Mary, Joan Thurston, Louise Marguerite.

d. 6 Dec. 1948, Umtali, Rhodesia.

Lucy Beatrice

b. 12 July 1871, Winchester. Winchester City Councillor (–1925).
d. unm. 22 Feb. 1941, Shawford.

Harriet Agatha

b. 3 Jan. 1873, Winchester. Nurse (*c.* 1899).

m. 23 Jan. 1906, Arthur Porcher Lance (Rev.) (*b.* 16 Apr. 1871, *d.* 16 Mar. 1957), son of Rev. William Harry and Charlotte Elisabeth Mildred Lance of Buckland St. Mary, Somerset. *Issue*: John Du Boulay, Arthur Hugh, Michael Ralph.

d. 8 Sept. 1971.

Winifred

b. 4 Oct. 1874, Winchester.
d. unm. 28 Apr. 1890.

Richard Francis

b. 23 Jan. 1877, Winchester. *Educ.* Winchester College. Farmer, Cape Colony, 1895–. Trooper Boer War. Gold mining, Transvaal, 1908–09. Farmer, Transvaal, 1909–17, 2nd Lt. R.A.S.C., Transvaal, 1914–19.

m. 28 Dec. 1911, Elizabeth Louise Douglass (*d.* 22 Nov. 1936), second daughter of Hon. A. Douglass of Heatherston Towers, Grahamstown, Natal. *No issue.*

d. 31 Jan. 1949, Durban.

Philip

b. 20 Mar. 1880, Winchester. *Educ.* Winchester College. The Egyptian Salt and Soda Co., 1899–1901. Egyptian State Railways and Telegraphs, 1901–07. Egyptian Govt. Service and Salt Concession, 1909–10. Farming Transvaal, 1910–11. Asst. Manager, United Egyptian Salt Co., 1911–27. Served in WWI (mentioned in dispatches, Order of the Nile (4th class)): Egyptian Labour Corps, Lt., Gallipoli, Alexandria, battle of Romani (1916), Capt., Suez, Desert Column branch of E.L.C., El Arish, Major (1917). Secretary, London firm of architects (1930).

m. 3 Nov. 1917, Mercy Tyrrell Friend (*b.* 6 Feb. 1889, *d.* 20 July 1986), elder daughter of Edward Coke Friend, of Woolett Hall, North Cray, Kent. *Issue*: Francis Robin, Edward Philip George.

d. 23 Feb. 1960, New Eltham, London.

Phyllis Susanne, S.S. St. J.

b. 25 Apr. 1883, Winchester. *Educ.* Winchester High School for Girls, Guy's Hospital. Nurse. Franciscan Nun. Mother Foundress, The Homes of St. Giles for Lepers, East Hanningfield, Essex (1914–). Nursing Sister of the Order of St John of Jerusalem (1931–)

d. unm. 4 June 1956, Winchester.

Appendix 2: *The Du Boulay Family Tree*

Benjamin François Houssemayne du Boulay 1724–1865 = Louise Lagier La Motte 1736–1825

François Jaques 1759–1828 = Elizabeth Paris 1775–1814

James Thomas (Rev.) 1801–36 = Susannah Maria Ward 1801–75

James Thomas (Rev.) 1832–1915 = Alice Mead Cornish 1841–1925

(1) Hubert (Dr) 1860– 1955 = Katherine Mary Young d. 1926	(2) Noel Wilmot (Brig. Gen.) 1861– 1949	(3) Isabel Aimée 1863– 1956 = Alfred Henry Evans 1858– 1934	(4) Alice Mary 1864– 1950	(5) George Pascal Keble (Rev.) 1866–95	(6) James (Sir) 1868– 1945 = Freda Elais Butts Howell 1874– 1957	(7) Ralph 1869– 1948 = Ethel Margaret Thurston 1875– 1961	(8) Lucy Beatrice 1871– 1941	(9) Harriet Agatha 1873– 1971 = Arthur Porcher Lance (Rev.) 1871– 1957	(10) Winifred 1874– 1890	(11) Richard Francis 1877– 1949 = Elizabeth Louise d. 1936	(12) Philip 1880– 1960 = Mercy Tyrrell Friend 1889– 1986	(13) Phyllis Susanne, S.S. St. J. 1883– 1956

Francis Robin 1920– 2008; Edward Philip George 1922– 2009

Index